Transdisciplinary
Knowledge
Co-production

Praise for this book

'This book is overflowing with insights on transdisciplinarity, co-production and methods to support learning across boundaries in urban communities. With case studies from both Africa and Europe, it covers a broad range of contexts. Unlike many authors who offer a supposedly "one best" methodology, this book sets aside any pretension that one approach can achieve everything we might need. Instead, it asks and answers the more difficult, but ultimately more fruitful, question: how can we best design local interventions in response to diverse issues, people, organizations, cultures, and environments? Nevertheless, the book is much more than a patchwork quilt of case studies: its achievement, and the achievement of the MISTRA Urban Futures research programme that underpins it, is to take all that local learning and draw out more general insights to inform transdisciplinary practice. In this sense, the "bottom up" learning in the local communities is mirrored in the structure of the book that narrates it. Dive in, explore, and then translate this learning into your own practice!'

Gerald Midgley, Professor of Systems Thinking and Co-Director of the Centre for Systems Studies, University of Hull, UK

'There is no greater need today than for integrating worlds of knowledge and practice in order to understand and deal with the complexities of changing environmental, social, and economic conditions which impact cities. This timely book does just that. It draws on lessons learnt from field-based research and practice and offers ideas and methods which are non-prescriptive, adaptable to the diversity of geographic and cultural differences globally. It will be, undoubtedly, a valuable resource for urban planning, for academics, practitioners, and policy makers.'

Nabeel Hamdi, Professor Emeritus, Oxford Brookes University

'What a treasure trove this book is! Over the last decade, Mistra Urban Futures has raised the bar for transdisciplinary projects by applying innovative methods and breakthrough thinking on co-production. This guide provides an array of tools and methods, illustrated by rich case studies from Kenya, South Africa, Sweden, and the UK. It is useful for everyone using transdisciplinarity to address complex societal issues.'

Gabriele Bammer, Professor of Research Integration and Implementation, Australian National University

Transdisciplinary Knowledge Co-production

A Guide for Sustainable Cities

Kerstin Hemström, David Simon, Henrietta Palmer,
Beth Perry, and Merritt Polk

Practical Action Publishing Ltd
25 Albert Street, Rugby,
Warwickshire, CV21 2SD, UK
www.practicalactionpublishing.com

© Kerstin Hemström, David Simon, Henrietta Palmer, Beth Perry, Merritt Polk and the Contributors, 2021

The moral right of the editors to be identified as editors of the work and the contributors to be identified as contributors of this work have been asserted under sections 77 and 78 of the Copyright Design and Patents Act 1988.

The PDF version of this book is distributed under a Creative Commons Attribution Non-commercial No-derivatives CC BY-NC-ND licence. This allows the reader to copy and redistribute the material; but appropriate credit must be given, the material must not be used for commercial purposes, and if the material is transformed or built upon the modified material may not be distributed. For further information see <https://creativecommons.org/licenses/by-nc-nd/4.0/legalcode>

Product or corporate names may be trademarks or registered trademarks, and are used only for identification and explanation without intent to infringe.

A catalogue record for this book is available from the British Library.

A catalogue record for this book has been requested from the Library of Congress.

978-1-788531-450 Paperback
978-1-788531-467 Hardback
978-1-788531-481 eBook

Citation: Hemström, K., Simon, D., Palmer, H., Perry, B., and Polk, M. (2021) *Transdisciplinary Knowledge Co-production: A Guide for Sustainable Cities*, Rugby, UK: Practical Action Publishing <http://dx.doi.org/10.3362/9781788531481>.

Since 1974, Practical Action Publishing has published and disseminated books and information in support of international development work throughout the world. Practical Action Publishing is a trading name of Practical Action Publishing Ltd (Company Reg. No. 1159018), the wholly owned publishing company of Practical Action. Practical Action Publishing trades only in support of its parent charity objectives and any profits are covenanted back to Practical Action
(Charity Reg. No. 247257, Group VAT Registration No. 880 9924 76).

The views and opinions in this publication are those of the author and do not represent those of Practical Action Publishing Ltd or its parent charity Practical Action. Reasonable efforts have been made to publish reliable data and information, but the authors and publisher cannot assume responsibility for the validity of all materials or for the consequences of their use.

Cover credit: RCO.design
Typeset by vPrompt eServices, India

The manufacturer's authorised representative in the EU for product safety is Lightning Source France, 1 Av. Johannes Gutenberg, 78310 Maurepas, France.
compliance@lightningsource.fr

Contents

vi Acknowledgements
vii Foreword
ix Boxes, figures, tables, and photos
xi Abbreviations
xii About the authors
xiv About the contributors

PART 1
02 Introduction
04 CHAPTER 1
    Why transdisciplinary urban knowledge co-production?
13 CHAPTER 2
    Methods for what? The strengths and limitations of transdisciplinary knowledge co-production

PART 2
60 Methods for transdisciplinary urban knowledge co-production
64 CHAPTER 3
    Creating co-productive spaces
100 CHAPTER 4
    Designing processes to integrate knowledge
135 CHAPTER 5
    Blurring boundaries to facilitate understanding

PART 3
164 Conclusions
166 CHAPTER 6
    Concluding reflections and recommendations
169 APPENDIX
    The contexts – Mistra Urban Futures Local Interaction Platforms

Acknowledgements

We gratefully acknowledge the core programme funding for Mistra Urban Futures from Mistra (the Swedish Foundation for Strategic Environmental Research); Sida (the Swedish International Development Cooperation Agency); and the Gothenburg Consortium comprising Chalmers University of Technology, the University of Gothenburg, City of Gothenburg, IVL (the Swedish Environmental Institute), Västra Götalandsregionen, The County Administrative Board of Västra Götaland, The Göteborg Region (GR), and RISE (Research Institutes of Sweden). This funding has also enabled the book to be made available for free electronic download on Open Access.

Some of the methods reported in this book have been developed or modified during the course of projects co-funded by research councils and other partners in the respective cities and countries. Our UK contributors acknowledge especially the Economic and Social Research Council (grant reference number ES/N005945/2) and the University of Sheffield. We also acknowledge the co-funding from each city platform, and the contributions of project participants too numerous to name in these processes beyond the respective author teams.

Compiling this book would not have been possible without the insights, experiences, and writing efforts of each contributing author. The complete list includes 49 names (in alphabetical order): Stephen Agong', Rikki Dean, Tove Derner, Catherine Durose, Mirek Dymitrow, Magnus Eriksson, Elin Andersdotter Fabre, Katie Finney, Margareta Forsberg, Daniel Gillberg, Birgitta Guevera, Jez Hall, Patrick Hayombe, Kerstin Hemström, John Holmberg, Johan Holmén, Karin Ingelhag, Sanna Isemo, Eva Maria Jernsand, Sophia Kaså, Helena Kraff, Johan Larsson Lindal, Åsa Lorentzi, Tim May, Per Myrén, Ithra Najaar, Barry Ness, Jonas Nässén, Michael Oloko, Lillian Omondi, George Mark Onyango, Franklin Otiende, Henrietta Palmer, Beth Perry, Merritt Polk, Amanda Preece, Ulf Ranhagen, Liz Richardson, Bert Russell, John Sande, Dianne Scott, Dan Silver, David Simon, Vicky Simpson, Rike Sitas, Warren Smit, Alice Toomer McAlpine, Sandra Valencia, and Sarah Whitehead. You will find contributing authors of specific sections indicated in the margins.

All the figures in the text have been designed by Erika Pekkari. We also thank Clare Tawney at Practical Action Publishing for seeing the value of making this guide available to the widest possible audience.

Foreword

Mistra Urban Futures ran for a decade. Over this time, the centre involved an enormous number of diverse people from civil society, the private and the public sectors, and academia in knowledge co-production. It did so to overcome what Horst Rittel called 'the symmetry of ignorance' among participants of transdisciplinary projects. This ignorance originates in our tendency to think and perceive the outside world from the perspective of our own bubble. Rittel used the expression some 40 years ago. I think, with the internet as a key source to find information and like-minded peers, the bubbles and the challenge to overcome the symmetry of ignorance is even more required nowadays. This is what makes Mistra Urban Futures so valuable. It explored ways to co-produce knowledge among those bubbles, with the 'desire to find new ways of working that also promote urban justice and inclusion' (Chapter 1, The contexts: Mistra Urban Futures – collaboration and co-production to realise just cities), in a variety of spaces in and around Gothenburg as well as in different spaces in the Global South and North.

Over the past few decades, the field of transdisciplinary research and co-production of knowledge has grown. Twenty years ago, one could safely say that the field was in an early stage of development and still exploring unknown ground. Today, I would consider such a statement to be wrong. Transdisciplinary scholars have now contributed to a variety of thematic fields, in shorter and smaller projects as well as longer and bigger ones. Mistra Urban Futures is one of the few longer and bigger transdisciplinary programmes. It is not yet the size of the projects Gabriele Bammer (2013) wants us to aim for – transdisciplinary projects that are massively funded and promise a next step for humanity like the genome project or the moon landing – but Mistra Urban Futures is still quite an achievement.

Transdisciplinarity and knowledge co-production programmes are expected to co-produce knowledge on complex, wicked problems with and for society. Some of the challenges the urban systems face should be addressed differently in the future because of the learning that has taken place in the spaces of co-production created by Mistra Urban Futures. Besides this main purpose of transdisciplinary research, there are other outcomes of Mistra Urban Futures to learn from. The present guide is written for those who run transdisciplinary processes of co-production and who want to learn from how others experienced and navigated co-production processes. I believe these experiences are an important element of the body of knowledge of transdisciplinary research and knowledge co-production. Such experiences need to be documented, critically reflected upon, and made available. I welcome this guide, which includes an excellent review and analysis of the methods, tools, and techniques used by Mistra Urban Futures. The following are three things I consider particularly well done in the book:

- The relaxed and pragmatic use of the different concepts that populate the field of co-production: Some transdisciplinary researchers spend their time 'doing boundary work' in the sense of defending a specific understanding of knowledge co-production as the right one. They argue, for example, that transdisciplinary research is in no way comparable to action research or claim that the inclusion of societal stakeholders is the sole identifier of transdisciplinarity. In this kind of boundary work, the plurality of understandings of knowledge co-production is a problem to be solved by a unifying definition, rather than a rich resource to be explored. My impression is that for the guide, the authors did not even think about entering this debate. Instead, they used and placed side-by-side whatever concept they considered helpful or what they were familiar with. Being pragmatic instead of doing boundary work will help us to further specify and adapt the transdisciplinary approach to different problem contexts.

- The consideration of the often-forgotten things that also influence knowledge co-production: the authors discuss ethics and emotional labour. They reflect on leadership, facilitation, intermediation, and administration. They discuss all of the different ways to engage with boundaries, be it through boundary objects, boundary work, or boundary organizations. Furthermore, I like the key role the authors give to reflexivity. My take on reflexivity is: On the individual level, transdisciplinarity and knowledge co-production force everyone to reflect on and explain what is taken for granted in her/his 'home discipline' or 'home societal sector'. On the collective level, co-production requires what Donald Schön (1991) calls 'reflection-in-action', the back and forth between co-producing knowledge and critically reflecting upon the process and its outcomes.

- The felicitous combination of conceptual clarifications, case studies from the Global South and North, and examples of how methods and tools were used, and co-production was facilitated: Going through the case studies, the one on fish cages at Miyandhe Beach in Kisumu, Kenya impressed me. 'With many stakeholders involved, the project could not control the effects' (Chapter 2, Box 2.13, 'Illustrating the need for reflective practice: co-production of fish cage farming'). The idea of the fish cages was too successful. I guess this might be a new challenge for projects of knowledge co-production, one we still have to learn how to cope with.

I recommend readers who are new to the field to start with Chapter 2, 'Methods for what?' to get an impression of the conceptual background of transdisciplinary research and knowledge co-production. Those more experienced, I assume, will dive into any of the cases, methods, or process experiences presented in Chapter 3. I am sure both groups of readers will find lots of inspiration and interesting reflections. Hopefully, they will also consider one of the authors' conclusions when building on the book's insights, specifically, 'don't be afraid of failure' (Chapter 6).

Christian Pohl
TdLab, ETH Zurich

References

Bammer, G. (2013) *Disciplining Interdisciplinarity: Integration and Implementation Sciences for Researching Complex Real-World Problems*, ANU E Press, Canberra.

Schön, D.A. (1991) *The Reflective Practitioner: How Professionals Think in Action*, Ashgate Publishing Ltd, Aldershot, UK.

Boxes, figures, tables, and photos

Boxes

- 15 **Box 2.1** The meaning of co-production
- 17 **Box 2.2** Considerations on whom to involve in the process
- 20 **Box 2.3** The necessity of clarifying assumptions: mapping rationalities of key stakeholders in the Urban Flooding CityLab
- 23 **Box 2.4** Challenges of transdisciplinary collaboration: co-production between PhD students and community members in an urban fishing village
- 29 **Box 2.5** Different types of reflexivity
- 34 **Box 2.6** Leading transdisciplinary co-production
- 38 **Box 2.7** Facilitation – bringing methods to life
- 41 **Box 2.8** Offering professional facilitation in Gothenburg
- 42 **Box 2.9** Flexible financing for transdisciplinary co-production
- 44 **Box 2.10** Formal engagements enabling co-production in Kisumu
- 45 **Box 2.11** Facilitating supportive administrative relationships for co-production
- 46 **Box 2.12** The point of boundary objects
- 53 **Box 2.13** Illustrating the need for reflective practice: co-production of fish cage farming
- 84 **Box 3.1** Methods, focus, and work modes used in the modules
- 123 **Box 4.1** Local co-production around the implementation of SDGs in Kisumu

Figures

- 10 **Figure 1.1** Locations of the main research arenas in Mistra Urban Futures
- 14 **Figure 2.1** A schematic image of a transdisciplinary co-production process, used in Pohl et al., 2017
- 18 **Figure 2.2** Four areas of consideration when setting boundaries for whom to involve in the transdisciplinary co-production process
- 80 **Figure 3.1** Illustration of the backcasting methodology used at Challenge Lab
- 93 **Figure 3.2** The first and second spaces are 'home spaces', and academics and practitioners move from these spaces into the third space of co-production and co-writing
- 104 **Figure 4.1** The five stages of the 'double diamond', illustrating the iterative process of design thinking in 'opening up' to include knowledge vs. 'narrowing down' to define and test
- 108 **Figure 4.2** Illustration of the re-conceptualization of worldviews resulting from changes in outlook
- 114 **Figure 4.3** An example of a scenario matrix showing four possible futures of urban development as a combination of two variables
- 116 **Figure 4.4** An example of a decision tree for the analysis of strategic choices
- 126 **Figure 4.5** How knowledge co-production between government and academia in the adaptation of a global sustainability agenda to the city level interplays with the implementation and monitoring of the agenda at other levels
- 139 **Figure 5.1** The Research Forum model with different forms of academic-practitioner interactions

Tables

37 **Table 2.1** Similarities and differences in viewpoints on good leadership in co-production

82 **Table 3.1** Learning outcomes for the doctoral course, Co-producing knowledge in transdisciplinary research – From practice to theory, 2017–2019

Photos

26 **Photo 2.1** Workshop with local tour guides, consisting of co-creative activities for developing a guided tour

68 **Photo 3.1** Using the Ketso method for participatory brainstorming on project ideas during the co-initiation phase of mini-ARC projects

75 **Photo 3.2** Body map representing different aspects of health and well-being in a local community

89 **Photo 3.3** Capacity building of Kibuye CBO members on briquette making process from market waste sourced from Kibuye Market in Kisumu

120 **Photo 4.1** Workshop activities involving the Method Kit decks of cards and the Block by Block-tool developed by UN-Habitat and Mojang, during step 2 of the Urban Girls method

131 **Photo 4.2** Visualization of the international policy exchange workshop, co-hosted with GMCA on 16 October 2019

143 **Photo 5.1** Photographs taken as part of the photovoice method showing everyday encounters of community researchers Saraswati Sinha, Jane Gregory, Pete Simms, and Tony Wright

148 **Photo 5.2** A playground working as boundary object bridging different interests and issues at Dunga beach

156 **Photo 5.3** Group of FunkTek pilots testing the city accessibility together with project co-ordinator Lisa Wahle, on the streets of Gothenburg, 2015

Abbreviations

- **ACC** African Centre for Cities
- **ARC** Action Research Collective
- **CCT** City of Cape Town
- **CP** co-production
- **DRMC** Disaster Risk Management Centre (Cape Town)
- **DT** design thinking
- **GM** Greater Manchester
- **GMCA** Greater Manchester Combined Authority
- **GMV** Gothenburg Centre for Sustainable Development
- **JOOUST** Jaramogi Oginga Odinga University of Science and Technology
- **KIWAN** Kisumu Waste Actors Network Co-operative
- **MCA** multi-criteria analysis
- **NGO** non-governmental organization
- **NUA** New Urban Agenda
- **R&D** research and development
- **RF** research forum
- **SDG** Sustainable Development Goal
- **SMLIP** Sheffield-Manchester Local Interaction Platform
- **SWOT** strengths, weaknesses, opportunities, and threats
- **TD** transdisciplinary
- **TD CP** transdisciplinary co-production
- **UCT** University of Cape Town
- **UGM** Urban Girls Movement
- **UN** United Nations
- **USC** Urban Station Communities project
- **WISE** Well-being in Sustainable Cities
- **WWF** World Wide Fund for Nature

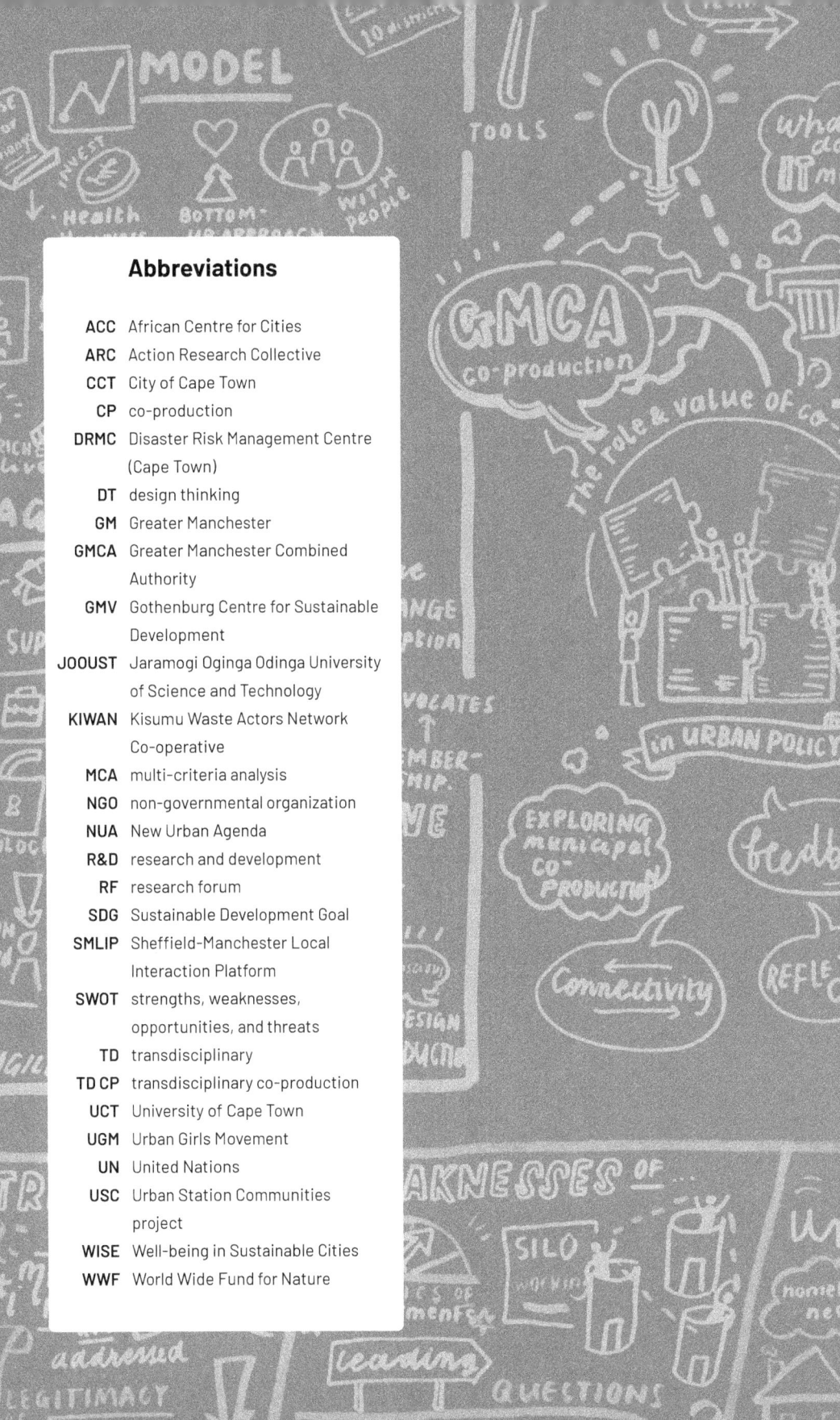

About the authors

Kerstin Hemström is a human ecologist and project leader at the Centre for Sustainable Urban Futures at Gothenburg Centre for Sustainable Development (GMV), co-hosted by Gothenburg University and Chalmers University of Technology. She was an in-house researcher at the Mistra Urban Futures platform (2017–2018) and international secretariat (2018–2019) in Gothenburg, focusing primarily on methods and tools to facilitate transdisciplinary co-production and collaborative research. Kerstin has a broad interdisciplinary background and holds a PhD in civil engineering. She has published within the areas of sustainable built environment, forestry, co-production, and transdisciplinary research. One of her key interests lies in understanding how collaborative research can contribute to sustainable development.

Henrietta Palmer is an architect and resesearcher. She was Artistic Professor of Urban Design at Chalmers University of Technology in Gothenburg, in parallel with being Deputy Scientific Director at Mistra Urban Futures from 2015 to 2019. She has a particular engagement in methodologies for transdisciplinary research, also developing and conducting a PhD course for transdisciplinary research. During 2005–15 she held a position as Professor of Architecture at the Royal Institute of Art, Stockholm, where she designed and conducted the transdisciplinary post-master's programme Resources, focusing on urban challenges with contextual studies across a number of cities globally. Her key research focus concerns just urban transformation processes stemming from social-spatial practices.

Professor Beth Perry is Co-Director at the Urban Institute at the University of Sheffield and Professor of Urban Knowledge and Governance. Her research focusses on processes and practices of urban transformation, co-productive urban governance, and 'just' knowledge-based transitions. Between 2012 and 2020 she was UK Platform Director for Mistra Urban Futures and led two ESRC projects — Jam and Justice: Co-producing Urban Governance for Social Innovation and Whose Knowledge Matters. She continues to lead a British Academy Sustainable Development Programme grant on cultural heritage and sustainable livelihoods in Cape Town and Kisumu. Beth has written widely with Professor Tim May on reflexive and participative methods and knowledge-based urban transformations. Together they have published two books, *Cities and the Knowledge Economy: Promise, Politics and Possibilities* (Taylor and Francis, 2018) and *Reflexivity: the Essential Guide* (Sage, 2017). They are finalizing the 5th edition of *Social Research: Issues, Methods and Process* (McGraw-Hill/Open University Press) to examine issues including post-truth, relativism, and power, and the impacts of participative and collaborative methods on social research practice.

Merritt Polk is a professor in Human Ecology at the School of Global Studies, University of Gothenburg, where she is currently Head of Department. Throughout her career, Merritt has worked collaboratively with practitioners in the fields of gender mainstreaming, sustainable transportation, and sustainable urban development. Her most recent research is on transdisciplinary methods for sustainable urban development. From 2010 to 2013, she was Co-Research Director at Mistra Urban Futures, where she was responsible for developing collaborative approaches to urban planning through different types of transdisciplinary knowledge co-production. Her most recent publications focus on describing, supporting, and evaluating different examples of transdisciplinary approaches. During 2017-2019, she and Henrietta Palmer developed and gave a PhD course on transdisciplinary co-production that targeted both doctoral students and practitioners by integrating their respective approaches to urban development. She is currently working on a project on the use of knowledge integration for understanding and mitigating urban planning conflicts in Gothenburg.

David Simon is Professor of Development Geography, Royal Holloway, University of London, and was also Director of Mistra Urban Futures, Gothenburg, Sweden from September 2014 until December 2019. A former Rhodes Scholar, he specializes in development-environment issues, with particular reference to cities, climate change, and sustainability, and the relationships between theory, policy, and practice, on all of which he has published extensively. He has also worked and published on the relationships between transport/mobility and development, and geopolitical transitions. At Mistra Urban Futures, he led the pioneering methodological research on comparative transdisciplinary co-production. Geographically, he has extensive experience across sub-Saharan Africa, South and Southeast Asia, the UK, Sweden, and USA. He is author, editor, and co-editor of many books and journal special issues on cities, development-environment challenges, and climate change adaptation, most recently *Rethinking Sustainable Cities: Accessible, Green and Fair* (Policy Press, 2016), *Urban Planet* (Cambridge University Press, 2018), *Holocaust Escapees and Global Development: Hidden Histories* (Zed Books, 2019), *Key Thinkers on Development* (2nd edn, Routledge, 2019), and *Comparative Urban Research from Theory to Practice: Co-production for Sustainability* (Policy Press, 2020).

About the contributors

Stephen Gaya Agong' is a Professor of Horticulture and Vice-Chancellor at Jaramogi Oginga Odinga University of Science and Technology, and Director of the Kisumu Local Interaction Platform. Previously he served as a Deputy Vice-Chancellor (Administration, Planning and Development) at Jomo Kenyatta University of Agriculture and Technology, Deputy Vice-Chancellor (Planning, Research and Extension Services) at Maseno University, and Executive Director at the African Academy of Science. He is an accomplished horticulturalist whose current focus is urban food security and sustainable urban development; and educator spanning over 30 years of university teaching, research, community outreach, management, and leadership.

Rikki Dean is a Postdoctoral Fellow in the Democratic Innovations Research Unit, Goethe University Frankfurt. His research interests encompass democratic theory, public administration theory, participatory policymaking, process preferences, and social exclusion. He worked with the Jam and Justice team on the leadership in co-production survey.

Tove Derner has a bachelor's degree in economics from Lund University, and she wrote her bachelor's thesis about how equality affects economic growth. She is currently studying for a master's degree in Global Political Economy at Stockholm University. During spring 2020 she was undertaking an internship at Global Utmaning.

Catherine Durose is Reader in Policy Sciences at the University of Birmingham's Institute of Local Government Studies. Catherine was a Co-Investigator on the Economic and Social Research Council / Mistra Urban Futures-funded project, Jam and Justice: Co-Producing Urban Governance for Social Innovation <https://jamandjustice-rjc.org>.

Mirek Dymitrow holds a PhD in Human Geography from the University of Gothenburg, Sweden, where he is a research fellow. Until the end of 2019, he also worked as research co-ordinator at the Gothenburg Platform of Mistra Urban Futures at Chalmers University of Technology. His research interests include social psychology and sociology of science with a focus on conceptual change and inertia, as well as problems and causes of social deprivation in the face of overarching sustainability goals.

Magnus Eriksson is a researcher at RISE Interactive in Gothenburg, conducting interdisciplinary research projects around civic technology, digital ethics, and participatory methods with technologists, arts and humanities, and civil society. He is also a PhD candidate at the Department of Sociology of Law at Lund University researching the role of digital technologies in the regulation of urban spaces.

Elin Andersdotter Fabre is the Programme Director for the Sustainable Cities Programme at the think tank Global Utmaning. She has broad experience of working with various development issues – democracy, human rights, gender equality, and security – from international organizations, government institutions, and civil society. Elin has previously worked with policy development and advocacy leading up to the UN 2030 Agenda Sustainable Development Goals and the Habitat III New Urban Agenda. Her academic background is in political science with degrees from Stockholm University, Sciences Po Paris, and King's College London.

Katie Finney brings together her love of facilitation and transformational leadership through working on projects linked to research, citizen engagement, and participation. She co-founded Amity CIC, was a member of the Jam and Justice Action Research Collective, and one of the facilitators of the Inquiry into Care at Home <https://amitycic.com/about-us>.

Margareta Forsberg has a PhD in Social Work and was the Director of the Gothenburg platform of Mistra Urban Futures until early 2019. For almost 30 years she has been working on co-ordination and management in different intersections between academia and practical organizations. She also has experience as a professional facilitator and sees the benefits of using facilitating methods in co-production research activities.

Daniel Gillberg is educated in culture heritage studies and currently works as a project manager at the Museum of Gothenburg. He has worked primarily with issues related to urban development, accessibility, and inclusive cultural experiences.

Birgitta Guevera has worked with issues related to integration and segregation for almost 20 years, first within the City of Gothenburg, later at the Public Employment Service, and for over 10 years within the County Administrative Board of Västra Götaland. Birgitta has also worked with segregation issues at the Government Office and at the newly inaugurated Anti-segregation Authority (Delegationen mot segregation). Guevara participated as project co-ordinator within KAIROS (Knowledge and Approaches for Fair and Socially Sustainable Cities).

Jez Hall is Director of Shared Future CIC. A committed community engagement practitioner based in Greater Manchester, Jez Hall helped set up Shared Future CIC and was an active participant in the Action Research Collective (ARC). He has been involved in many co-production projects over the years, including facilitating a number of citizens' juries and supporting participatory budgeting projects <https://sharedfuturecic.org.uk/director/jez-hall/>.

Patrick Odhiambo Hayombe is Associate Professor and, currently, the Dean of School of Spatial Planning and Natural Resource Management at Jaramogi Oginga Odinga University of Science and Technology (JOOUST). His research interests include whose heritage matters, social-cultural track, ecotourism, food culture, green planning, geospatial solutions, planning standards, and urban mobility. He also consults for Pre-envero Consultants in Spatial and Environmental Planning.

John Holmberg is Professor of Physical Resource Theory at Chalmers University of Technology and also holds Sweden's first UNESCO chair in Education for Sustainable Development. His current research focuses on navigating sustainability transitions and he is the founder of Challenge Lab. He is active as an adviser and expert at the United Nations: to the headquarters in New York related to the Agenda 2030; to UNESCO in Paris for higher education for sustainable development; and to UNEP in Nairobi.

Johan Holmén is a doctoral student in physical resource theory. He conducts inter- and transdisciplinary research on and for sustainability transitions. Key research interests include methodological development for navigating transitions in practice, transformative social learning, and education.

Karin Ingelhag is a project manager within business development and former educator. Karin's recent and current engagements include running the EU-project 'Urban Rural Gothenburg' as well as co-ordinating research in collaboration between the City of Gothenburg and Chalmers University of Technology. Karin's academic background in psychology and behavioural sciences recurs in her ongoing work with sustainability transitions.

Sanna Isemo is a project leader at the Gothenburg Centre for Sustainable Development, Chalmers University of Technology and University of Gothenburg. She worked as Platform Co-ordinator for Mistra Urban Futures' Gothenburg Local Interaction Platform between 2016 and 2019 and has been involved as project participant in several Mistra Urban Futures projects with specific focus on urban justice, social sustainability, and participatory governance.

Eva Maria Jernsand is a researcher in marketing at the Centre for Tourism and School of Business, Economics and Law, University of Gothenburg. Eva Maria conducted her PhD studies in collaboration with Mistra Urban Futures' platform in Kisumu, developing tourism in Dunga by Lake Victoria. Her research interest revolves around learning, inclusiveness, participation, and co-creation in place branding and destination development. Eva Maria has published in journals such as *Place Branding and Public Diplomacy*, *Tourism Recreation Research*, and *Action Research Journal*.

Sophia Kaså started her own business, Katalysator (Catalyst), in 1999. Since then she has been working with co-creation in city planning and organizational development, primarily with the public sector. During 2019 she worked part-time as an in-house facilitator supporting the co-production processes in the different research projects at Mistra Urban Futures in Gothenburg. Sophia has a degree in social work.

Helena Kraff has a PhD in Design and is a researcher in design at the Faculty of Fine, Applied and Performing Arts at the University of Gothenburg. Her main research interests include participatory and inclusive forms of tourism and place development. Her thesis, entitled 'Pitfalls of participation and ways towards just practices: through a participatory design project in Kisumu, Kenya', explores a number of challenges related to participatory research practices. She has published in international journals and edited books, and written reports in the areas of participatory design, tourism, place branding, and transdisciplinary research.

Johan Larson Lindal is a research engineer previously based at the Royal University of Technology, Stockholm and research assistant at Mistra Urban Futures' Stockholm Node. There he produced a report on sustainable co-creation methods in the Stockholm region 2018–2019. Since September 2019 he has been a PhD student at Linköping University.

Åsa Lorentzi has worked with development in municipalities for 30 years with issues related to education, integration, and social sustainability. Most of this time has been spent in the City of Gothenburg in different strategic positions in local city districts. Åsa is also a trainer in participatory leadership, approaches, and methods for a more co-creative way of working and handling complex challenges in society. From 2012 to 2016 Åsa was one of two project leaders in Mistra Urban Futures' KAIROS project (Knowledge and Approaches for Fair and Socially Sustainable Cities).

Tim May is a Professorial Fellow at the University of Sheffield. He worked for the Mistra foundation to advise them on setting up Mistra Urban Futures prior to its conception and he has written widely on research methodology and methods, universities as sites of knowledge production, urban change, and the philosophy of the social sciences.

Per Myrén, Head of Development at Change Maker AB in Gothenburg, has facilitated a large number of workshops and conferences/seminars as a hired process and workshop leader. He has initiated, developed, and projected a number of IT and game development projects for public organizations and institutions. He has developed and been responsible for various types of competence development programmes for companies, organizations, teachers, and students in Sweden and internationally.

Ithra Najaar is the Finance and Operations Manager of the African Centre for Cities (ACC) at the University of Cape Town. Ithra has a BCom degree from the University of the Western Cape and a Postgraduate Diploma in Strategic Business Project Management from the University of Cape Town. Ithra's work focuses on the management of research finance, to provide a high-level financial, strategic, systems, and operational perspective to shape the direction of the ACC in alignment with university objectives and the centre's strategic direction.

Jonas Nässén is a senior researcher in Physical Resource Theory at Chalmers University of Technology. His main research interest is the development of societal consumption patterns and how they can be transformed towards long-term climate targets. He was part of the co-production WISE project at Mistra Urban Futures' Gothenburg platform.

Barry Ness was, until the end of 2019, the Director of the Skåne Local Interaction Platform for the Mistra Urban Futures programme and a project researcher on its solid waste comparative project. Barry is an associate professor in Sustainability Science at the Centre for Sustainability Science at Lund University where his present research interests focus on promoting and understanding sustainability in the craft beer sector through bottom-up, participatory approaches.

Past research themes have included sustainability assessment, the diffusion of simple, more sustainable innovations in Africa, and large land acquisitions in Africa, among others.

Michael Oloko is a senior lecturer and researcher at Jaramogi Oginga Odinga University of Science and Technology (JOOUST) and was Deputy Director of the Kisumu Local Interaction Platform. He is also the Dean of the School of Engineering and Technology at JOOUST. His current research interests include environmental engineering, integrated water resources management, renewable energy technology, urban agriculture, and solid waste management.

Lillian Omondi is Lecturer at Maseno University's Department of Sociology and Anthropology, Kenya. Her research interests include social capital and its influence on community action, migration and migrant networks, engendering research and community action, and community-led climate change adaptation. Her latest publications pick up on social capital and climate change perception in the Mara River Basin, Kenya, and the role of gender within transdisciplinary integration.

George Mark Onyango is Professor of Urban and Regional Planning at Maseno University. He has been an initiator and team leader in the Market Places pilot project and Transit Oriented Development and researcher on Urban Knowledge, Urban Governance, and Urban Change at the Kisumu Local Interaction Platform. He has been engaged in a number of projects in the city and has written articles and book chapters on co-production in Kisumu based on local experiences.

Franklin Otiende Awuor is a lecturer at Jaramogi Oginga Odinga University of Science and Technology, a postdoctoral researcher in food security, and was assistant Socio-ecological Track leader at Kisumu Local Interaction Platform. His research interests lie in food security, solid waste governance, and wildlife management.

Amanda Preece is an experienced qualitative and quantitative researcher, working closely with public and third sector clients to identify community assets, develop community links, and collect needs-based information. She is an associate of Shared Future CIC, founder of Mill Research, and was one of the facilitators of the Inquiry into Care at Home <https://www.linkedin.com/in/amandamillresearch/>.

Ulf Ranhagen, PhD, is senior Professor at Dalarna University, former professor at KTH Royal Institute of Technology, and senior chief architect at Sweco. Ulf was a process leader of the Mistra Urban Futures project Urban Station Communities and has developed approaches, methods, and tools for sustainable urban development. He has long professional experience in urban planning, urban design, and architecture in Sweden and internationally.

Liz Richardson is Professor of Public Administration at the University of Manchester. Her research interests are in governance, public policy, and citizen participation. Her work has appeared in journals such as *Governance, Environment and Planning, British Journal of Politics and International Relations, Social Policy and Administration*, and *Policy & Politics*.

Bert Russell, PhD, is a research associate at the University of Sheffield's Urban Institute. His interests include municipalism (with a recent paper in *Antipode* entitled 'Beyond the local trap: new municipalism and the rise of the fearless cities' and a forthcoming paper in *Soundings*) and new models of economic democracy (with a recent co-authored policy report published by Common Wealth entitled *Public-Common Partnerships: Building New Circuits of Collective Ownership*). He is an editorial community member of Minim, and has published recently in *Open Democracy, Red Pepper, ROAR, Citymetric, Novara*, and *The Conversation*.

John Sande is Deputy Director at the County Government of Kisumu's City Directorate of Environment and Natural Resources. He is also a member of the secretariat implementing the Kisumu Urban Project (KUP), a French-funded project within the city addressing issues of solid waste management, transport infrastructure improvement, and upgrading of commercial infrastructure. He is a social safeguards officer for the Kenya Urban Support Programme (KUSP) and the Kenya Devolution Support Programme (KDSP), both World Bank-funded projects being implemented by the County Government of Kisumu.

Dianne Scott is Associate Professor at the African Centre for Cities, University of Cape Town. Dianne has been part of two co-production projects, namely, FRACTAL working with academics and officials in southern African cities, and Knowledge for Coastal Change, working with a variety of urban stakeholders in Durban. Dianne is the lead editor of the book *Mainstreaming Climate Change in Urban Development: Lessons from Cape Town* (2019).

Daniel Silver is a Lecturer in the Department of Politics at the University of Manchester. His research focuses on critical social policy and research methods.

Vicky Simpson, PhD, is a research manager at the Urban Institute, University of Sheffield specializing in the administrative design and delivery of transdisciplinary research. She was Programme Coordinator for the Sheffield–Manchester Local Interaction Platform of Mistra Urban Futures and the ESRC Jam and Justice project between 2016 and 2019, and is a member of the Association of University Administrators.

Rike Sitas straddles the academic world of urban studies and creative practice, and is fascinated by the intersection of culture with cities, and more specifically on the role of art, culture, and heritage in urban life. Linked to this has been exploring the impact of the creative economy and cultural policy in producing more just and sustainable cities. A large part of her research focus has meant unpacking the notions of public space and public life in Southern cityness. Until the end of 2019, Rike was the Co-ordinator of the Cape Town Local Interaction Platform for Mistra Urban Futures and is a researcher at the African Centre for Cities at the University of Cape Town.

Warren Smit is the Research Manager at the African Centre for Cities, University of Cape Town, South Africa, and was the Director of the Mistra Urban Futures Cape Town Local Interaction Platform from 2016 to 2019. He has a PhD in urban planning and has been a researcher on urban issues for over 25 years. His main areas of research include urban governance, urban health, and housing policy, with a particular focus on African cities.

Alice Toomer-McAlpine is a community organizer, adult educator, and media practitioner based in Manchester. She is a co-editor and founding director of The Meteor media co-operative and was a member of the Jam and Justice Action Research Collective.

Sandra Valencia is a researcher at Gothenburg University. She was lead researcher at Mistra Urban Futures (Chalmers University of Technology) of a comparative project on city-level implementation of Agenda 2030 in seven cities on four continents. She has an interdisciplinary background with a PhD in Sustainability Science from Lund University, a BSc in Physics and an MSc in Development Management. She has worked as a research scientist at NASA Goddard Space Flight Center for the Micro-pulse Lidar Network project, which consists of the collection and analysis of atmospheric data. Then she worked for several years developing and managing climate change adaptation projects in Latin America and the Caribbean at the Inter-American Development Bank.

Sarah Whitehead is the Global Innovator of Social Change and Inclusion at Salford-based Community Pride CIC. She is a single mother with a working-class background who uses her lived experience of poverty and the educational tools of Paulo Freire to increase participation and build resilient communities that are reactive to the issues that affect them daily.

Transdisciplinary
Knowledge
Co-production

PART 1
Introduction

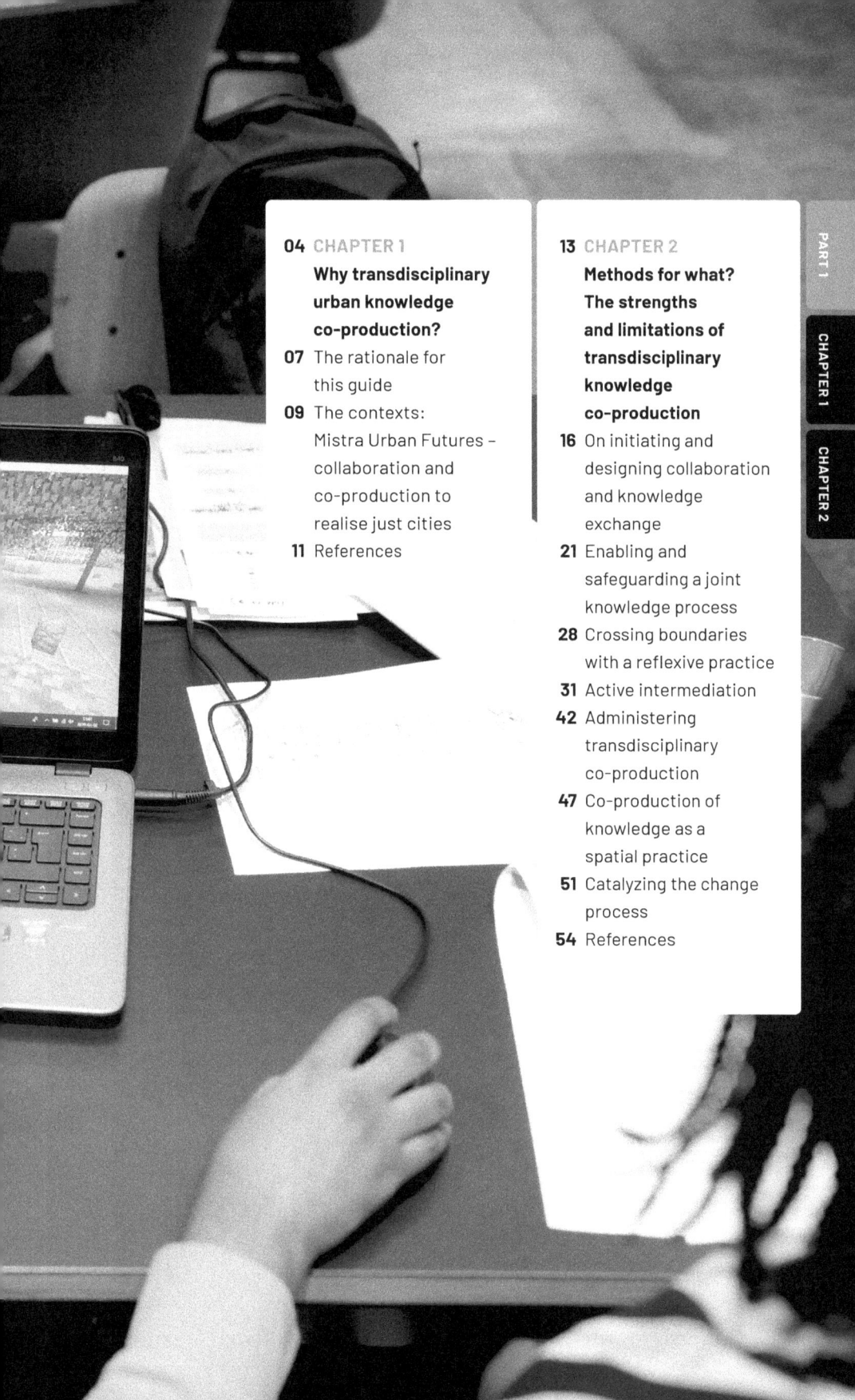

04 CHAPTER 1
Why transdisciplinary urban knowledge co-production?
07 The rationale for this guide
09 The contexts: Mistra Urban Futures – collaboration and co-production to realise just cities
11 References

13 CHAPTER 2
Methods for what? The strengths and limitations of transdisciplinary knowledge co-production
16 On initiating and designing collaboration and knowledge exchange
21 Enabling and safeguarding a joint knowledge process
28 Crossing boundaries with a reflexive practice
31 Active intermediation
42 Administering transdisciplinary co-production
47 Co-production of knowledge as a spatial practice
51 Catalyzing the change process
54 References

PART 1
CHAPTER 1
CHAPTER 2

CHAPTER 1
Why transdisciplinary urban knowledge co-production?

keywords
transdisciplinary research, knowledge co-production, methods, tools, sustainable urban development, local interaction platforms

Increasingly, socially relevant research requires stakeholder participation and interaction. Transdisciplinary co-production is an approach that aims to create new cultures and practices for research collaboration that better mirror the complexities we are facing. The core idea is to expand who is involved in generating new knowledge and address real-world problems through collaborative processes that include a wide variety of knowledge and expertise.

Kerstin Hemström and Merritt Polk

ALL OVER THE WORLD, COMMUNITIES, researchers, and decision-makers are trying to come to grips with the serious challenges involved in realizing sustainable development.

The impacts of climate change, widening inequalities, decreasing biodiversity, and untenable consumption levels are just some examples of global issues that are jeopardizing life as we know it. Typically, these problems defy not only geographical and organizational borders, but also the expertise and problem-solving capabilities of politicians, practitioners, researchers, and civil society. Many of them are also 'wicked'. Not only are they complex, but also often highly contested, involve unclear problem definitions, have uncertain and unpredictable trajectories, and no given or testable solutions (Rittel and Webber, 1973; Brown et al., 2010).

Cities sit at the intersection of many of these challenges. While they provide basic services, transport, employment, education, and health care, they also must deal with climate change, crime and violence, poverty, environmental degradation, segregation, and economic depression. On the one hand, cities are platforms where highly diverse actors can come together to catalyse new ideas and transformations. On the other, cities are characterized by specific types of complex problems with often high degrees of fragmentation in administrations, sectors, and decision-making levels. They embody hard infrastructures as well as social, economic, cultural, and political structures that are difficult to change, even when the need to do so is imperative (Ramadier, 2004; Muñoz-Erickson et al., 2017). All of these issues together pose great challenges to sustainable urban transformations (Polk, 2015b; May and Perry, 2018).

In addition, 'sustainability' itself is a vague, ambiguous, and highly contested term. It allows unlimited possibilities for context- and actor-dependent interpretations of what changes are necessary, in what direction, and how to reach them (Robinson, 2004). In urban arenas, different actors are likely to bring competing views of what 'sustainability' is – from the profit-generated needs of short-term development schemes to the long-term building of societal infrastructures. The ways in which 'sustainability' is applied in the urban arena are thus continually adapted and revised to fit the needs and underlying worldviews of the respective stakeholders, be they politicians, researchers, civil servants, representatives from community-based organizations, or business developers (Owens and Cowell, 2002).

The challenges faced by cities in creating more sustainable and resilient futures not only affect and engage a variety of stakeholders, decision-making levels, disciplines, and sectors. They also exceed the limits of traditional academic research and conventional notions of science-society and science-policy interactions, where knowledge production and decision-making happen independently from one another in a linear manner. These challenges thus point to the need for approaches to knowledge production and problem solving that are able to harness and engage the different values, knowledge, and expertise of the involved stakeholders effectively (Polk, 2015a; May and Perry, 2016). Achieving truly relevant and usable knowledge for urban transformations requires stakeholder participation and interaction (Lang et al., 2012; Polk, 2015b; Van der Hel, 2016).

Knowledge is a claim, idea or belief that someone holds true enough to guide his or her reasoning and actions (Muñoz-Erickson et al., 2017). As such, 'knowledge' is deeply intertwined with values and beliefs about the order of the world. These values and worldviews not only result in different framings of sustainable urban development, they also determine what is regarded as valid or legitimate knowledge for decision-making (Petts et al., 2008; Simon, 2016). To be viable over longer periods, any attempt to realize urban development that is socially, economically, and environmentally sustainable must meet a diversity of values and needs from various interest groups while recognizing and mediating contradicting or incommensurable perspectives (Brugmann, 2009). In this process, different actors, holding different knowledges, need to engage in conversations with one another on what sustainability should be, and how to achieve it. One could even go so far as to say that to be successful, the imagining, designing, planning, and building of liveable and inclusive cities and urban systems *must* include a broad and situated knowledge base to create solutions that are sufficiently tailored for and anchored in each local context. This need for diversity of knowledge is a direct consequence of the multifaceted social challenges and environmental constraints that exist in urban areas and the number and variety of actors involved. Broadly, this is motivated by three interrelated concerns regarding:

- who has the right to participate in defining problems and developing solutions;
- the need to engage and blend several types of knowledge and experiences to identify and adequately address the complex societal problems of our time; and
- the need to make science and scientific institutions more accountable for, and relevant to, society (Felt et al., 2015; Kläy et al., 2015).

Transdisciplinary co-production is one answer to such concerns. Focusing on real-life problems, the overall rationale is to stretch beyond academic disciplines and pre-defined levels of decision-making to include the voices, perspectives, and know-how of those necessary to address the issue in practice. Instead of moving knowledge from research to society, learning is co-generated in context, in a process that recognizes that knowledge is carried by diverse actors. The aim is to create new cultures and practices of research collaboration that better mirror the complexities we are facing, in which all those involved are engaged as knowledge carriers, knowledge producers, and knowledge users (Polk, 2015a):

> *Transdisciplinary co-production refers to collaboratively based processes where academic researchers and other actors and groups come together to share and create knowledge that can be used to face the sustainability challenges of today, while increasing capacity to societal problem-solving in the future* (adapted from Polk, 2016: 35).

Transdisciplinary co-production constitutes a promising approach for generating usable knowledge for sustainable urban futures in several ways. Linking knowledge to action by combining the theoretical and cumulative foundations of scientific knowledge with other types of knowledge, know-how, and practical expertise from lay people, businesses, civil society, practitioners, and politicians reduces the risk of generating knowledge that cannot be applied in urban decision-making (Wuelser et al., 2012). Including the multiple realities and perspectives of a complex problem implies better opportunities to understand the conditions and constraints for sustainable change and to explore solutions to the problem at hand. Through doing so, new insights can be reached that do not easily emerge from working within a single disciplinary or professional logic (Jahn et al., 2012). In the urban context, this creates both actionable knowledge that can be applied to concrete problem-solving, as well as scientific knowledge that can refine and contribute to the empirical and theoretical bases of research work.

The circumstances underlying this type of collaboration among different stakeholders are generally context-specific (Clark et al., 2016; Perry et al., 2018).

Each city presents its own opportunities and barriers to linking knowledge and action and what is radically new in one context may be the norm in another. For example, despite great diversity, significant differences exist between the material and social conditions of what is sometimes referred to as the global North and South. In the North, urban systems are often formally regulated, and research institutions can engage with diverse formalized, legitimate, and institutional stakeholders and actors. In the South, urban areas tend to be more heterogeneous and complex, with diverse formal and informal services, and a more fluid and dynamic social situation, including informal communities (Van Breda and Swilling, 2019). The application of transdisciplinary co-production thus needs to be exposed to and based on experience of the local situation (Muñoz-Erickson et al., 2017). Not only is it necessary to understand the problem context and the conditions for change, but the new knowledge generated is more likely to be effective in influencing action if perceived to be salient, credible, and legitimate by the larger local stakeholder community (Schuttenberg and Guth, 2015; Hansson and Polk, 2018).

The rationale for this guide

Transdisciplinary co-production offers an opportunity for diverse actors to reflect collectively on, and propose robust solutions to, reality-based challenges. As such, it is a powerful framework for guiding transformations to more sustainable and just cities. However, as a general approach to doing science with and in society, the idea of transdisciplinary co-production alone does not provide the sort of practical guidance that supports academic researchers and other participants or funders when they seek knowledge on how to go about it.

There is no ideal or universal method for cross-fertilizing different worlds of knowing. In dealing with the richness of the real world, it is best to go beyond single recipes to combine several, in whole or in part, to achieve what is possible and necessary in a given situation (Mingers and Brocklesby, 1997). Hence, specific methods for transdisciplinary co-production developed in one context cannot merely be replicated and transferred to others (Van Breda and Swilling, 2019). The approach needs to be locally contextualized and tailored to fit the specific reality-based problem and the situated conditions of the research endeavour (Polk, 2015a; Schneider and Buser, 2018). Doing this is methodologically challenging.

Terms like 'methods' or 'tools' are open to various interpretations, but generally apply to some sort of structured set of guidelines or activities that assist people in achieving a specific aim (Mingers and Brocklesby, 1997). Often, they are about doing or performing certain tasks and procedures in a particular manner for a particular purpose, reflecting assumptions about what is helpful or needed to develop the work. In research, an 'approach' or 'process' is a structured set of activities to assist people in undertaking research or interventions. Tools, methods or 'techniques' are specific activities that have a clear purpose within a specific approach (Mingers and Brocklesby, 1997). Alternatively, a 'method' can also refer to a unique process as it manifests, seeing there is some purposeful and discernible pattern in the decisions and actions that takes it forward (Jordan, 2014). This is evidenced, for example, in the methods undertaken by the facilitators of group processes on complex issues. In these situations, conditions vary from case to case, and methods have unfolded in response to the needs in the contexts and situations in which they have evolved (ibid.). Often, it is only in retrospect that their primary value can be discerned.

This book sets out the challenges and opportunities posed by transdisciplinary co-production, with practical examples of methods in action, underpinned by a reflexive approach to learning about limitations and opportunities (May and Perry, 2017). In Chapter 2, we identify some important considerations when undertaking transdisciplinary co-production as a research approach. We base this on our experiences of methodological and institutional challenges, what we have found necessary to enable transdisciplinary co-production to take place, and the current literature. Some of these experiences, and particularly those distinct for a specific urban context, are highlighted in text boxes. In Chapters 3-5, the main body of this book, we illustrate how transdisciplinary co-production can be operationalized through a selection of method descriptions. These descriptions have been crowdsourced from among the research projects enabled under the umbrella of Mistra Urban Futures – an international centre for sustainable urban development (see 'The contexts: Mistra Urban Futures – collaboration and co-production to realise just cities', below). Reflecting the Centre's ethos and commitment to transdisciplinary co-production, they have mainly been authored by people who themselves have been involved in the research process.

By sharing these examples, we offer readers ways to integrate transdisciplinary co-production in their work and inspire those interested in addressing urban challenges to find, develop, and playfully combine the collaborative methods that are suitable to a specific reality-based challenge. Many of the examples are not text-book methods but means of collaboration that have evolved during research practice to help participants navigate the challenges of transdisciplinary co-production. Since these are not complete case studies, we have been careful to give sufficient background information so that readers can better understand the conditions and circumstances under which each example was developed and applied. They have unfolded *from* and *within* different urban contexts and research conditions. No set of methods for transdisciplinary co-production can ever be universal or completely comprehensive. However, learning from and reflecting on the insights of others, starting from wherever you are and adapting the tools to fit your own particular situation, enables the development of suitable means that are tailored for each unique research situation (Midgley et al., 2017).

The contexts: Mistra Urban Futures – collaboration and co-production to realise just cities

Simon

> *Co-produced research, like the co-production of services, can sometimes also be transdisciplinary. Although this latter term is sometimes used synonymously with interdisciplinary to refer to the crossing of academic disciplines, here we adopt the more conventional current usage denoting the collaboration of academics and practitioner/practice-oriented researchers from different disciplines and/or backgrounds. ... As such, it involves a team made up of practitioners and academics, creating a fundamentally different epistemology of social science knowledge production from the conventional linear, positivist and expert-led model that still underpins most urban research worldwide* (Simon et al., 2018: 482).

Mistra Urban Futures was a unique international research centre from 2010 to 2019, working through formal city-based partnerships, so-called Local Interaction Platforms, between different combinations of academic, local authority, other public sector, civil society, and private sector organizations (see Appendix). Underpinning the Centre's idea of partnerships was the reciprocal exchange and generation of new knowledge among these stakeholder groups. Establishing such relations to enable transdisciplinary co-production – the Centre's hallmark methodological approach – required the creation of liaisons on several levels so that the work could pave the way for organizational change. The platforms became arenas for Mistra Urban Futures' approach to knowledge co-production at the interface between science and society in each city context.

By 2017, research partnerships ultimately comprised Gothenburg, Malmö–Lund (Skåne), and Stockholm in Sweden, Sheffield-Greater Manchester in the UK, Cape Town in South Africa and Kisumu in Kenya (see Figure 1.1). Teams in Buenos Aires in Argentina and Shimla in India (not shown in Figure 1.1) also participated in a comparative project. These cities are intentionally diverse on most criteria, which provided a valuable basis for testing the potential influences of location, size, urban form, climate and environment, socio-cultural factors, political context, and other variables. While the original four cities were all secondary or intermediate in their national urban systems, the addition of Stockholm and Buenos Aires introduced two capital cities which are also the largest in their respective countries. What motivated the teams in each to form or join Mistra Urban Futures was a shared realization that conventional approaches based around top-down expert knowledge were not working and had become increasingly discredited. The desire to find new ways of working that also promote urban justice and inclusion therefore united the city teams. Accordingly, Mistra Urban Futures created arenas where a diversity of different understandings and approaches to sustainable urban futures could meet and interact constructively and creatively.

As will become evident from the individual summaries in the Appendix, each platform or partnership was constituted differently according to local preferences and priorities. The motivations behind co-production in the respective cities stemmed from diverse combinations of political, practical, and academic considerations. Local needs, challenges, and governance structures influenced the approach to co-production formulated in each partnership. Sometimes, especially initially, existing methods were adopted but, more commonly, as reflected in this guide, such methods were adapted, or new ones developed for that specific context and purpose when no existing method met the requirements. Approaches differed according to the urban sector, activity, and range of stakeholders involved, the extent of shared or divergent perspectives and value systems needing to be accommodated, and the like. Sometimes there were North–South differences in such parameters but the Centre's approach to transdisciplinary co-production enabled simplistic binary divides to be transcended in the sharing and joint refinement of mutually appropriate methods to promote urban justice and social inclusion as essential prerequisites for sustainability (Perry et al., 2018; Simon et al., 2018, 2020).

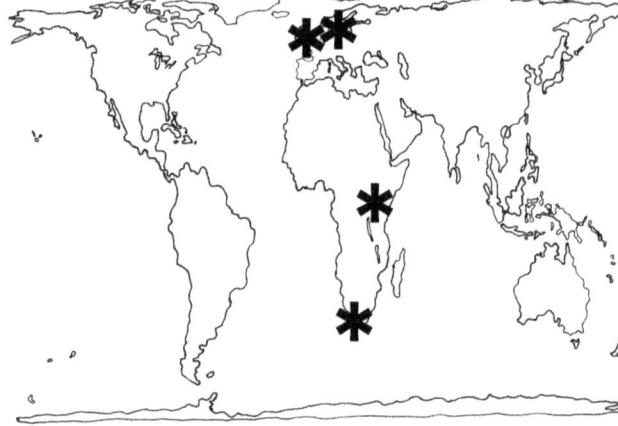

Figure 1.1
Locations of the main research arenas in Mistra Urban Futures: Gothenburg, Malmö–Lund, and Stockholm (Sweden), Sheffield–Greater Manchester (UK), Cape Town (South Africa), and Kisumu (Kenya). Throughout this book, a map icon will indicate to which city or cities the text relates.

References

Brown, V. A., Harris, J. A. and Russell, J.Y. (eds) (2010) *Tackling Wicked Problems: Through the Transdisciplinary Imagination*, Earthscan, New York.

Brugmann, J. (2009) *The Urban Revolution: How Cities are Changing the World*, Bloomsbury Press, London.

Clark, W. C., van Kerkhoff, L., Lebel, L. and Gallopin, G. C. (2016) 'Crafting usable knowledge for sustainable development', *Proceedings of the National Academy of Sciences* 113(1): 4570-8 <https://doi.org/10.1073/pnas.1601266113>.

Felt, U., Igelsböck, J., Schikowitz, A. and Völker, T. (2015) 'Transdisciplinary sustainability research in practice: between imaginaries of collective experimentation and entrenched academic value orders', *Science, Technology & Human Values* 14(4): 732-61 <https://doi.org/10.1177/0162243915626989>.

Hansson, S. and Polk, M. (2018) 'Assessing the impact of transdisciplinary research: the usefulness of relevance, credibility, and legitimacy for understanding the link between process and impact', *Research Evaluation* 27(2): 132-44 <https://doi.org/10.1093/reseval/rvy004>.

Jahn, T., Bergmann, M. and Keil, F. (2012) 'Transdisciplinarity: between mainstreaming and marginalization', *Ecological Economics* 79: 1-10 <https://doi.org/10.1016/j.ecolecon.2012.04.017>.

Jordan, T. (2014) 'Deliberative methods for complex issues: a typology of functions that may need scaffolding', *Group Facilitation: A Research and Applications Journal* 13: 50-71.

Kläy, A., Zimmermann, A. B. and Schneider, F. I. (2015) 'Rethinking science for sustainable development: reflexive interaction for a paradigm transformation', *Futures* 65: 72-85 <https://doi.org/10.1016/j.futures.2014.10.012>.

Lang, D. J., Wiek, A., Bergmann, M., Stauffacher, M., Martens, P., Moll, P., Swilling, M. and Thomas, C. J. (2012) 'Transdisciplinary research in sustainability science: practice, principles, and challenges', *Sustainability Science* 7(suppl. 1): 25-43 <https://doi.org/10.1007/s11625-011-0149-x>.

May, T. and Perry, B. (2016) 'Knowledge for just urban sustainability', *Local Environment: The International Journal of Justice and Sustainability* 22(suppl. 1): 23-35 <http://dx.doi.org/10.1080/13549839.2016.1233527>.

May, T. and Perry, B. (2017) *Reflexivity: The Essential Guide*, Sage, London.

May, T. and Perry, B. (2018) *Cities and the Knowledge Economy: Promise, Politics and Potentials*, Routledge, Oxford.

Midgley, G., Nicholson, J. D. and Brennan, R. (2017) 'Dealing with challenges to methodological pluralism: the paradigm problem, psychological resistance and cultural barriers', *Industrial Marketing Management* 62: 150-9 <https://doi.org/10.1016/j.indmarman.2016.08.008>.

Mingers, J. and Brocklesby, J. (1997) 'Multimethodology: towards a framework for mixing methodologies', *Omega* 25(5): 489-509 <https://doi.org/10.1016/S0305-0483(97)00018-2>.

Muñoz-Erickson, T. A., Miller, C. A. and Miller, T. R. (2017) 'How cities think: knowledge co-production for urban sustainability and resilience', *Forests* 8: 203 <https://doi.org/10.3390/f8060203>.

Owens, S. E. and Cowell, R. (2002) *Land and Limits: Interpreting Sustainability in the Planning Process*, Routledge, London.

Perry, B., Patel, Z., Bretzer, Y. N. and Polk, M. (2018) 'Organising for co-production: local interaction platforms for urban sustainability', *Politics and Governance* 6(1): 189-98 <https://doi.org/10.17645/pag.v6i1.1228>.

Petts, J., Owens, S. and Bulkeley, H. (2008) 'Crossing boundaries: interdisciplinarity in the context of urban environments', *Geoforum* 39: 583-601 <https://doi.org/10.1016/j.geoforum.2006.02.008>.

Polk, M. (2015a) 'Transdisciplinary co-production: designing and testing a transdisciplinary research framework for societal problem solving', *Futures* 65: 110-22 <https://doi.org/10.1016/j.futures.2014.11.001>.

Polk, M. (2015b) *Co-producing Knowledge for Sustainable Cities: Joining Forces for Change*, Routledge, New York.

Polk, M. (2016) 'How to manage complexity: co-producing knowledge for urban change', in H. Palmer and H. Walasek (eds), *Co-production in Action: Towards Realising Just Cities*, pp. 34-45, Mistra Urban Futures, Gothenburg.

Ramadier, T. (2004) 'Transdisciplinarity and its challenges: the case of urban studies', *Futures* 36: 423-39 <https://doi.org/10.1016/j.futures.2003.10.009>.

Rittel, H.W.J. and Webber, M.M. (1973) 'Dilemmas in general theory of planning', *Policy Sciences* 4(2): 155-69 <https://doi.org/10.1007/BF01405730>.

Robinson, J. (2004) 'Squaring the circle? Some thoughts on the idea of sustainable development', *Ecological Economics* 48: 369-84 <https://doi.org/10.1016/j.ecolecon.2003.10.017>.

Schneider, F. and Buser, T. (2018) 'Promising degrees of stakeholder interaction in research for sustainable development', *Sustainability Science* 13: 129-42 <https://doi.org/10.1007/s11625-017-0507-4>.

Schuttenberg, H. Z. and Guth, H.K. (2015) 'Seeking our shared wisdom: a framework for understanding knowledge coproduction and coproductive capacities', *Ecology and Society* 20(1): 15 <http://dx.doi.org/10.5751/ES-07038-200115>.

Simon, D. (ed.) (2016) *Rethinking Sustainable Cities: Accessible, Green and Fair*, Policy Press, Bristol.

Simon, D., Palmer, H., Smit, W., Riise, J. and Valencia, S. (2018) 'The challenges of transdisciplinary co-production: from unilocal to comparative research', *Environment and Urbanization* 30(2): 481-500 <http://dx.doi.org/10.1177/0956247818787177>.

Simon, D., Palmer, H. and Riise, J. (2020) 'Assessment: learning between theory and practice', in D. Simon, H. Palmer, and J. Riise (eds), *Comparative Urban Research from Theory to Practice: Co-production for Sustainability*, pp. 155-172, Policy Press, Bristol.

Van Breda, J. and Swilling, M. (2019) 'The guiding logics and principles for designing emergent transdisciplinary research processes: learning experiences and reflections from a transdisciplinary urban case study in Enkanini informal settlement, South Africa', *Sustainability Science* 14(3): 823-41 <https://doi.org/10.1007/s11625-018-0606-x>.

Van der Hel, S. (2016) 'New science for global sustainability? The institutionalisation of knowledge co-production in Future Earth', *Environmental Science & Policy* 61: 165-75 <https://doi.org/10.1016/j.envsci.2016.03.012>.

Wuelser, G., Pohl, C. and Hirsch Hadorn, G. (2012) 'Structuring complexity for tailoring research contributions to sustainable development: a framework', *Sustainability Science* 7: 81-93 <https://doi.org/10.1007/s11625-011-0143-3>.

CHAPTER 2
Methods for what? The strengths and limitations of transdisciplinary knowledge co-production

keywords
facilitating transdisciplinary co-production, active intermediation, reflexivity, knowledge integration, boundary space

Putting transdisciplinary co-production into practice involves different types of challenges. In this chapter, we elaborate on the general process of transdisciplinary co-production and on the considerations involved when initiating and designing this type of collaboration. We outline the importance of practising reflexivity and what leading, participating in, and administering transdisciplinary co-production research involves for participants and their organizations. Finally, we discuss the meaning of a co-productive 'boundary space'. The discussions presented here provide essential background reading to the issues which inform the application of different methods and processes detailed in Part 2, Chapters 3–5.

Kerstin Hemström and Merritt Polk

HISTORICALLY, 'KNOWLEDGE PRODUCTION' has been seen as a task for scientific institutions, commonly ordered by scientific disciplines. The traditional relationship between science and society has been one where society uses science to provide practical solutions to problems. Science, in turn, uses societal problems to pursue its own disciplinary development (Jahn et al., 2012). Academic perspectives typically dominated traditional processes of generating new knowledge for society, where scientists developed 'objective' knowledge for practitioners to apply and implement in practice.

In contrast, transdisciplinary co-production aims for an open knowledge-production process, where traditional types of linear knowledge production are replaced by co-owned, co-led, and co-produced processes that are based on continual and in-depth collaboration between different actors (see Box 2.1 for a conceptual overview). As noted in the Introduction, the core idea is to expand the process of generating new knowledge and addressing real-world problems by including a variety of types of knowledge and expertise in the process. Here, academic know-how is but one perspective among others.

Typically, such collaborative processes are described as proceeding through three successive phases, each posing different tasks and situations for leaders and participants (Figure 2.1). In the first, different stakeholders come together around a real-world challenge to jointly formulate and frame the problem and research questions. Following this, the problem is analysed, and relevant knowledges are integrated to reach new and more comprehensive knowledge in relation to the problem. In the third and final phase, the results are evaluated in terms of their relevance and impact in relation to both the problem being addressed and the different fields of science and practice (Bergmann et al., 2005; Pohl and Hirsch Hadorn, 2008; Krütli et al., 2010; Jahn et al., 2012; Lang et al., 2012).

These phases are usually revisited in an iterative manner. The team typically engages in several stages of deliberation, mutual learning, and intentional reflection, in which different perspectives and ways of knowing intersect and become relevant to one another in a process that emerges and develops over time. The participants inform each other regarding the problem in focus, and ways to address it. They thereby increase their understandings of both their own positions and those of others, as the team matures, builds trust, and builds a joint knowledge base. Some of these situations may call for lower intensities of interaction between the participants than others. The required nature and degree of interaction depends on, for example, the diversity of and difference between involved actors and their interests, their history of collaboration, the level of contestation around the issues addressed, and the intended contributions of the research endeavour (Stauffacher et al., 2008; Steelman et al., 2015; Schneider and Buser, 2018). In other words, the approach allows continual re-contextualization of both practical and scientific contexts throughout the entire knowledge-production and problem-solving process.

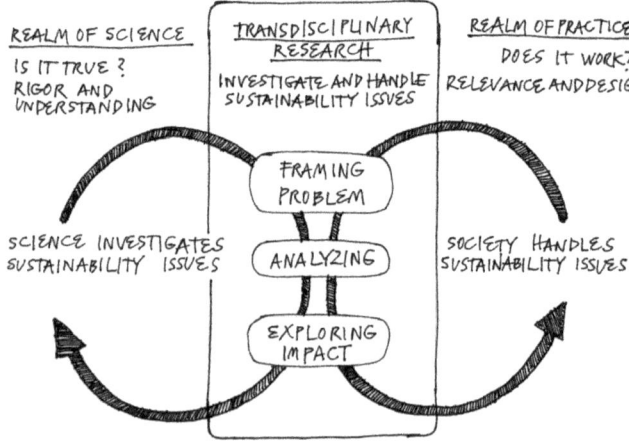

Figure 2.1
A schematic image of a transdisciplinary co-production process, used in Pohl et al., 2017. (Based on Bergmann et al., 2005; Pohl and Hirsch Hadorn, 2008; Krütli et al., 2010; Jahn et al., 2012)

Although this image of a transdisciplinary co-production process is an attempt to generalize and capture the global essence of the approach, some critics suggest that it implicitly assumes the existence of certain social and material conditions, including formal or legitimized stakeholders or actors who can engage with academic experts on an equal footing. They argue that this research has emerged largely in the global North, under very different social and material conditions from those prevalent in many urban environments in the global South (Steelman et al., 2015; Van Breda and Swilling, 2019). For example, in some urban areas of the South, there are limited formal leadership and authorities to engage with. Instead, acknowledging and working with informal social actors and networks is fundamental to developing context-relevant solutions. To that end, critics question whether the current literature on the approach has sufficiently generated a set of guiding logics and principles that are relevant in diverse contexts (Steelman et al., 2015; Van Breda and Swilling, 2019).

Clearly, the prospects for stakeholder participation in research activities and the circumstances under which different groups can collaborate are shaped by circumstances such as pre-existing power relations and hierarchies, and their specific democratic, demographic, and political conditions. The composition and nature of these circumstances can vary widely between different urban contexts. Pivotal questions therefore remain regarding the extent to which this simplified model of transdisciplinary co-production, free from the detailed complexities of reality, is valid in all settings (Scholz and Steiner, 2015; Steelman et al., 2015). Nonetheless, and as exemplified throughout this book, many co-production processes have evolved precisely because of informality and limited opportunities for formal engagement with the problem. Through these processes, poor urban communities have been able to secure significant improvements to their living environments under conditions where there have been no other ways of addressing the problems effectively (Watson, 2014). As such, highly uncertain and intricate urban settings can also make up perfect examples of why transdisciplinary co-production is needed.

Box 2.1 The meaning of co-production

Co-production is a term that has a long history of use within both academic and practice-based settings. There are two main categorizations that are often made regarding its use, and a variety of sub-categories and uses (Bremer and Meisch, 2017). Here we will outline the two main uses that are most relevant for the work with transdisciplinary co-production highlighted in this book.

The first categorization includes co-production being used to describe different types of collaboration between diverse groups to attain a specific goal such as service provision or knowledge production. This is called *the normative use* because it focuses on co-production being used to achieve normative goals. The second use includes co-production being used to describe the relationships between science, society, and nature. This is called *the descriptive use* because it focuses on using co-production as a way to understand, describe, and analyse how science, society, and nature are mutually constituted (Jasanoff, 2004).

The normative use of the term focuses on different types of collaboration for societal problem solving for example in concrete applications for service provision initiated by citizen groups or governmental agencies (Mitlin, 2008; Watson, 2014). The normative use also includes participatory approaches to solving societal problems such as action research, participatory rural appraisal, transdisciplinary research, sustainability science, and other types of participatory social science (Lang et al., 2012; Wiek et al., 2014).

It is important to note that different actor groups are included in these different approaches. Some focus on co-production within and between citizen organizations and governmental agencies, and others on co-production between researchers/universities and practice-based actors and organizations from citizen groups, administration, and business. The goals of the collaboration also vary greatly, from concrete applications for service provision, empowerment, and learning, to a more cognitive focus on jointly co-designing and co-creating different forms of knowledge that can be used in different policy and scientific settings and contexts. The descriptive use of co-production focuses on interpreting and describing how our understandings of science, society, and nature are co-produced through the interactions of science with different cultural and social practices (Nowotny et al., 2001; Jasanoff, 2004). This approach sees the creation of scientific knowledge about different natural and societal states and processes as inseparable from those processes themselves. While this is an important foundation for how nature-society relationships can be understood, the dominant use of co-production in the work compiled in this guide is its use for achieving different societal goals, the normative one. We therefore use 'co-production' as the umbrella term throughout the book, although you will find some authors referring to the process as *co-creation*.

On initiating and designing collaboration and knowledge exchange

A key purpose of transdisciplinary co-production research is forming a team of both academic researchers and other societal actors who can work effectively together and engage in mutual learning to integrate the best available knowledge in response to a real-world problem (Pohl and Hirsch Hadorn, 2008; Lang et al., 2012). This process of eliciting, searching, selecting, and engaging relevant perspectives to jointly set up goals and criteria in relation to a real-world problem is commonly referred to as 'problem framing' (Pearce and Ejderyan, 2019). In theory, everyone who has something to say about a real-world problem and is willing to participate can play a role.

Keeping real-life change in focus, it is important to include as many viewpoints and types of expertise as possible right from the beginning, to allow the problem to be identified in its complexity (Herrero et al., 2019). The initial trimming of the content and scope of the research process sets the stage for how the problem is framed, whose knowledge matters, and what is important to include or consider in addressing it. No research can, however, include everything or everyone who might possibly be relevant. In practice, the recruiting of participants and extent to which they can be involved is often limited by practical constraints such as time frames, budget, availability of personnel, specifications by funders, ethical or political considerations, or contextual conditions such as the geographical distance between potential team members. To avoid loss of interest and drop-outs later in the research process, it is important to find a manageable level and scale of participation that can be maintained throughout (Lang et al., 2012; Perry and Russell, 2020). Box 2.2 offers some overall guidance on considerations relevant to this process.

Box 2.2   Considerations on whom to involve in the process

Regardless of the practical constraints, there are clear benefits to setting transparent criteria and clear rationalizations regarding the relationships between the real-world problem being addressed and who is involved in the transdisciplinary co-production process. By doing so, earlier decisions can be reviewed and altered when needed. Ideally, the recruiting of participants should be based on considerations of the broader context of the problem and what actors, perspectives, values, and decision-making it involves. These include reflections on the significance of one's own as well as others' views of the problem, and on whose interests should be served, what sources of power need to be included, what should count as relevant knowledge, and what should the consequences of the research be (Bammer, 2008; Herrero et al., 2019). At an early stage, however, the initiators of the research may only have a vague idea of who needs to be engaged to address the problem at hand, and it may be difficult to shake off preconceived ideas about the relevance of different expertise, or about who can affect or may be affected by the problem under study. Even with carefully designed standards for selecting team members, changes to the context of the research or in individual situations and work conditions, or new insights reached through the research process may change the roles and responsibilities of participants, result in reduced inputs or drop-outs, or justify engaging additional participants (Lang et al., 2012; Norris et al., 2016).

Based on Ulrich (2005), Bammer (2008) highlights four areas to consider when thinking about whom to involve in the collaboration (Figure 2.2). These areas are coupled with key questions to help set boundaries:

1. The motivation for the collaboration: Whose interests are and ought to be served, what should the consequences of the research process be, and how should success be measured?
2. The sources of power in the collaboration: Who can or should decide, and what conditions need or need not be in place for decision-makers?
3. The sources of knowledge for the collaboration: What should count as relevant knowledge and what should be its role, who should be involved, who or what needs to be involved to guarantee real-life change?
4. The sources of legitimation for the collaboration: Who should argue for those who are affected by the research but cannot speak for themselves, and how are those treated and related to in the research (Ulrich, 2005; Bammer, 2008)?

Figure 2.2
Four areas of consideration when setting boundaries for whom to involve in the transdisciplinary co-production process. (Based on Ulrich, 2005; and Bammer, 2008)

Given the role of the participants in co-production processes, it is important that decisions are, as much as possible, made explicitly and openly so that the sense of shared ownership and enthusiasm for continuing the process are maximized (Polk, 2015). Our experience in diverse settings shows that this helps to reduce subsequent losses of motivation and withdrawals.

In co-production processes there are no predefined rules for who should take on what role or task. Rather, once a team has been set up, it is important to allocate time to explore the problem and potential research questions together. The project group together needs to clarify the key assumptions and prerequisites of the different participants as well as discuss and define the purpose and rules of the collaboration. This includes exploring power relations and potential power asymmetries or conflicts among members of the team and clarifying the roles and responsibilities of participants. Doing so is often fundamental to sustaining engagement in the research process, building trust among team members, and developing broader understandings of, and responses to, the problem in focus (Lang et al., 2012; Klenk and Meehan, 2015; Schuttenberg and Guth, 2015; Herrero et al., 2019). There is a general need to make more visible the 'hidden politics' of co-production (Flinders et al., 2016) and its potential risks, costs, and limits. The literature around these processes often focuses on the positives of greater inclusion, without adequate consideration of the challenges that can arise (Oliver et al., 2019).

While transparency is important throughout the research process, it is imperative at an early stage, so that everyone involved feels that the process mirrors their concerns and needs (Lang et al., 2012). Collaboration tends to benefit from recognizing the heterogeneity and clarifying key differences between the individuals involved (Lang et al., 2012; Lux et al., 2019). The description in Box 2.3 exemplifies how this played out in a research project in Cape Town. This concerns not only the obvious differences that motivated the collaboration in the first place, for example, between academic researchers and other societal actors, but also those that are incidental to the collaboration. For example, each team member not only brings their own perspective on the issue addressed and the collaborative process, and what it needs to involve. They also bring their individual skills, experiences, professional identities, ways of working, forms of expression, worldviews, interests, motivations, and personalities. Recognizing these differences from the beginning of the process can prevent them from causing unnecessary tensions and frustration and interfering with the commitment to and effectiveness of the collaboration (Bammer 2008; Palmer and Walasek, 2016; Thompson et al., 2017; Herrero et al., 2019).

Generally, effective interaction rests on having enough time and willingness to understand, communicate, and contribute to a process. The ideal research process is often described as one that creates an oasis where all participants are given an equal voice, and where trust, creativity, and understanding can develop despite power imbalances in the broader social context (e.g. Schuttenberg and Guth, 2015). However, building participants' trust and commitment to the collaboration and gaining access to their knowledge is highly challenging and often takes considerable time. Finding the means to do so is always an exploratory, experimental, and emergent process. The outcome of different decisions and of the knowledge process can never be fully predicted. Ultimately, the specific nature and methods of the collaboration need to be flexible enough to be continually tailored to fit the problem focus and context conditions, as well as the individuals involved.

Box 2.3   The necessity of clarifying assumptions: mapping rationalities of key stakeholders in the Urban Flooding CityLab

Warren Smit

In the Urban Flooding CityLab in Cape Town (see Chapter 3, 'The CityLab programme in Cape Town'), dealing with the conflicting rationalities of the participants was a major challenge, but also an opportunity for integrating different perspectives and different types of knowledge. The Lab brought together different stakeholders to share insights and undertake collaborative research on the flooding of informal settlements in Cape Town. The focus of the research was on interviewing key stakeholders involved in the governance of urban flooding in order to identify their rationalities with regards to the causes of, and possible solutions to flooding, and the technologies and resources they mobilized. Drawing on the work of Michel Foucault (1997), rationalities can be described as the socially and contextually shaped ways in which people see, interpret, and act in the world. The mapping of different rationalities, through interviews and analysis of documentation, showed that the officials of different local government departments had very different understandings of the nature of the problem and the solutions, which were closely aligned to the disciplinary backgrounds of the officials in each department.

The officials of the Disaster Risk Management Centre (DRMC), who came from a disaster risk science background, largely viewed the city in terms of hazards and risks posed to residents, infrastructures, and service delivery by natural phenomena or human activities. With their disaster risk reduction lens on the flooding issue, DRMC staff identified the source of the problem as simultaneously one of people living in unsuitable locations and of excessive rainfall and high water levels. In practice, the focus of DRMC officials was on disaster risk relief. Roads and Storm Water officials were from a civil engineering background and saw the problem of flooding as essentially too much water in certain places, which needed to be disposed of through better storm water drains (and better maintenance of storm water drains). Informal Settlements Management officials, who were mainly housing practitioners, saw flooding of informal settlements in Cape Town as mainly a problem of people being in the wrong place rather than as a problem of excess water; this is because the flooding problems they have to deal with are generally caused by people occupying low-lying, poorly drained areas that are not (in their present state) suitable for residential use. They thus saw the issue as a socio-political problem, with the solution as relocation and/or informal settlement upgrading.

These different rationalities can potentially be an obstacle to collaboration, but through mapping these different perspectives and through bringing together different stakeholders to integrate the different perspectives into a more holistic understanding of the flooding of informal settlements, it was possible to identify synergies and opportunities for collaboration and co-ordination. This was done through a series of workshops that brought together different stakeholders (mainly various government departments and various civil society groups) and allowed space for presentations from participants and for one-on-one networking. The approach was also institutionalized through working with the City of Cape Town's Task team, a structure on which all the local departments involved with flooding were represented.

Suggested readings

Shearing, C. and Wood, J. (2003) 'Nodal governance, democracy, and the new "denizens"', *Journal of Law and Society* 30(3): 400-19 <http://dx.doi.org/10.2307/1410537>.

Ziervogel, G., Waddell, J., Smit, W. and Taylor, A. (2016) 'Flooding in Cape Town's informal settlements: barriers to collaborative urban risk governance', *South African Geographical Journal* 98(1): 1-20 <http://dx.doi.org/10.1080/03736245.2014.924867>.

Enabling and safeguarding a joint knowledge process

Perry
Tim May

Given that transdisciplinary co-production differs from traditional research processes, specific dynamics and issues emerge. Joint knowledge processes represent a coming together of different institutional and cultural settings and raise new challenges and opportunities. Despite the emphasis on knowledge co-production, there is still little consensus on what it means, why it is undertaken or how to undertake it (Oliver et al., 2019). Successful transdisciplinary co-production will not 'occur spontaneously simply because substantial benefits could be achieved' (Ostrom, 1996: 1082).

The ethics and emotional labour of transdisciplinary co-production

A critical issue is the 'hidden politics' of co-production (Flinders et al., 2016: 261). Universities remain powerful actors at the centre of efforts to support and innovate in transdisciplinary approaches. This endows academics with power and privilege in often unacknowledged ways. The need to navigate, negotiate, and manage across boundaries in collaborative work leads to a number of specific challenges for researchers. It is important here to distinguish between ethics and morality. Where morals are personal standards and beliefs that enable individuals to differentiate between what they see as 'right' or 'wrong', ethics refers to the systematized codes and standards defined by specific groups.

Standard ethical processes undertaken within universities can be unsuited to dealing with deep, collaborative research. Traditional assumptions do not always hold: instead of privacy, the emphasis is on publicness, disclosure, and intimacy; instead of informed consent, researchers need to plan for the unknown; instead of discrete and planned periods of data collection, everything is potentially data; instead of avoiding harm, the emphasis is on doing good.

Institutional ethical standards presume a distance between subject and object, researcher and researched that does not reflect the realities of collaborative work (Kesby, 2007). Ethical dilemmas are plentiful: to what extent can anonymity be guaranteed in projects where partners' identities are publicly known? What are the limits and boundaries of confidentiality, when researchers may have unprecedented and privileged access to the inner workings of partner organizations? What are the implications of university rules on data protection and intellectual property, in projects where knowledge produced collectively should properly be a common good? As transdisciplinary co-production depends on personal relationships of trust and reciprocity, there is increased possibility for individual and institutional standards to conflict over the appropriate moral or ethical approach.

These conflicts require additional emotional labour in transdisciplinary co-production. UK researchers in Mistra Urban Futures held a workshop with early career researchers in December 2018 to reflect on these issues (see May et al., 2019). A key theme was the crisis of identity that transdisciplinary researchers may experience in belonging both within and outside the university. This crisis is exacerbated where institutional incentives and reward structures continue to value traditional work over more collaborative forms of research. Funders of the Mistra Urban Futures centre placed equal emphasis on academic writing and outputs for diverse audiences; however, when this balance is not reflected in researchers' home institutions, a clash of expectations can occur. This leads many to question whether co-produced research is 'good' for careers in a context where academic publication in peer-reviewed journals continues to be the hallmark of success, apart from specific innovative funding programmes, which remain rare.

Existential doubt arises when there are irreconcilable tensions between how we judge ourselves and how we are judged by others. Researchers undertaking this kind of work are motivated by being useful, making a difference or the quality and longevity of relationships, for instance. Rather than detached 'experts', researchers are positioned deeply within research contexts, often working on behalf of their partners rather than seeking to further their own agendas. This immersion in the contexts and lives of research partners blurs the boundaries between personal and professional identities and requires constant attentiveness and an increased ethics of care. This is especially the case when working with vulnerable or marginalized groups. At the same time, researchers need to manage competing pressures, with differential amounts of time, capacity, and positions to commit to long-term partnerships. The example of PhD collaborations in Dunga Beach highlights that the impact of the institutional power of the university can even be exacerbated in international collaborations, where Swedish researchers had greater antecedent power to shape relations than local Kenyan researchers (see Box 2.4).

Many of these concerns are not new to the process and practice of research. However, transdisciplinary co-production exacerbates and heightens such issues. A case in point relates to the concern around co-optation. Power is manifest not only within and by the university but by privileged research partners who may mobilize their position to undermine access for others to research processes. Researchers need to be aware of how others, such as elite decision-makers, may be 'gaming' processes of transdisciplinary co-production, creating path dependencies that reinforce their access to resources.

Confronting the privilege and politics of transdisciplinary research is a daily task for many researchers undertaking this kind of work while simultaneously working across multiple boundaries. Although not unique, the risk is that the high levels of resulting emotional labour will lead to burn out, particularly in the context of concerns over precarity for contract research staff (Gill and Pratt, 2008). Transdisciplinary co-production can leave researchers feeling vulnerable and exposed, adrift or homeless. Yet many argue that if researchers don't feel uncomfortable, they aren't doing it right (Cribbin, 2019)! It is only by challenging ourselves, through and with others, that we can truly co-produce. At the same time, it is important to recognize not only emotional labour, but also emotional payback: from personal satisfaction, feelings of joy and privilege, and a sense of usefulness that comes from positioning oneself clearly as part of ongoing processes of social change.

Box 2.4 Challenges of transdisciplinary collaboration: co-production between PhD students and community members in an urban fishing village

Helena Kraff and Eva Maria Jernsand with Franklin Otiende and Patrick Hayombe

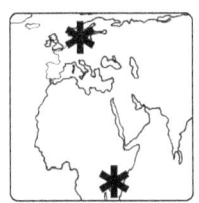

In the Dunga fishing village on the outskirts of Kisumu, Kenya, a team of four Kenyan and Swedish doctoral students undertook transdisciplinary action research to develop the benefits of small-scale ecotourism in the area. The main collaborating actors were a group of local tour guides. There were also collaborations with a local NGO, the local beach management unit, and residents in the community.

To improve local livelihoods, the tour guides wanted the village to become a more attractive and sustainable ecotourism destination. The main problems addressed concerned the low ranked position of local guides in relation to larger private tour operators and a low diversity of tourism offerings. Accordingly, female community members and a specific group of women were highly affected by the tourism business taking place in their village but over which they had little power or influence.

The aim of the project was twofold:

- to produce practical and directly implementable results in the local context; and
- to produce academic outputs in the form of co-produced publications on inclusive tourism and action-based research methodologies.

The practical implementation, as part of the design-based research approach, included development of guided tours; infrastructural improvements regarding waste collection and signage; the design and execution of a cultural day; initiation of a county-wide association aiming to strengthen the position of local guides; and initiation of a female guide group, breaking into the male-dominated profession of tour guiding.

Methods and tools
The methods and tools used during the project were inspired by participatory design and service design practices, as well as by methods found in participatory rural appraisal projects. Characteristic of these is that they rely heavily on visualizations (e.g. sketches, drawings, photos) and tangible prototyping (e.g. small-scale models) (see Photo 2.1). These make participation easier in projects where there are language barriers, as well as aiding idea generation in group work. These methods were mixed with more business and management-oriented methods aiming to develop the tour guiding business, adapted to the specific situation and local context throughout.

The main knowledge co-production emerged between the PhD students and members of the guide group, as well as between the PhD students of different disciplinary origin. As a result of collaborative evaluation and refinement, the guided tours, for instance, expanded to include more storytelling and the cooking of food. The guides, having participated in several workshops, strengthened their confidence and skills in using visual tools and took on the responsibility to lead workshops in the later stages of the project. They were further asked by other tour guide groups to come and teach them how to develop their own sites. This was noteworthy since it indicated that other tour guides perceived value in the co-produced activities at the beach.

An important factor was the long duration of the process, which led to deeper collaborations and possibilities to plan subsequent steps together. A mutual trust developed through working as partners with the guides. A communicative approach with open presentations, sharing of work, discussions, written reports, an available project space, and social media communication also contributed to knowledge co-production.

Challenges
While there were various positive outputs from the knowledge co-production and practical implementation of solutions, several challenges also emerged. Many of these were connected to the North–South collaboration and the power relations and inequalities between actors that this led to.

The different university systems created unjust preconditions between the PhD students, leaving the Swedish students in a more beneficial situation, having more time to write their theses than their Kenyan colleagues, who constantly had to chase time. There was also unequal access to knowledge resources between the researchers and the community actors, which can become highly problematic in projects where the aim is to produce knowledge together.

The claims for community empowerment frequently made in participatory projects provided a challenge because of diversity within the Dunga community. The participants often belonged to already strong groups within the community, while marginalized groups found it difficult to take part or to express themselves adequately if they did join in. The project group addressed this by reflecting critically on people's different possibilities to participate, taking into consideration aspects such as time, language, and place.

Takeaways from the experienced co-production

- A transdisciplinary and action-oriented approach served as an example of how it is possible to combine research and development practice.
- The use of multiple and visual methods and tools gave opportunities to involve a broad set of stakeholders.
- Other development projects and disciplinary constellations could make use of this approach.
- The identified challenges can help others engaged in participatory forms of research to pinpoint issues of power and inequalities between actors. This includes for example discussions on how to build collaborative and respectful environments between academia and practice and exploring power and inequalities within transdisciplinary co-production.

Photo 2.1 Workshop with local tour guides, consisting of co-creative activities for developing a guided tour. The workshop method is inspired by service design methods such as a desktop walkthrough, in which a visual overview of, for example, a service is created. (Photos by Eva Maria Jernsand)

Suggested readings

Jernsand, E.M. (2016) *Inclusive Place Branding: What it is and How to Progress Towards it* [online], PhD dissertation, University of Gothenburg <https://gupea.ub.gu.se/handle/2077/49535> [accessed 15 July 2020].

Jernsand, E.M. and Kraff, H. (2015) 'Participatory place branding through design: the case of Dunga beach in Kisumu, Kenya', *Place Branding and Public Diplomacy* 11(3): 226–42 <https://doi.org/10.1057/pb.2014.34>.

Kraff, H. (2018) *Exploring Pitfalls of Participation and Ways Towards Just Practices Through a Participatory Design Process in Kisumu, Kenya*, PhD dissertation, University of Gothenburg, ArtMonitor 66 <https://gupea.ub.gu.se/handle/2077/56078> [accessed 15 July 2020].

Crossing boundaries with a reflexive practice

Beth Perry and Tim May

Transdisciplinary co-production requires crossing disciplines, sectors, organizations, and social and personal worlds, and this has to be underpinned by a reflexive practice. Reflexivity means analysing and understanding the conditions and processes through which knowledge is produced. This requires reflecting critically on the tools with which we work and the pre-understandings we bring to research. While we would argue that reflexivity is necessary for any research practice, it is particularly so for collaborative research. Others have noted the key role of reflexive practice in negotiating the 'swampy lowlands' of research (Schön, 1983). Researchers need to be clear about their own positionality and standpoint as a precondition for engaging with others (Hartsock, 1987). In working across boundaries, a constant questioning of what we take for granted is needed in order to be sensitive to the challenges that emerge.

Reflexivity is different from reflection. Whereas the latter involves looking back on past experiences in order to capture learning, the former constitutes a process of meta-learning – reflection not only *in* but *on* action. Reflection entails 'in-the-moment reflective episodes', whereas reflexivity is 'a conscious cognitive process whereby knowledge and theory are applied to make sense of remembered reflective episodes' (Dallos and Stedmon, 2009: 4).

Reflexivity is centred in the production, justification, and application of social scientific knowledge in contemporary societies. Reflexivity allows a process of deepening awareness of the production of valid and reliable data, strengthening a commitment to the value of this awareness and generating a willingness to be open to 'hostile information' (Gouldner, 1971: 494). This means paying attention to the dimensions of *endogenous and referential reflexivity* and their dynamic interaction in shaping social scientific practice in an era of ambivalence and risk (see Box 2.5).

Box 2.5 Different types of reflexivity

Tim May and Beth Perry

When we think about the need for reflexivity, we usually rely on specific disciplinary or cultural norms as the basis for understanding the limits to our ways of knowledge and modes of investigation. Specific expectations, often latent and unarticulated, are made up of the practices and forms of knowledge that are deployed in particular fields of endeavour.

Endogenous reflexive practice refers to how we practise within our own social and cultural milieus, including academic disciplines, crafts, and professional settings as a whole.

Referential reflexivity, on the other hand, is required when we work outside or across these boundaries. When transdisciplinary researchers work across cultures of knowledge production and reception, a different form of reflexive practice is required that includes consideration of different epistemological assumptions generated by the meeting of two or more types of knowledge.

This means reflecting on how both our own assumptions and limits and those of others impact on the production of social scientific knowledge. The cultures in which people work shape the 'multiple reflexivities' they exhibit (see Lynch, 2000; Mruck and Mey, 2007).

Increasingly scholars are calling for 'inter-relational reflexivity' (Gilbert and Sliep, 2009: 468) which includes 'a concern for moral agency and the negotiation of accountability and responsibility for action, as social action requires a joint deconstruction of power in the voices and relationships operating between the stakeholders within a performative space'. The relational approach highlights the need for regular reflexive dialogues as part of the research process to facilitate new possible realities and relations (Hosking and Pluut, 2010: 59).

Methods that help
There is no such thing as a method for reflexivity. The issue is whether existing methods are or are not deployed reflexively. This is an essential point: no method can be a guarantee of reflexivity – it is not what method you choose but how you to choose to approach it.

Writing is a common approach to aid reflexivity in the research process, whether in diaries, letters, essays or working with transcripts. For Diane Watt (2007), writing notes iteratively throughout the research process is one approach which allows researchers to discover things they did not know were there. For others reflexivity infuses the research process only when researchers explicitly 'think differently' in rejecting the categories/language that is available. In all cases, the danger is that such writings turn too far into confessional, indulgent or 'narcissistic' endeavours (Patai, 1994; Denzin, 1997).

Many authors have sought to add nuance to the different ways in which reflexivity can be applied to the processes of research. Denzin (1997) identifies five different types of reflexivity: methodological, intertextual, standpoint, queer, and feminist. Ryan (2005) focuses on dimensions of reflexivity which are focused on introspection, deconstructing praxis, considering presuppositions, theories and methods, and beliefs and assumptions. Finlay (2002) offers 'maps' for five variants of reflexivity: introspection, intersubjective reflection, mutual collaboration, social critique, and discursive deconstruction. At the same time, processes of reflexivity should also lead to self-change and be transformative at the level of the individual. Within such distinctions is the idea that it is not even possible to be reflexive during a study, as such perspective and distance can only be born over time rather than in the immediate context of the field.

There are multiple choices – what matters for those involved in transdisciplinary co-production is how the reflexive application of methods and tools can lead to more honest and mature practices.

Key messages
By being 'vigilant about our practices' (Spivak, 1985: 184) we can produce better research. Reflexivity is also about knowing limits and practising modesty – it is not placing the individual at the centre as being all knowing. The emphasis is upon changing practice and not just paying lip service to reflexivity to justify our actions. It is not easy and requires the development of supportive cultures of inquiry where we find a willingness to learn, assist others, and understand limits and potentials. Some of our own experiences provide ample opportunity to remain sceptical as to the success of such a strategy. However, we maintain an aspiration to contribute to the possibility of knowledge with transformative outcomes that improves collective capacities to create more just and sustainable futures.

Suggested reading

May, T. and Perry, B.
(2017) *Reflexivity: The Essential Guide*, Sage, London.

Active intermediation

Perry im May

Working across boundaries requires a vigilant practice. Even where entry has been negotiated and codified in formal partnership agreements or memoranda of understanding, the waters of collaborative research are muddy. Research is rarely linear and requires constant boundary work in managing expectations. Working across boundaries does not mean that they no longer exist or are relevant; on the contrary, the practice of the deeper forms of collaborative research, such as co-production, require boundary maintenance and even reinforcement in order to ensure that muddy waters don't descend into stagnant swamps.

Co-productive research is characterized by active management of these boundaries. It is also characterized by the need for compromise and making-do in changing and variable research settings. As more participatory forms of collaborative research means leaving decisions and resources on the table, to be determined collectively by those involved, so participants need to develop the ability to be highly flexible, adaptive, and creative in contrast with the usual delivery of pre-planned research tasks.

These practices can be time-consuming and are layered on top, not instead of, traditional elements of the research process. They can be characterized by variable levels of tension and the need for conflict resolution and expectation management, depending on the interactions between culture, time, space, and politics. Boundary work requires understanding and working with the grain of different institutional cultures characterized by different processes, organizations, and practices of undertaking research. These can vary strongly even within academic institutions, for instance, between a traditional department and an inter-disciplinary or geographically defined cluster, section or centre. Culture varies internationally as the setting for collaborative research is shaped and constrained by different national political economies of research and systems of higher education.

The cultures and organizations of knowledge production have often been criticized as not 'fit for purpose' in meeting the increasing demands of societal and economic relevance, leading to a one-sided deficit model which pushes universities to adapt to external circumstances. However, cultures of knowledge reception are equally significant in shaping the context for collaborative research. Numerous studies have pointed to the value of collaborative research for the individuals involved, but a larger challenge is embedding learning within wider organizational settings and forms of classification.

Time is an additional feature. Universities have often been characterized as out-of-sync or too far behind the decision frames of policymaking and implementation to be relevant. Academic researchers and practitioners alike are increasingly urged to 'speed up' in order to keep pace. Time, or the lack of it, is often cited as the key issue in different forms of collaborative research impacting on the type, scale, and quality of interactions. Yet time and a preparedness to learn, rather than repeat mistakes of the past, are also key ingredients. Co-production is seen as a particularly time-consuming process, as the standards of participation to which such approaches aspire lead to lengthy decision-making and set up periods. Expectations that co-production is a quick fix, or way of securing cheap or even free academic consultancy, need to be managed carefully in terms of when and how specific impacts may be seen.

Paradoxically, while researchers are often encouraged to accelerate to keep pace with the supposed demands and needs of society, the value of collaborative research is often said to lie in the space it provides for those involved to think differently and reflect on their practice. This slowing down is precisely one of the reasons why deep collaborative practices tend to take a long time. Boundary work is needed to ensure that such spaces are conducive to all involved. This does not mean managing out, but managing with, conflicts that will inevitably arise in the negotiation of interests in collaborative research.

The nature of these conflicts can vary and are often unearthed through the process of research, with unanticipated consequences. Participants may believe they are entering into a co-productive relationship and have sought to identify shared interests, goals, and values at the outset, only to realize that there are clear ideological differences between them. Many people have different ideas, for instance, about the means and modes of collaboration and this raises the possibility of conflict and tension. Such issues are not necessarily problematic, but can become so if group processes are captured, or co-opted by particular interests. For all these reasons, appropriately skilled and diplomatic leadership and facilitation is invaluable (see Boxes 2.6, 2.7, and 2.8).

Different forms of knowledge can be considered and mediated through a collaborative process of working with city officials and communities to exchange knowledge, learn, and inform actions. The cultures of both knowledge production and reception can become open to reflexive scrutiny and with that, the possibility for transformation. 'Active intermediation' is a concept we developed based on extensive experience in working across boundaries in transdisciplinary research projects.

Active refers to the movement away from passive ideas about knowledge transfer towards iterative, complex, and messy concepts of knowledge exchange. *Active* means paying attention to the continuous and interactive relationship between research participants, in which differences in divisions of labour are recognized, negotiated, tolerated, and acted upon for mutual benefit according to changes in the environments we occupy. This is not an easy process. Active commitment, work, and institutional support to be effective are necessary. The result is that research feeds practice and vice versa, with an emphasis on learning. Knowledge needs to be actively received, understood, and interpreted.

Intermediation refers to the work of being and moving between different cultures of knowing and acting. Knowledge exchange does not take place between two separate spheres of activity but is a space of communication where different cultures of enquiry and reception can engage. This space of communication and willingness to enter into dialogue is frequently absent. Without intermediation – working across sites where knowledge is produced and used – there is a missing middle between the contexts in which knowledge is produced and received. This means that expectations may be unrealistic or unarticulated, with no mutual understanding between parties.

'Active intermediation' (May and Perry, 2017) is not a simple solution or model to be implemented. It is a set of practices in the interstitial spaces between research and practice. It represents the active and constant 'agonism' (Mouffe, 2005) of engaged social scientific research: there is no state of resolution, rather a set of practices that inform the possibility of producing 'excellent-relevant' knowledge. It means working at the boundaries which inform the conduct, context, and consequences of the research and shape its transformative potential. It is not only the multi-dimensional reflexivity of the researcher that comes into play, but that of all knowledge producers in the process – and of how they interrelate.

In our fragmented, fast-speed, time-poor, high-pressured societies, where policy proceeds at a startling pace in the absence of learning, collective spaces for reflection are needed even more. As epistemic permeability challenges the boundaries between and within disciplines and the social world, the task is to design spaces for collectively producing knowledge with a reflexive ethos, without collapsing into group therapy, while maintaining concern to contribute to the possibilities of transformation of the world to which we belong.

Box 2.6 Leading transdisciplinary co-production

Catherine Durose, Beth Perry, Liz Richardson, and Rikki Dean

Interest in co-production reflects a growing demand and interest for a more socially accountable form of knowledge production. Yet the challenges presented by co-production are often underplayed in comparison to its potential, and the question of leadership in co-production is often marginalized as a 'second order' question. It is critical to ask: who leads, for what purpose, and how? Where leadership is discussed, particular leadership strategies for co-production are often assumed or extolled. Critical perspectives about power and positionality in co-production – and what this means for leadership – are rarely reflected upon.

On leadership
It is often argued that co-production must be flexible and recognize diverse forms of leadership according to the relationships among the different participants and their respective involvement at different stages of co-production (Bussu and Galanti, 2018; Simon et al., 2020). This diversity includes the opening up of leadership to involve actors from different backgrounds (Hartley and Allison, 2000). But what would this wealth of diverse forms look like in practice? Co-production necessarily brings together people with not only different forms of expertise, but probably also different interests and views. This raises substantive questions of power, and the purpose and practices of leadership.

We asked what does 'good' leadership in co-production look like? What different views do those involved in transdisciplinary projects have about leadership? And how do they differ? Are there trade-offs in managing different pressures, for instance, between being directive and inclusive, innovative and accountable, open to what emerges and sharing power? Do the existing models reflect leadership practice in co-production projects?

What we did
We interviewed 17 people involved in the Jam and Justice Action Research Collective and identified some key themes. The interviews helped us develop ideas, which we supplemented with academic theories. We then tested these ideas using an innovative and systematic technique, called Q methodology (McKeown and Thomas, 2013). We then undertook a survey of key informants with prior experience of transdisciplinary research projects,

involving a university partner and self-identifying as using 'co-production'. The full results of the study have been published in an academic journal (Durose et al., 2020).

Developing co-productive leadership models

We found that people had strong agreement on characteristics of 'bad' leadership. They also agreed that leadership needs to take questions of power seriously.

But there were different views on what 'good' leadership looks like; for instance, in terms of what power differentials actually mean or how much direction people need. We identified four viewpoints on good leadership in co-production: creative leadership, outcomes-focused leadership, visionary leadership, and egalitarian leadership.

- Creative leadership should be flexible and focused on group dynamics and relationships in order to support people's creativity.

Creative leadership is marked by the presence of creativity, and the ability of a group to move. It is premised on the underlying relationships between those involved in co-production. Those advocating creative leadership focus on relationships as a precondition for creativity, allowing for unexpected outcomes, and also enabling co-production to adapt to changing circumstances. Leadership should respond to group dynamics and preferences and address inequities in power within the group. Flexibility is important: even in the same process, different stages are recognized to need different approaches and styles. This viewpoint emphasizes that co-production is nearly always messy. Lower priority is placed on having clear processes and outcomes.

- Outcomes-focused leadership is about having clear structures and finding the best person for the job at hand in order to deliver outcomes.

Outcomes-focused leadership defines the purpose of leadership as ensuring activity towards an outcome. Proponents are concerned that without this focus, processes can become meaningless and people get disappointed. This viewpoint takes a more instrumental view on relationships than creative leadership, seeing them as a means to understand the different strengths each party brings. Good leadership in co-production is about getting things done, rather than focusing on group decision-making and collective voice. Decisions should be taken by whoever has the most appropriate skills and capacities. Relationships of trust, clear structures, and transparent processes support this priority. Lower priority is placed on addressing inequalities in power.

- Visionary leadership is about having the discretion to support people in following their passions in order to achieve a vision.

Visionary leadership emphasizes being visible and articulating a vision, but also being prepared to listen to people and to modify that vision. It focuses on having empathy and awareness and holding people to the sense of purpose. While clarity on roles is deemed important, fixed processes are eschewed in favour of leaders' discretion to act, improvise, and not be overly constrained by structure. Power dynamics are treated pragmatically and with honesty. This viewpoint highlights the importance of 'soft skills' in enabling people to act creatively and start thinking for themselves. Loose structures are often preferred that enable flexibility, so long as things can be pulled back together again.

- Egalitarian leadership is about finding consensus and sharing power within the group in order to reach towards equity.

Egalitarian leadership in co-production focuses on creating a shared, inclusive process for a collective purpose or identity as an outcome in its own right. This means the group taking ownership of the process so that decision-making is shared. The primary route to achieve this is through clear and transparent structures for decision-making, which constrain the power of well-resourced members of the groups and ensure that the process is genuinely shared by all. Empowering structures are coupled with actively including all members of the group. Structure and transparency are seen as important to limit the exercise of arbitrary power, so that co-production is not hijacked by those with hidden agendas.

Each viewpoint has a unique emphasis regarding questions of purpose, practice, power, structure, and decision-making in co-production leadership, as summarized in Table 2.1. There is agreement across viewpoints, for instance, that acknowledging power dynamics between participants in co-production is crucial, but they differ on how far leadership should transform power relations. Viewpoints are divided differentially on the importance of structure; for instance, whether leadership is exercised through formal structures or a more relational leadership approach. There were also complex differences between the viewpoints on how decision-making is exercised and by whom.

Implications for practice
Thinking about leadership is valuable for those interested in co-production. We eschew a 'one size fits all' approach to leadership in co-production and instead understand leadership as a 'situated practice'. We are not proposing an either/or approach and recognize that contexts demand different responses. These viewpoints are not mutually exclusive. Nonetheless, the Q method revealed clear differences and tendencies held by individuals in terms of their underlying orientation to power, practices, and politics.

Table 2.1 Similarities and differences in viewpoints on good leadership in co-production

Viewpoint on leadership in co-production	Creative	Outcomes-focused	Visionary	Egalitarian
Purpose	Creativity	Outcomes	Vision	Equality
Practice	Building relationships and group resilience	Identifying and incorporating all relevant expertise	Enabling individuals to take responsibility for what they feel passionate about	Maintaining group cohesion and consensus
Power	Redistributing power	Working with power	Working with power	Redistributing power
Structure	Flexible and relational	Clear and formal	Flexible and relational	Clear and formal
Decision-making	Emergent	Leaders by expertise	Leaders by discretion	Group by consensus

Source: Durose et al., 2020. Based on 'What is good leadership in co-production?' survey, funded by ESRC Jam and Justice project.

Practitioners should acknowledge the specific leadership demands posed by co-production. What those demands may be in any given context requires further conversation about the fundamental question of who leads in co-production and how. Each process will generate its own response; the key is that the question is asked.

The viewpoints identified in this box – *creative, outcomes-focused, visionary*, and *egalitarian* leadership – provide a useful framework for such conversations within co-production. Differences in the purpose of leadership (facilitating creativity, delivering outcomes, offering vision or ensuring inclusivity) and how to handle unequal power dynamics, have real implications for how we approach co-production. There is a need to bring leadership to the fore in future conversations.

Box 2.7   Facilitation – bringing methods to life

Katie Finney   The role of the facilitator has emerged as critical in multiple settings where people have come together seeking to create positive change in the world. Many now acknowledge the impact that an individual with the knowledge and skills of facilitation can have in guiding a group towards a shared goal:

> *The facilitator is an aware and conscious listener, and a clear communicator, who understands group dynamics and provides process expertise, usually in the form of questions and suggestions. She/he grows meaningful relationships, participation, and collaboration, focuses a group on its purpose, and guides its development through organic cycles, using cooperative processes and collective decision-making (Hunter, 2007: 20).*

The idea of co-production recognizes the potential of bringing together different voices and forms of expertise and this 'often needs to find or create different ways to have a conversation that brings out the best of what everyone has to offer' (Perry et al., 2019: 6). Given that co-production aims to support more open processes, make participation meaningful through valuing people's knowledge and skills and move towards fairer outcomes (ibid: 14), facilitation has a central role to play, especially given the emphasis on the values of equal worth, full participation, and balancing consensus with celebration of difference (Hunter, 2007: 25).

Facilitation in action

One of the Jam and Justice mini-projects developed within the Action Research Collective (ARC) was called 'GM Decides' (see Chapter 3, 'Designing the Action Research Collective'). GM Decides started as a project inspired by digital democratic innovation across the world, particularly Decidim in Barcelona – a digital platform for participatory decision-making. The GM Decides team wanted to know whether and how such an innovation could be realized in Greater Manchester (GM) and specifically how such a platform could be co-designed with and for women. A Partnership Group of women working in digital, community, and participation across Greater Manchester was formed by co-researcher members of the ARC. This Group quickly recognized the importance of deeply understanding women's participation in urban decision-making before thinking about the technical considerations and practical applications of digital democratic participation.

The process included:

- *A Landscape Review*: an exploration of what is going on in Greater Manchester, the UK, and the world in relation to digital democratic participation.
- *'Listening Sessions'*: one-to-one and group conversations in which we heard from women across GM about their experiences of participation on and offline.

- *A Gathering*: an event to which we invited those connected to the project, or interested in it, to explore what was emerging.

We used principles, methods, and frameworks from Community Organizing and Human Centred Design. Community Organizing is the work of bringing people together to take action around their common concerns and overcome social injustice. Human Centred Design is a process that starts with the people you're designing for and ends with new solutions that are tailor-made to suit their needs. The GM Decides story (Finney and Toomer McAlpine, 2019) was captured using creative documentation (see Toomer McAlpine and Perry, Chapter 5, 'Closing the co-productive cycle: creative documentation for multi-vocal representation').

There is no single method
One important outcome of the Jam and Justice mini-project GM Decides was insight into the facilitation of processes that enable participation in decision-making. These insights relate not to the methods used, but to the vital *invisible* understanding through which a facilitator chooses appropriate tools and methods and delivers them with powerful impact.

Facilitators need to know *what* tools and methods they can use and *how* to develop the skills to deliver them, especially when groups of people often articulate competing agendas. However, there are numerous skills and options, which no individual or group of facilitators can ever hope to develop or work their way through. A simple search on search engine Ecosia brings up 63,400,000 results for 'facilitation methods', and 18,900,000 'facilitation training' options are discoverable online. Given this, it is an understandable response for facilitators to pick and choose their trusted approaches and prioritize the importance of one method or skill over others.

Valuing what we cannot see
This means that facilitators should not be overly focused on the application of a method, but on understanding how our experiences are created, and on our innate skills and capabilities. In his work on social innovation, Otto Scharmer points to the importance of understanding what we cannot see, noting that 'the success of an intervention depends on the interior condition of the intervenor' (Scharmer, 2003: 2).

The GM Decides project illuminated how facilitation is impacted by the innate qualities people hold, and the separate experience of each person involved in a collective process. Understanding what lies behind our human experiences is how a facilitator brings methods to life.

When a facilitator knows how human psychology works – that our experience of life is created from the inside out through thought in the moment and that all people have innate mental health (Pransky, 2019) – they can be freed up to be responsive in the moment. This means they can serve the needs of the group to achieve their purpose. Realizing how experience is created shifts our state of mind; hence facilitators are better able to know when they are *inside or outside the logic*. Facilitators can work without taking group dynamics and tensions personally. They can draw from the facilitator toolbox the most appropriate tools and methods to use in a given context – throwing the plan out of the window if needed.

Learning to let go
Using this logic in facilitating the GM Decides process, we avoided taking changes in project direction and differing levels of participation personally. This experience demonstrated that, with clarity of mind, facilitators are able to let go of their own preconceived ideas of what a project should look like and set their own agendas aside, welcoming and supporting diversity of participation.

The methods used were creative, and outcomes unexpected. By emphasizing that the answers to the issues being examined lay with each of the GM Decides participants, it was possible to appreciate the expertise and contribution of each person. Holding this as true means that, in co-production practice, the roles of people from communities and all sectors become clearer, more constructive, and equally valued.

Taking it forward
Facilitation and co-production value expertise in its many and varied forms. Truly understanding that each person has innate capacity to contribute removes any personal or professional pressure. What we realize is that the facilitator is never really doing the work. It becomes clear that, as a facilitator, you are not responsible for, or concerned with, the outcome. When a facilitator knows that each person has innate capacity, they know that their true task is to consistently point people towards this fact – so that when people show up to tackle tricky challenges or develop new solutions, they apply their unique learned skills to maximum effect.

Acquiring the skills and knowledge of facilitation in co-production can be a great asset. For facilitators and all practitioners of social change, it is vital to look more closely in the direction of the invisible factors which bring life and effectiveness to the methods we choose.

Suggested readings

Banks, S. (1998) *The Missing Link*, International Human Relations Inc., Vancouver.

Bettinger, D. and Swerdloff, N. (2016) *Coming Home: Uncovering the Foundations of Psychological Well-being*, CreateSpace Independent Publishing Platform, Scotts Valley, CA.

Neill, M. (2013) *The Inside Out Revolution*, Hay House, London.

Box 2.8 Offering professional facilitation in Gothenburg

Margareta Forsberg and Sophia Kaså

Urban co-production can be a hotbed for misunderstandings, frustration, distrust, and conflicts, motivating support in professional facilitation. A professional facilitator is skilled in fostering and encouraging collaboration in diverse groups and to forestall and address problems that may emerge. The level of facilitation needed depends on what the participants bring to the situation and the complexity of the task to be achieved. Above all, facilitation is a skill to host and create a safe space and to scaffold a group to make the most of its potential. Thereto, it is a skill to select and combine appropriate methods to support this work and create the best possible learning conditions among participants. Based on these insights and with the purpose to develop the capacity for co-production in research projects and among administrative staff in Gothenburg, a professional facilitator was hired. This was an intrepid initiative, considering the absence of affirmative proof of the benefits involved. Often, academic researchers involved in this type of research are expected to take on a facilitating role, in addition to other competencies/responsibilities.

Among the leaders of ongoing local research projects, the initiative met two dominant reactions. Approximately half of them welcomed the initiative, while the other half was hesitant. The latter did not see professional facilitation as necessary or could not manage to involve additional persons in the project work. For the affirmative project leaders, the offering of professional facilitation meant getting assistance in addressing facilitation needs that had already been identified, identifying new needs, developing the project design or ongoing work, and/or developing the within-project reflective learning.

Over a year, the professional facilitator carried out about 30 interventions, support in designing project plans, identifying research topics, collecting community data, designing structures and methods for joint analysis of findings and reflection on the learning, and communicating results. The facilitator also trained project leaders in basic facilitation skills and in hosting meetings. Those who received facilitation assistance referred to it as a core benefit of being part of the platform. Based on this experience, we believe that the need for facilitation should be evaluated and integrated in the project design at an early stage.

Administering transdisciplinary co-production

Kerstin Hemström

Bringing together diverse stakeholders in transdisciplinary co-production carries with it many practical challenges and administrative burdens. When several institutions and organizations are involved, such as universities and public authorities, the details of the process often do not fit any of their institutional structures, routines or established practices. Some examples are inflexible management structures, rules on how to allocate time, funding mechanisms, and reward systems within the organizations to which participants belong (Djenontin and Meadow, 2018). This is more than a conceptual issue. Actors who desire to participate often feel hindered by the institutional framework in which they work. They may be embedded in several roles and situations parallel to the research work, which involve different timelines and logics. All of these influence their attitude towards the process and ability to be engaged. If participants experience friction between the desire to participate in transdisciplinary co-production and the constraints of their daily work, they may not commit fully (Thompson et al., 2017).

Working within existing systems and finding windows of opportunity for a different approach requires creativity. Recurrently, new administrative and financial relations need to be invented within and between the scope of the participating organizations and institutions, to enable transdisciplinary co-production to take place. It is important to set up a reliable structure for the collaboration and sort out necessary formal partnership and contractual agreements. Different contextual conditions will require different strategies to enable this to happen. Groups and individuals work by various logics, have diverse needs for participation in the collaboration, and may require different forms of engagement. Generally, because these research endeavours vary and develop in the form and intensity of collaborations and partnerships, adaptability and flexibility are key. Ideally, the set-up should be flexible enough to allow changes deemed necessary later in the research process, such as taking on skills and expertise that could not be anticipated at an early stage (Djenontin and Meadow, 2018). We share some examples of how transdisciplinary co-production has been facilitated at an administrative level within Mistra Urban Futures in Boxes 2.9–2.11.

Box 2.9   Flexible financing for transdisciplinary co-production

Ithra Najaar and Warren Smit

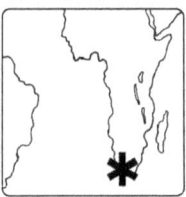

Research participation is often associated with costs: for example, for travel and in-kind contributions of labour. For transdisciplinary co-production to take place, enough time, labour, and financial resources must be made available to enable different individuals to participate. However, most research funding is fairly rigid in terms of specific budget lines and tight time frames. Shifts between budget lines ('virements')

are tightly restricted. By contrast, knowledge co-production processes are often very flexible and open-ended. It is often not clear from the start what the time frames and activities will be. Being co-produced by the participants, the process can also change over time. Co-production processes, therefore, ideally require fairly flexible funding that can be shifted between budget lines and, when necessary, extended in terms of time frames.

Working with multiple partners on co-production projects may involve complex flows of funds, as there may be other partners making financial and in-kind contributions to the project. In such cases, it is important that formal legal agreements exist between the relevant parties that set out the amounts to be transferred, the purpose of the funding, and how (and by whom) the expenditure will be monitored and reported on. International comparative co-production work, such as that of Mistra Urban Futures, involves international transfers of funds. Before the funds are received, it is important to update the expenditure reports and budgets regularly to reflect the current exchange rate. Once the funds have all been received, the actual exchange rate at which the funds were received must then be used.

Although flexible funding is required for co-production processes, regular monitoring of expenditure is essential to ensure that overall budget parameters are followed. It is also vital that all audit requirements are closely adhered to, such as keeping originals of all supporting documentation and following appropriate procurement processes for the acquisition of goods and services. Large institutions are likely to have financial procedures that meet international standards, but smaller organizations may need to develop new systems and procedures. The main challenge in funding co-production processes is being able to secure long-term flexible funding. Although obtaining funding for co-production has often been difficult (given its open-ended nature and focus on long-term process rather than on immediate outputs), many funding agencies and government organizations are starting to recognize the importance of co-production, and there are increasing numbers of funding calls that accommodate co-production approaches.

A Cape Town example of flexible funding
When the African Centre for Cities set up its first knowledge co-production CityLab programme in Cape Town (see Chapter 3, 'The CityLab programme in Cape Town'), funds from a range of sources (local government, provincial government, a parastatal, and the private sector) were pooled to form a flexible fund. The main item of expenditure was the salaries of the programme co-ordinators. These were full-time researchers recruited to facilitate, and be resource people for, the CityLabs. Other major items of expenditure were costs for seminars and field trips to expose the CityLabs' participants to a range of perspectives, and publication costs for co-produced written outputs. Each CityLab co-ordinator budgeted on an annual

basis for their CityLab, but significant amounts were also set aside for contingencies, for example, travel.

The same model of flexible funding with annual budgeting was used for local co-production work within Mistra Urban Futures. An overall strategic plan was drawn up for each five-year period, while detailed plans and budgets were done for each year. CityLabs wanting to undertake new collaborative research projects generally needed to apply for additional project-specific funding with specified deadlines and outputs.

Detailed analysis of expenditure was undertaken every four months. Being based at a university (as many co-production intermediary organizations are), many university-wide financial processes had to be complied with in terms of authorization, procurement, and so on. Therefore, although flexibility is required in terms of funding, high levels of monitoring and control over expenditure are necessary. In the case of funding flows between the African Centre for Cities and the City of Cape Town, a committee consisting of equal numbers of members from both parties was set up to oversee the jointly funded projects.

Box 2.10 Formal engagements enabling co-production in Kisumu

Michael Oloko and Stephen Agong'

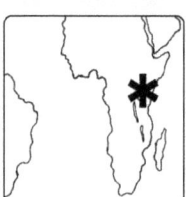

Co-production involves collaboration between stakeholders of different mandates and interests to reach desired goals. In Kisumu, Kenya, these have included university researchers, the City of Kisumu, the County Government of Kisumu, civil society organizations, co-operatives, and private companies. Several forms of formal document have been necessary to enable these various organizations to participate in, and foster their commitment to, the co-production process. These include temporary occupation licences, memoranda of understanding, recognition letters and letters of representation, and certificates of registration.

As a first step in setting up these relationships, leading local researchers communicated formally by letter with relevant city and county departments, presenting the research idea and seeking collaboration and representatives in the research team. The City Manager then appointed a director as a formal representative in the research project. Having secured formal participation of the City, other formal necessities were revealed in the research processes. For example, *Memoranda of Understandings* have served as formal agreements of goodwill and specified the details of the collaboration between different formal actors. *Temporary Occupation Licences*, issued by the City, have been necessary to secure public space to conduct research in the proximity of relevant community actors. *Certificates of registration* and *recognition letters* have been pivotal to secure relationships to previous informal actors, and to foster their commitment to the research process.

Altogether and in various ways, these formal documents have served to justify and enable the co-production research. They have been particularly important to secure the participation of, and improve the relations between, formal and informal actors when there has been a history of mistrust between them. In most cases, they have served to establish working relationships between different stakeholders that continue even after the end of the research.

Box 2.11 Facilitating supportive administrative relationships for co-production

Vicky Simpson and Sanna Isemo

Depending on the size of the research group and scope of the collaboration, co-production research sometimes necessitates administrative brokers who work at the interface between different organizations to make sure that things run smoothly. This involves fostering meaningful contractual relations, funding arrangements, generating supportive documents of different sorts, and ensuring the mundane but important work gets done of making sure people are paid on time. The role of professional services within this process is to keep many plates spinning simultaneously, to ensure that relationships have a firm foundation, and that approaches are designed to support the research. This may involve institutional innovation, for instance, generating 'boundary objects' to constitute understanding (see Box 2.12), such as developing mini-project agreements ensuring that all participants know what they need to produce and by when, how and when they will get paid, and how this will be done.

As administrators who have supported co-production research in the Sheffield-Manchester region and Gothenburg, respectively, we have identified three key elements which have been essential to ensuring healthy relationships among the partners involved:

- *Communication: Accurate, simple, and repetitive.* In addition to the crucial competences of a professional service function within any organization – such as clear and simple communication, helpfulness, and accessibility – other skills are needed to support co-production. These include sensitivity, responsiveness, and mediation among different (or conflicting) needs, interests, and conditions. Ongoing, transparent communication with research participants is essential. Friendliness, being approachable, and giving accurate and clear information that is easy to understand are all important to ensure consistency of experience for multiple partners and support in navigating institutional barriers that could inhibit effective transdisciplinary work.

- *Adaptation: No single model fits all.* A co-production administrator needs to be creative. This includes negotiating, tailoring processes, and, when necessary, introducing new practices. This can also necessitate going the extra mile and understanding partners' needs to ensure that all can easily engage with the research, regardless of their size, sector or organizational requirements. The administrator is expected, on the one hand, to ensure compliance with existing university norms, practices, and rules and acts as the day-to-day representative of the host organization. On the other hand, the co-production administrator needs to be flexible and responsive to differences in needs and prerequisites among the different stakeholders and their respective organizations. Questioning established rules of conduct may be needed to bring about necessary structural change. Examples include financial innovation and reform to develop light-touch and less bureaucratic processes for accessing resources to support smaller self-funding organizations, from the voluntary or charitable sectors.

- *Trust: Respect, transparency, and patience.* Trust must be earned from all participants. Trust is built by mediating among different needs, interests, expectations, and conditions and by contributing to a culture of openness, respect, and mutual understanding. Co-production research frequently involves interactions that are 'outside the norm' of established institutions. This can sometimes create unease. A pivotal role lies in understanding the needs of the research processes while, at the same time, ensuring that it complies with formal rules and requirements. Over time, the once unusual request becomes familiar. It is important to keep expectations transparent among participating institutions, be patient, and gradually support and embed new routines.

Box 2.12   The point of boundary objects

Kerstin Hemström   The main purpose of transdisciplinary co-production is knowledge integration; the act of combining and integrating different perspectives and expertise to generate comprehensive and solution-oriented knowledge in relation to a real-world problem. The first step in achieving this comes with recognizing a diversity of perspectives on the problem at hand and accepting their significance and difference (Pohl and Hirsch Hadorn, 2008). Ideally, the knowledge of different participants is integrated in a fair and rigorous way that does not privilege one understanding over another, creating a favourable learning situation for all. As explained in this chapter, this however, is difficult to achieve in practice. Often, exploring issues together through in-depth interactions, where each participant is given equal voice, takes considerable time, resources, and skills.

One way of expediating communication and understanding between participants is to meet around a *boundary object*. The term is used in various contexts to signify a tool or catalyst for a process. In general, boundary objects are phenomena (e.g. physical objects, places, concepts, and maps) that represent something that can be understood by everyone involved but are open and flexible enough to accommodate several understandings and embody different meanings. Thereby, the boundary object can help diverse participants to communicate and learn from one another on flat grounds.

Sometimes, the real-world issue around which a transdisciplinary team gather to co-produce, is itself referred to as a boundary object. In this book, the term is used to refer to something more delimited within the transdisciplinary co-production process, that is shaped by those who participate while at the same time representing their common understanding. In this way, the boundary object enables interactions between individuals of different knowledge and backgrounds (Lang et al., 2012; Wyborn, 2015).

Co-production of knowledge as a spatial practice

Jetta Palmer

The role of space is pertinent to consider, both consciously and critically, when setting up a transdisciplinary co-production research process. 'Space' is frequently referred to in the literature on transdisciplinary research, with several conceptual connotations and attributed characteristics that explain its importance and relevance. Space is interwoven with the knowledge production process, as something necessarily 'present' for a process to achieve good results, or as a successful 'outcome' of the process itself. It is also attributed as 'support' that creates fruitful preconditions for transdisciplinary co-production, or thereover as something truly catalytic, embodying the setting, the process, and the outcomes.

In spatial theory, there is a long tradition of debating the difference between 'space' and 'place' (Agnew, 2011). Even though transdisciplinary literature dwells on space primarily, 'place' is infused in the arguments. The increased importance of the 'place-specific' in the sustainability discourse also makes it worthwhile to understand these two concepts in parallel. In broad terms, place is geographically distinct and bound to a location, history, culture, and social and economic processes, which all contribute to embedded meanings (Norberg-Schulz, 1980). Space, on the other hand, is the intellectual appreciation of an environment created through relationships formed by humans, physical objects or abstract phenomena. The world is described as increasingly 'placeless', following from the expansion of globally branded shopping districts, streamlined business centres, and seemingly identical hubs of international transport (Augé, 1995; Agnew, 2011). In parallel there is an ongoing localization of abstract *space*, as in 'cyber space', 'media space', or the 'space of politics'. Thus, to some degree the connotations of the two concepts have shifted. Space has taken on meaning and locality, while place has lost its authenticity and specificity.

As space and place are often used interchangeably, our focus here is on the notion of 'space' as it appears in transdisciplinary and co-production research. Three dimensions of space are particularly relevant for transdisciplinary research: relational, physical, and institutional.[1] In all three dimensions, space fills an important role in bridging knowledge production processes with the transformations necessary for overcoming institutional constraints for urban transformation and development. Our experience leads us to argue that one key outcome of transdisciplinary co-production is the creation of new urban spaces of inclusiveness.

The relational space of transdisciplinary co-production

A transdisciplinary co-production process needs to allow for learning and knowledge integration to happen (Pohl et al., 2010; Pohl, 2011). Therefore, the process itself is sometimes referred to as a 'learning space'. Learning spaces are often discussed in conceptual terms, connoting the relationship between participating actors and their mutual agreements, or as 'spaces for action' in terms of attention or setting aside resources such as time and funding, or assuring the legitimacy of participation. This learning situation is sometimes also described as a 'safe space', as in safe from judgements and pre-set power arrangements and hierarchies, opening for learning to happen independently of stakeholders' everyday roles and perspectives, and for trust to be established among the participants (Palmer and Walasek, 2016; Perry et al., 2018). The notion of a 'safe' space refers both to the constructed precondition for a successful process and to the definition of the process itself. In this way, transdisciplinary co-production is understood as a *relational* space with certain inter-relational characteristics and requirements that need to be acknowledged, agreed upon, and set up to enable knowledge integration and learning to happen.

The physical space for transdisciplinary co-production

While the relational space lies at the core of the transdisciplinary co-production process, the importance of the *physical* space is often neglected. It is rather assumed that the collaborative enthusiasm of a transdisciplinary co-production endeavour overshadows any specific spatial requirements, allowing transdisciplinary research to take place 'anywhere'. But certainly, transdisciplinary co-produced research implies a specific physical space for collaborative workshops, meetings, learning, and training. Space, then, has the capacity to support different means of coming together through its form, size, proportions, organization, light, materiality, and other designed and cared for features. These qualities are sometimes referred to as 'scaffolding' (Jordan, 2014), meaning a set of arrangements which enhance positive outcomes of collaboration. Spatial scaffolding equals classic architectural knowledge of the relationship between space, function, human behaviour, and well-being. Many have elaborated on the oppressive (Foucault, 1977) versus the enabling agency of space (Price, 2003; Hamdi, 2004, 2010). With such awareness, consideration needs to be given to how physical spaces should be designed or arranged to support processes of trustful openness, collaborative meta-reflection, and learning.

Physical space further occupies a specific *location* (as with the meaning of 'place') which makes the notion of space in transdisciplinary co-production research critical and political, as space takes on a role of accessibility, representation, and manifestation in relation to involved stakeholders and other urban actors and urban conditions. Because much transdisciplinary co-production research is university-based (this differs clearly from other kinds of co-production initiatives originating from civil society or existing within the public sector), the location of transdisciplinary practice at the university campus tends to be unquestioned. However, the spatial separation of transdisciplinary spaces from the immediate university campus as well as from public agency corridors could be crucial. Many public officials participating in transdisciplinary urban knowledge co-production emphasize the importance of having access to a space to interact that is located outside or at the edge of a city university campus, promoting easy entry from their everyday engagements in the city.

With spaces and locations separate from specifically 'claimed' environments, different stakeholder groups can come together in a far more unaffected collaborative mood, without the feeling of 'intruding' into spaces owned by others, nor having to take on the role of 'hosting' or even 'defending' space of one's own. Participants sometimes experience and describe such spaces as 'neutral' (Hansson and Polk, 2017). This term may not be fully accurate considering that all physical space is marked by the politics of its creation and of its attendant social practices. The experience and intention, though, is to see this type of space as symbolically 'unaligned' to any of the involved institutions or stakeholders. It thereby allows participants to step out of formal and daily roles to act in new constellations, unburdened by institutional bounds.

The institutional space generated through transdisciplinary co-production
Because transdisciplinary co-production often involves interactions between different organizations and mandates, it is regularly referred to as 'boundary work',

and the processes as such as 'boundary conditions' (see 'Active intermediation' on page 31). The term 'boundary organization' is used to describe organizations belonging to neither the realm of science nor politics but with a mediating capacity to negotiate the relationship between the two. This is different from the transdisciplinary co-production process, bridging not only the realms of science and policy but also overlapping and blurring the knowledge borders and professional roles of the two (see Pohl et al., 2010). The latter overlapping realm is defined as an open, social, and 'permeable space', and sometimes described as an 'agora', using the symbolic image of a classical ancient Greek urban public space, in which science can meet the public and the public can speak back to science (Nowotny et al., 2001 in Pohl et al., 2010).

Both in the situation of boundary organization and of the agora of transdisciplinary research, *knowledge is produced together with social order* by redrawing the boundaries between academic and non-academic communities (Pohl et al., 2010). The difference is that boundary organizations with their intermediate presences are stabilizing new boundaries between the realm of science and policy, while the boundaries between science and policy in the agora are provisionally blurred, as a necessary condition for changed perceptions and behaviours to occur (Pohl et al., 2010). This gives the agora a radical potential, not only inviting individual participants to step out of their daily roles but also for the diverse organizations to act in new manners. With mandates from participating organizations, the agora, or the *boundary space*, could facilitate new structures to challenge power relations, leadership, and decision-making in a collaborative way. When new practices, technologies, and rules are eventually established, new 'proto-institutions' could emerge from these collaborative practices (Lawrence et al., 2002).

The institutional merging of public, private, academic, and civil society organizations is also sometimes described as a 'hybrid space'. The term 'hybridity' is often associated with the cultural critic Homi Bhabha (1993). For Bhabha, 'hybridization' is not a merging of two different cultures into one, but an ambiguous negotiation between the differences of the two. Arguing that there are always unequal power relations in the meeting of cultures, Bhabha insists that hybridization offers opportunity for the powerless to 'speak back to power' (Bhabha, 1994). Therefore, hybridization can never equate to a merging of differences but is the permission of different voices to co-exist without claims for fusion or consensus. With such a critical consciousness, boundary spaces as institutional spaces could be cared for as constantly emerging, making them both creative and sensible to changing circumstances and needs.

Space enables transdisciplinary co-production and urban change
The argument here is that relational and material conditions of space need to be strongly present in the processes of knowledge integration if they are to happen

successfully, and that space in this context should be practised, experienced, and represented.

Understanding transdisciplinary co-production as a public space – an agora – is intriguing, liberating the process from becoming an isolated institutional experiment. In discussions regarding how universities need to embrace transdisciplinary research (Gibbons, 1997), and thereby also change pedagogical structures, the location of transdisciplinary spaces should be taken into particular account, since institutional spaces are marked by ownership and inherent power. Taking this seriously, transdisciplinary spaces could remodel both the fringes of the campus and the institutional contours of the university, creating new physical and institutional spaces for transformation.

Transdisciplinary co-production will then exist, not only as a mode of knowledge production and joint social production but also as a mode of spatial production. Space is not merely a precondition for a collaborative research process and a possible institutional emergence, but the formation and outcome of both. Being critically conscious of this potential, involved actors could engage in urban transformation, creating inclusive spaces as urban commons, linking collective knowledge production to new spatial production. These then, could be urban spaces as a collective practice of pluralism and egalitarian difference.

Catalyzing the change process

in Hemström

The knowledge emanating from transdisciplinary co-production can be carried, expressed, and inform action in multiple ways, for example, as materialized products, tools or guidelines in relation to specific issues, or manifested in increased capacities and deepened insights at individual, organizational or community levels. As has been explained in this chapter, what is useful knowledge for promoting urban change on the local level depends on what is meaningful for the specific purposes of the action. This knowledge need not be entirely 'new'. It may intend to make better and more creative use of the existing knowledge in relation to a real-world problem to better facilitate sustainable change (West et al., 2019). Similarly, the participants of transdisciplinary co-production need not necessarily reach consensus around the issues addressed or the possible solutions suggested. They may very well engage in mutual learning and knowledge integration, each setting something into motion that has significance for the real-world problem at hand.

Having a broad range of actors involved in transdisciplinary co-production opens multiple pathways to change (Belcher et al., 2019; West et al., 2019). An underlying motivation for pursuing transdisciplinary co-production in the first place is the reciprocal relationship between knowledge and action. This means that the knowledge we carry does not necessarily precede our actions but is constantly put into use either consciously or subconsciously. Similarly, through our actions, our knowledge is in constant development (Jasanoff, 2004; West et al., 2019). This implies that, when relevant stakeholders are involved, the knowledge they co-produce is not 'applied' to action, but used interchangeably, regenerated, and used within the situation at hand to better act upon it (West et al., 2019). It informs the usual manner of thinking and acting by everyone involved and can generate considerable personal rewards through, for example, feelings of inclusion, empowerment, and involvement in social change (Thompson et al., 2017). Frequent interactions among the participants of transdisciplinary co-production can also generate longstanding relationships, networks, and alliances, making it easier for disparate actors to approach one another again. This can mean, for example, that subaltern knowledges, such as those of poor or indigenous community members, achieve greater legitimacy and influence to address structural injustices in urban development (Marshall et al., 2018).

As detailed throughout this chapter, relevance is not automatic but closely tied to how the transdisciplinary co-production process and interactions between participants unfold. It is crucial to the process that the participants learn to be reflective and responsive and develop means to reveal what matters and is relevant to them, while keeping flexibility to allow for the unfolding of solutions different from their original purposes (Van Breda and Swilling, 2019). Critical reflection on the interests, concerns, roles, and responsibilities different participants assume in the co-production process, while paying attention to the frictions and tensions that the interactions provoke, is key to achieving societally relevant outcomes (Hoffmann et al., 2017; Lux et al., 2019). Here, the question of how to best tailor change and the search for solution-oriented outputs and actions need to be continually integrated, sensitive to changes in the real-life context that may open windows for change or call the research focus into question (Klein, 2008; Steelman et al., 2015; Lux et al., 2019). Box 2.13 on the failure of a fish-cage farming project in Kisumu illustrates just how critical this type of reflective practice can be.

Practising reflexivity (see 'Crossing boundaries with a reflexive practice' on page 28) in a transdisciplinary team is a way of checking up on the relevance and validity of the research activities and results that accommodate multiple perspectives. Meanwhile, doing so jointly can itself induce change. The process of examining, questioning, and revising taken-for-granted perspectives and assumptions helps to identify disparate expectations and objectives and facilitates exchange of ideas, arguments, and information. This opens doors for a peer-to-peer learning that can promote and empower participants to contribute more actively to change (Lang et al., 2012; Popa et al., 2015; Boström et al., 2018; Herrero et al., 2019). As will be evidenced in several of the respective method descriptions in the next chapter, many participants in transdisciplinary co-production processes are challenged in a manner that transforms their way of thinking and acting. This learning can itself enhance their decision-making capacities, to better approach the real-world issue at hand.

Box 2.13 Illustrating the need for reflective practice: co-production of fish cage farming

Michael Oloko and Patrick Hayombe

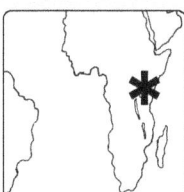

At Miyandhe Beach in Kisumu, Kenya, research on the potential to improve local food security through alternative fishing methods and fish cage farming quickly presented unanticipated challenges. As a result of uncontrolled fishing activities, the fish stock in Lake Victoria had been declining rapidly, making traditional fishing methods unreliable. The local fishermen's co-operative society had previously introduced fish cage farming to improve the situation but with minimal success. To find new means of livelihood, local researchers wanted to investigate fish cage farming and alternative fishing methods further, through co-production with the community. In the absence of official guidelines on fish cage farming, the project could only proceed as a research pilot project through the university.

Lessons learned

Ten fish cages were introduced in agreement with the Miyandhe Beach Management Unit. Nine cages belonged to the research group and one to the community. Community members participated in all activities in developing, testing, and undertaking fish cage farming. The community-owned cage provided motivation for them to commit, including to feed the fish and watch over all cages. With the first harvest, the community discovered a more reliable source of livelihood and started replicating the cages off nearby beaches. They had quickly learned the technology and developed a network to manufacture and sustain fish caging. Thousands of cages were soon anchored in the lake, drawing further interest from individuals, youth and women's groups, politicians, and even government officials looking for ways to improve local livelihoods.

With many stakeholders involved, the project could not control the effects. Co-production proved an effective way of developing knowledge that responded well to the critical needs of the local community, but the rapid community uptake presented acute challenges. The research activities needed quickly to be redefined to instead focus on emergent issues such as policies, guidelines, and regulations for the fast-growing fish cage farming, in addition to concerns of, for example, lake pollution, fish mortality rates, and effects of storms, water hyacinth invasion, and underwater currents. At this stage, the research had not progressed enough to make recommendations on how to carry out fish caging sustainably within the lake. Thereto, alternative technologies, such as land-based fishing and closed lake fishing systems, still needed to be considered. These experiences point to the need for specific care and reflexivity in taking up community co-production in this way.

Suggested reading

Njiru, J.M., Aura, C.M. and Okechi, J.K. (2019) 'Cage fish culture in Lake Victoria: a boon or a disaster in waiting?', *Fish Management Ecology* 26: 426-34 <https://doi.org/10.1111/fme.12283>.

Notes

2.1 This text draws in part on Palmer et al. (2020).

References

Agnew, J. (2011) 'Space and place', in J. Agnew and D. Livingstone (eds), *Handbook of Geographical Knowledge*, Sage, London.

Augé, M. (1995) *Non-places: Introduction to the Anthropology of Supermodernity*, Verso, London.

Bammer, G. (2008) 'Enhancing research collaborations: three key management challenges', *Research Policy* 37: 875-87 <https://doi.org/10.1016/j.respol.2008.03.004>.

Belcher, B.M., Claus, R., Davel, R. and Ramirez, L.F. (2019) 'Linking transdisciplinary research characteristics and quality to effectiveness: a comparative analysis of five research-for-development projects', *Environmental Science and Policy* 101: 192-203 <https://doi.org/10.1016/j.envsci.2019.08.013>.

Bergmann, M., Brohmann, B., Hoffmann, E., Loibl, M.C., Rehaag, R., Schramm, E. and Voss, J-P. (2005) *Quality Criteria of Transdisciplinary Research: A Guide for the Formative Evaluation of Research Projects* [online], Institut Fuer Soxial-Oekologische Forschung (ISOE) <https://doi.org.1007/s11625-016-0360-x> [accessed 12 May 2020].

Bhabha, H.K. (1993) 'Culture's in between', *Artforum*, September 1993.

Bhabha, H.K. (1994) *The Location of Culture*, Routledge, London.

Boström, M., Andersson, E., Berg, M., Gustafsson, K., Gustavsson, E., Hysing, E., Lidskog, R., Löfmarck, E., Ojala, M., Olsson, J., Singleton, B.E., Svenberg, S., Uggla, Y. and Öhman, J. (2018) 'Conditions for transformative learning for sustainable development: a theoretical review and approach', *Sustainability* 10(12): 4479 <https://doi.org/10.3390/su10124479>.

Bremer, S. and Meisch, S. (2017) 'Co-production in climate change research: reviewing different perspectives', *WIREs ClimChange* 8: e482 <https://doi.org/10.1002/wcc.482>.

Bussu, S. and Galanti, M.T. (2018) 'Facilitating coproduction: the role of leadership in coproduction initiatives in the UK', *Policy and Society* 37(3): 347-67 <https://doi.org/10.1080/14494035.2018.1414355>.

Cribbin, T. (2019) *Classphemy*, Empire Publications, Manchester.

Dallos, R. and Stedman, J. (2009) 'Flying over the swampy lowlands: reflective and reflexive practice', in R. Dallos and J. Stedman (eds), *Reflective Practice In Psychotherapy and Counselling*, Open University Press, Maidenhead, UK.

Denzin, N.K. (1997) *Interpretive Ethnography: Ethnographic Practices for the 21st Century*, Sage, London.

Djenontin, N.S. and Meadow, A.M. (2018) 'The art of co-production of knowledge in environmental sciences and management: lessons from international practice', *Environmental Management* 61: 885-903 <https://doi.org/10.1007/s00267-018-1028-3>.

Durose, C., Perry, B., Richardson, L. and Dean, R. (2020) 'What is leadership in co-produced research: a Q-method study', Working Paper <https://www.academia.edu/44942989/What_is_leadership_in_the_co_production_of_research_A_Q_methodology_study>.

Finlay, L. (2002) 'Negotiating the swamp: the opportunity and challenge of reflexivity in research practice', *Qualitative Research* 2(2): 209-30 <https://doi.org/10.1177%2F146879410200200205>.

Finney, K. and Toomer McAlpine, A. (2019) 'GM Decides: the story' [online] <https://www.sutori.com/story/gm-decides-final--ppANRaQrZfkM8zvRHm2NU398> [accessed 28 February 2020].

Flinders, M., Wood, M. and Cunningham, M. (2016) 'The politics of co-production: risk, limits and pollution', *Evidence & Policy* 12(2): 261-79 <https://doi.org/10.1332/174426415X14412037949967>.

Foucault, M. (1977) *Discipline and Punish: the Birth of the Prison*, Random House, New York.

Foucault, M. (1997) 'On the government of the living', in P. Rabinow (ed.), *Ethics: Subjectivity and Truth. The Essential Works of Michel Foucault 1954-1984*, vol. 1 (R. Hurley, Trans.), pp. 81-5, The New Press, New York (original work published 1980).

Gibbons, M. (1997) 'What kind of university? Research and teaching in the 21st century', *1997 Beanland Lecture*, Victoria University of Technology. Also published in: K. Elstrøm, J.E. Kristensen, M. Pedersen, H., Sørensen, J.V.O. Nielsen, and B.V. Sørensen (eds) (2007) *Ideer om et universitet. Det moderne universitets idehistorie fra 1800 til idag*, Aarhus Universitetsforlag, Aarhus.

Gilbert, A. and Sliep, Y. (2009) 'Reflexivity in the practice of social action: from self- to inter-relational reflexivity', *South African Journal of Psychology* 39(4): 468-79 <https://doi.org/10.1177/008124630903900408>.

Gill, R. and Pratt, A. (2008) 'In the social factory? Immaterial labour, precariousness and cultural work', *Theory, Culture & Society* 25(7-8): 1-30 <https://doi.org/10.1177/0263276408097794>.

Gouldner, A. (1971) *The Coming Crisis of Western Sociology*, Heinemann, London.

Hamdi, N. (2004) *Small Change*, Routledge, London.

Hamdi, N. (2010) *The Placemaker's Guide to Building Community*, Earthscan Ltd, London and Washington, DC.

Hansson, S. and Polk, M. (2017) *Evaluation of Knowledge Co-production for Sustainable Urban Development. Part I: Experiences from Project Leaders and Participants at Gothenburg Local Interaction Platform 2012-2015*, Mistra Urban Futures, Gothenburg.

Hartley, J. and Allison, M. (2000) 'The role of leadership in the modernization and improvement of public services', *Public Money and Management* 20(2): 35-40.

Hartsock, N. (1987) The feminist standpoint: developing the ground for a specifically feminist historical materialism', in S. Harding (ed.), *Feminism and Methodology*, Open University Press, Milton Keynes.

Herrero, P., Dedeurwaerdere, T. and Osinski, A. (2019) 'Design features for social learning in transformative transdisciplinary research', *Sustainability Science* 14: 751-69 <https://doi.org/10.1007/s11625-018-0641-7>.

Hoffmann, S., Pohl, C. and Hering, J.G. (2017) 'Methods and procedures of transdisciplinary knowledge integration: empirical insights from four thematic synthesis processes', *Ecology and Society* 22(1): 27 <https://doi.org/10.5751/ES-08955-220127>.

Hosking, D.M. and Pluut, B. (2010) '(Re) constructing reflexivity: a relational constructionist approach', *The Qualitative Report* 15(1): 59-75 <http://bettinepluut.nl/wp-content/uploads/2010/09/reconstructing-reflexivity.pdf>.

Hunter, D. (2007) *The Art of Facilitation: The Essentials for Leading Great Meetings and Creating Group Synergy*, 2nd edn, Jossey-Bass, San Francisco.

Jahn, T., Bergmann, M. and Keil, F. (2012) 'Transdisciplinarity: between mainstreaming and marginalization', *Ecological Economics* 79: 1-10 <https://doi.org/10.1016/j.ecolecon.2012.04.017>.

Jasanoff, S. (2004) *States of Knowledge: The Co-production of Science and Social Order*, Routledge, London and New York.

Jordan, T. (2014) 'Deliberative methods for complex issues: a typology of functions that may need scaffolding', *Group Facilitation: A Research and Applications Journal* 13: 50-71.

Kesby, M. (2007) 'Spatialising participatory approaches: the contribution of geography to a mature debate', *Environment and Planning A* 39: 2813-31 <https://doi.org/10.1068/a38326>.

Klein, J. (2008) 'Evaluation of interdisciplinary and transdisciplinary research: a literature review', *American Journal of Preventive Medicine* 35(2): 116-23 <https://doi.org/10.1016/j.amepre.2008.05.010>.

Klenk, N. and Meehan, K. (2015) 'Climate change and transdisciplinary science: problematizing the integration imperative', *Environmental Science & Policy* 54: 160-7 <https://doi.org/10.1016/j.envsci.2015.05.017>.

Krütli, P., Stauffacher, M., Flüeler, T. and Scholz, R.W. (2010) 'Functional-dynamic public participation in technological decision-making: site selection processes of nuclear waste repositories', *Journal of Risk Research* 13(7): 861-75 <https://doi.org/10.1080/13669871003703252>.

Lang, D.J., Wiek, A., Bergmann, M., Stauffacher, M., Martens, P., Moll, P., Swilling, M. and Thomas, C.J. (2012) 'Transdisciplinary research in sustainability science: practice, principles, and challenges', *Sustain Science* 7(Supplement 1): 25-43 <https://doi.org/10.1007/s11625-011-0149-x>.

Lawrence, T.B., Hardy, C. and Phillips, N. (2002) 'Institutional effects of interorganizational collaborations: the emergence of proto-institutions', *The Academy of Management Journal* 45(1): 281-90 <https://doi.org/10.5465/3069297>.

Lux, A., Schäfer, M., Bergmann, M., Jahn, T., Marga, O., Nagy, E., Ransiek, A-C. and Theiler, L. (2019) 'Societal effects of transdisciplinary sustainability research—How can they be strengthened during the research process?' *Environmental Science and Policy* 101: 183-91 <https://doi.org/10.1016/j.envsci.2019.08.012>.

Lynch, M. (2000) 'Against reflexivity as an academic virtue and source of privileged knowledge', *Theory, Culture and Society* 17(3): 26–54 <https://doi.org/10.1177/02632760022051202>.

Marshall, F., Dolley, J. and Priya, R. (2018) 'Transdisciplinary research as transformative space making for sustainability: enhancing propoor transformative agency in periurban contexts', *Ecology and Society* 23(3): 8 <https://doi.org/10.5751/ES-10249-230308>.

May, T. and Perry, B. (2017) *Reflexivity: The Essential Guide*, Sage, London.

May, T., Perry, B. and Spring, C. (2019) 'Methodological issues and emotional labour in co-produced research' [blog], Realising Just Cities <https://realisingjustcities-rjc.org/blog/methodological-issues-and-emotional-labour-co-produced-research> [accessed 12 May 2020].

McKeown, B. and Thomas, D. (2013) *Q Methodology*, 2nd edn, SAGE Publications Ltd, London.

Mitlin, D. (2008) 'With and beyond the state: Coproduction – a route to political influence, power and transformation for grassroots organizations', *Environment and Urbanization* 20: 339–60 <https://doi.org/10.1177/0956247808096117>.

Mouffe, C. (2005) *On the Political*, Routledge, London.

Mruck, K. and Mey, G. (2007) 'Grounded theory and reflexivity', in A. Bryant and K. Charmaz (eds), *The SAGE Handbook of Grounded Theory*, Sage, London.

Norberg-Schulz, C. (1980) *Genius Loci: Towards a Phenomenology of Architecture*, Rizzoli International Publications, New York.

Norris, P.E., O'Rourke, M., Mayer, A.S. and Halvorsen, K.E. (2016) 'Managing the wicked problem of transdisciplinary team formation in socio-ecological systems', *Landscape and Urban Planning* 154: 115–22 <https://doi.org/10.1016/j.landurbplan.2016.01.008>.

Nowotny, H., Scott, P. and Gibbons, M. (2001) *Re-thinking Science: Knowledge and the Public in an Age of Uncertainty*, Policy Press, Cambridge.

Oliver, K., Kothari, A. and Mays, N. (2019) 'The dark side of coproduction: do the costs outweigh the benefits for health research?', *Health Research Policy and Systems* 17: 33 <https://doi.org/10.1186/s12961-019-0432-3>.

Ostrom, E. (1996) 'Crossing the great divide: co-production, synergy and development', *World Development* 24(6), 1073–88 <https://doi.org/10.1016/0305-750X(96)00023-X>.

Palmer, H. and Walasek, H. (eds) (2016) *Co-production in Action: Towards Realising Just Cities*, Mistra Urban Futures, Gothenburg, Sweden.

Palmer, H., Polk, M., Simon, D. and Hansson, S. (2020) 'Evaluative and enabling infrastructures: supporting the ability of urban co-production processes to contribute to societal change', *Urban Transformations* 2: 6 <https://doi.org/10.1186/s42854-020-00010-0>.

Patai, D. (1994) (Response) 'When methods become power', in A.D. Gitlin (ed.), *Power and Method: Political Activism and Educational Research*, Routledge, New York.

Pearce, B.J. and Ejderyan, O. (2019) 'Joint problem framing as reflexive practice: honing a transdisciplinary skill', *Sustainability Science* 15: 683–98 <https://doi.org/10.1007/s11625-019-00744-2>.

Perry, B. and Russell, B. (2020) 'Participatory cities from the outside in: the value of comparative learning', in D. Simon, H. Palmer and J. Riise (eds), *Comparative Co-production from Theory to Practice*, pp. 133–54, Policy Press, Bristol.

Perry, B., Patel, Z., Bretzer, Y.N. and Polk, M. (2018) 'Organising for co-production: local interaction platforms for urban sustainability', *Politics and Governance* 6(1): 189-98 <https://doi.org/10.17645/pag.v6i1.1228>.

Perry, B., Durose, C. and Richardson, L. with the Action Research Collective (2019) *How Can we Govern Cities Differently? The Promise and Practices of Co-production* [pdf], Jam and Justice Project report, Greater Manchester, Creative Concern <https://jamandjustice-rjc.org/publications-jam-and-justice> [accessed 28 February 2020].

Pohl, C. (2011) 'What is progress in transdisciplinary research?', *Futures* 43: 618-26 <https://doi.org/10.1016/j.futures.2011.03.001>.

Pohl, C. and Hirsch Hadorn, G. (2008) 'Methodological challenges of transdisciplinary research', *Natures Sciences Sociétés* 16: 111-21 <https://doi.org/10.1051/nss:2008035>.

Pohl, C., Rist, S., Zimmermann, A., Fry, P., Gurung, G.S., Schneider, F., Ifejika Speranza, C., Kiteme, B., Boillat, S., Serrano, E., Hirsch Hadorn, G. and Wiesmann, U. (2010) 'Researchers' roles in knowledge co-production: experience from sustainability research in Kenya, Switzerland, Bolivia and Nepal', *Science and Public Policy* 37(4): 267-81 <https://doi.org/10.3152/030234210X496628>.

Pohl, C., Krutli, P. and Stauffacher, M. (2017) 'Ten reflective steps for rendering research societally relevant', *Gaia* 26(1): 43-51 <https://doi.org/10.14512/gaia.26.1.10>.

Polk, M. (2015) 'Transdisciplinary co-production: designing and testing a transdisciplinary research framework for societal problem solving', *Futures* 65: 110-22 <https://doi.org/10.1016/j.futures.2014.11.001>.

Popa, F., Guillermin, M. and Dedeurwaerdere, T. (2015) 'A pragmatist approach to transdisciplinarity in sustainability research: from complex systems theory to reflexive science', *Futures* 65: 45-56 <https://doi.org/10.1016/j.futures.2014.02.002>.

Pransky, J. (2019) *Hope For All*, CCB Publishing, British Columbia.

Price, C. (2003) *Cedric Price – The Square Book (Architectural Monographs 7)*, Wiley-Academy, Chichester, UK.

Ryan, T.G. (2005) *The Reflexive Classroom Manager*, Temeron Books/Detselig, Calgary.

Scharmer, O. (2003) *The Blind Spot of Leadership: Presencing as a Social Technology of Freedom*, Habilitation thesis [online] <https://www.ottoscharmer.com/sites/default/files/2003_TheBlindSpot.pdf> [accessed 28 February 2020].

Schneider, F. and Buser, T. (2018) 'Promising degrees of stakeholder interaction in research for sustainable development', *Sustainability Science* 13: 129-42 <https://doi.org/10.1007/s11625-017-0507-4>.

Scholz, R.W. and Steiner, G. (2015) 'The real type and ideal type of transdisciplinary processes: part I— theoretical foundations', *Sustainability Science* 10(4): 527-44 <https://doi.org/10.1007/s11625-015-0326-4>.

Schön, D.A. (1983) *The Reflective Practitioner: How Professionals Think in Action*, Basic Books, New York.

Schuttenberg, H.Z. and Guth, H.K. (2015) 'Seeking our shared wisdom: a framework for understanding knowledge coproduction and coproductive capacities', *Ecology and Society* 20(1): 15 <http://dx.doi.org/10.5751/ES-07038-200115>.

Simon, D., Palmer, H. and Riise, J. (2020) 'Assessment: learning between theory and practice', in D. Simon, H. Palmer, and J. Riise (eds), *Comparative Urban Research from Theory to Practice: Co-production for sustainability*, pp. 155-72, Policy Press, Bristol.

Spivak, G.C. (1985) 'Criticism, feminism and the institution', *Thesis Eleven* 10(11): 175-89.

Stauffacher, M., Flüeler, T., Krütli, P. and Scholz, R.W. (2008) 'Analytic and dynamic approach to collaboration: a transdisciplinary case study on sustainable landscape development in a Swiss prealpine region', *Systemic Practice and Action Research* 21(6): 409-22 <https://doi.org/10.1007/s11213-008-9107-7>.

Steelman, T., Nichols, E.G., James, A., Bradford, L., Ebersöhn, L., Scherman, V., Omidire, F., Bunn, D.N., Twine, W. and McHale, M.R. (2015) 'Practicing the science of sustainability: the challenges of transdisciplinarity in a developing world context', *Sustainability Science* 10(4): 581-99 <https://doi.org/10.1007/s11625-015-0334-4>.

Thompson, M.A., Owen, S., Lindsay, J.M., Leonard, G.S. and Cronin, S.J. (2017) 'Scientist and stakeholder perspectives of transdisciplinary research: early attitudes, expectations, and tensions', *Environmental Science and Policy* 74: 30-9 <https://doi.org/10.1016/j.envsci.2017.04.006>.

Ulrich, W. (2005) *A Brief Introduction to Critical Systems Heuristics (CSH)* [pdf], website of the ECOSENSUS project, Open University, Milton Keynes, UK <http://projects.kmi.open.ac.uk/ecosensus/publications/ulrich_csh_intro.pdf> [accessed 26 February 2020].

Van Breda, J. and Swilling, M. (2019) 'The guiding logics and principles for designing emergent transdisciplinary research processes: learning experiences and reflections from a transdisciplinary urban case study in Enkanini informal settlement, South Africa', *Sustainability Science* 14(3): 823-41 <https://doi.org/10.1007/s11625-018-0606-x>.

Watson, V. (2014) 'Co-production and collaboration in planning - the difference', *Planning Theory and Practice* 15(1): 62-76 <http://dx.doi.org/10.1080/14649357.2013.866266>.

Watt, D. (2007) 'On becoming a qualitative researcher: the value of reflexivity', *The Qualitative Report* 12(1): 82-101.

West, S., van Kerkhoff, L. and Wagenaar, H. (2019) 'Beyond "linking knowledge and action": towards a practice-based approach to transdisciplinary sustainability interventions', *Policy Studies* 40(5): 534-55 <https://doi.org/10.1080/01442872.2019.1618810>.

Wiek, A., Talwar, S., O'Shea, M. and Robinson, J. (2014) 'Towards a methodological scheme for capturing societal effects of participatory sustainability research', *Research Evaluation* 23(2): 117-32 <https://doi.org/10.1093/reseval/rvt031>.

Wyborn, C. (2015) 'Connectivity conservation: boundary objects, science narratives and the co-production of science and practice', *Environmental Science & Policy* 51: 292-303 <https://doi.org/10.1016/j.envsci.2015.04.019>.

PART 2

Methods for transdisciplinary urban knowledge co-production

Produced by workshop participants in the Healthy Cities CityLab, African Centre for Cities.

64 CHAPTER 3
Creating co-productive spaces
65 Designing the Action Research Collective: embracing incompleteness
72 The CityLab programme in Cape Town
76 Establishing communities of trust through panels
79 A space for learners to lead and leaders to learn: Challenge Lab
81 Exploring TD methods in a PhD course: creating a TD 'learning space'
86 Space-enabling co-production on solid waste management
91 Academics and municipal officials co-writing in third space
96 Conclusion
97 References

100 CHAPTER 4
Designing processes to integrate knowledge
101 Symmetrical leadership and participation for cross-learning in WISE
103 Joint problem formulation and solution through iterative practice: design thinking
106 Study circles and co-writing of boundary-breaking 'changes in outlook'
111 Methods and tools for co-creation of urban station communities
117 A method for participatory public space planning and design: Urban Girls Movement
122 A framework for comparative transdisciplinary co-production around the Sustainable Development Goals
129 Exchange as method: the value of trans-local learning
134 References

135 CHAPTER 5
Blurring boundaries to facilitate understanding
136 Building transdisciplinary capacities through the Knowledge Transfer Programme
138 A model for co-production of knowledge: creating a Research Forum
141 A method for making the everyday visible: photovoice and everyday politics
146 Playing for social inclusion
150 Tapping hidden expertise: the model of the Inverted Citizens' Jury
154 Engaging people of different needs to create a better city for all: FunkTek
159 Closing the co-productive cycle: creative documentation for multi-vocal representation
163 References

Methods for transdisciplinary urban knowledge co-production

HOW CAN TRANSDISCIPLINARY URBAN KNOWLEDGE co-production be operationalized in research practice? In recent years, the number of tools, methods, and approaches offered to address complex issues through participation has burgeoned. However, as tools reflect a diversity of research traditions, scientific disciplines, professions, and worlds of practice, they tend to be highly distributed in disconnected ways across the intellectual landscape. This makes it difficult to locate methods when you need them (O'Rourke, 2017). Furthermore, many descriptions of methods and tools are largely decontextualized, leaving limited insights as to what they can help achieve, or how they can be combined with other methods or tools, in different situations or contexts. Alternatively, they report on single case studies, from which it is difficult to discern what the specific recipe used has to offer in other situations.

A multiplicity of methods is used in transdisciplinary co-production. As outlined in previous chapters their use needs to fit and be sensitive to the specific context and circumstances of the real-life issue and associated research endeavour. In the following chapters, we explain and illustrate varied methods and techniques that have been applied to operationalize transdisciplinary co-production in response to real-world urban issues. Reflecting the diversity of problem areas and contextual conditions that cities face worldwide, the 22 methods presented throughout Chapters 3–5 exemplify a breadth of techniques and tools. This diversity is part of the strength of transdisciplinary co-production.

Each description derives from research projects undertaken by transdisciplinary teams to address urban issues. These, however, differ in how they have been initiated and who has taken the lead, involve different stakeholders in different constellations across different geographical scales, and mirror varying opportunities for face-to-face and deliberated meetings. Some methods have close ties to specific research traditions, while others have emerged from practice-based contexts or from within the transdisciplinary research process itself. Originating from different authors with different backgrounds, the descriptions are also presented differently in terms of what is described, and how. Each author has attempted to describe procedures in a concrete manner. Symptomatic for collaborative research methods in general, however, these methods are more or less systematic, more or less context dependent, more or less abstract and concrete (O'Rourke, 2017). Yet all have sought to combine scientific knowledge with other types of knowledge, such as know-how and practical expertise from residents, businesses, community organizations, planners, administrators, and politicians, to build new and combined knowledge of relevance for urban sustainability. Several of them have evolved intentionally to strengthen often marginalized perspectives, such as those of unprivileged community members, in relation to more powerful ones in the research process.

Emulating the diversity referred to above, the methods are loosely categorized into three headings: 'Creating co-productive spaces' (Chapter 3), 'Designing processes to integrate knowledge' (Chapter 4), and 'Blurring boundaries to facilitate understanding' (Chapter 5). These are not indisputable and watertight divisions, nor do they reflect an analytically sophisticated and comprehensive framework for organizing methods in terms of what they can be used for or help achieve. All the projects that have informed this book focus on creating new meeting places, based on different types of knowledge integration and boundary crossings. Still, the descriptions have been categorized to highlight the main focus of the example. Each chapter is opened by a short introduction, explaining the category theme and its relevance for enabling collaboration, to open windows of opportunity for sustainable urban change.

CHAPTER 3
Creating co-productive spaces

keywords
action research collective, CityLab, communities of trust, Challenge Lab, transdisciplinary learning space, solid waste management, co-writing

One of the challenges in transdisciplinary co-production is bringing partners from different organizations together in a way that makes them comfortable and encourages them to explore their differences and then to collaborate productively. This kind of experimental work is difficult to undertake in participants' normal workplaces. 'Space' plays a fundamental role, in setting the relational and material conditions which characterize, and may facilitate, collaboration among diverse stakeholders and actors. While diverse in other respects, the contributions of this chapter each draws attention to different ways in which co-productive spaces have been established and utilized effectively under varied urban circumstances. Each involves the design or enabling of some type of physical or abstract space, creating favourable environments for interactions, learning, and knowledge integration.

THE CHAPTER OPENS WITH A DESCRIPTION of the creation of the Action Research Collective in Sheffield-Manchester, designed to create new learning and relational spaces among researchers, decision-makers, civil society, and citizens. We then learn how the CityLab programme in Cape Town and the Panels in Skåne enabled new relations and knowledge integration among diverse actors around different urban themes. The two subsequent descriptions, on the Challenge Lab and the Open Research School in Gothenburg, both involve creating learning spaces for transdisciplinary capacity-building, where academic and non-academic participants collaboratively investigate complex real-life problems. Next, we learn how the concentration of research activities at a physical site in Kisumu enabled different stakeholders to come together and form longstanding empowered relations. The chapter concludes with the description of co-writing in a Cape Town circle on how a virtual 'third' space can function as a heuristic tool to enable meaningful interaction. The co-writing of outputs is a crucial element in several processes described in this book, to facilitate learning and reflection among participants with different forms of knowledge. In each of these descriptions, the creation of an appropriate space played a critical role in establishing favourable conditions for productive encounters among different stakeholders and perspectives.

Designing the Action Research Collective: embracing incompleteness

Beth Perry, Liz Richardson, and Catherine Durose

Greater Manchester, in the North of England, is a city-region with 2.8 million people. It was the first English city-region outside London to agree a deal for greater devolved powers from central government. In 2017, residents elected their first Mayor to head a new strategic Combined Authority, integrating the 10 local authorities. The deal was criticized for being made behind closed doors. Many people asked how devolution could be an opportunity for greater citizen participation in addressing substantive policy concerns.

We wanted to know if co-production could offer a way to address this question by building local democracy, valuing knowledge and expertise, and producing fairer outcomes (May and Perry, 2018). We wanted to test ways to connect decision-makers, civil society, and citizens ('the jam'), specifically involving those usually excluded from such processes to address wider issues ('justice').

In 2016 we started a project called *Jam and Justice: Co-producing Governance for Social Innovation* with funding from the UK Economic and Social Research Council and Mistra Urban Futures (Perry et al., 2019). The main partners receiving funding were the Universities of Sheffield, Manchester, and Birmingham with the Greater Manchester Centre for Voluntary Organisation (GMCVO). The co-investigator team involved three academics and the Chief Executive of the GMCVO.

About the Action Research Collective

Our aim was to explore the value and practice of co-production to address complex urban problems and understand how to achieve fairer and more inclusive outcomes for all. Our approach was to create an Action Research Collective (ARC) as an extended peer community – a critical, reflexive space where diversity is embraced, and concepts of authority and expertise are blurred (see Chapter 2, 'Crossing boundaries with a reflexive practice'). We wanted to create a diverse ARC that crossed sectoral boundaries, where people with different experiences and modes of thinking shared a common desire for positive social change. Our ambition was to assemble a rich set of networks and partnerships, so we could draw on multiple forms of expertise, think creatively across sectoral and hierarchical boundaries, and have great reach for our findings and impacts.

The ARC initiated and developed a set of test-and-learn projects – on topics including spatial planning, energy policy, procurement, local democracy, youth engagement, political engagement, health and social care, digital innovation, and the solidarity economy. Our design developed the idea of hybridity as a way to facilitate hands-on social science (Richardson et al., 2018). This meant having multiple action research projects based in a single place.

Transdisciplinarity was a key concept underpinning the design of the ARC. We wanted to learn by doing through a research design that accepted the messy, fragmented social world and worked with these dynamics in an inclusive and participatory format.

This meant that 'incompleteness' was a vital ingredient and allowed co-contributors to influence the research. It was important to avoid a situation where all the details of what we would do were decided in advance. The project tried to embrace adaptation, creativity, and uncertainty, working across organizational, sectoral, and technical boundaries to catalyse social innovation and change.

Designing incompleteness

Our process had a broad structure and timeline but evolved and adapted over the four years of the project (2016-2020). At the beginning of the process, certain decisions were left on the table for the ARC to be able to wield genuine influence over the direction of the project. The process was characterized by openings and closings, cycles of uncertainty and certainty, and an unfolding of the journey in different directions from those originally anticipated.

Academic initiation. The idea for Jam and Justice was developed in a collaborative workshop and set of meetings which established a common problem space. However, given the nature of the academic funding and application process, the first phase of the project was inevitably shaped by decisions made by the academic researchers during the bid writing process. The first goal for the co-investigator team was to select members for the ARC. We held an Open Evening with interactive activities to share information and discuss what participation would involve. We also had three taster workshops to let people get a feel for how the ARC might operate. The co-investigator team held an open application process, with over 50 people from Greater Manchester applying. The team then focused on finding people with diverse expertise and connections across Greater Manchester. Fifteen people were selected to join the ARC, with professional roles in national and local charities, consultancies, community interest and benefit organizations, and public sector bodies. Importantly, none of those joining the ARC had been involved in the collaborative workshops. This meant that ARC members inherited decisions made by others.

Co-decision making. Once the ARC was formed, we held several different meetings to get to know people. For instance, during the first ARC meeting we ran 'speed dating' and ARC members shared a photograph or object that was important to them. At the second ARC meeting we introduced key ideas and undertook a World

Café exercise. During the third meeting we brainstormed what principles we wanted to guide participation in the project and how we wanted to select projects. These sessions were supplemented by an open workshop on participatory urban governance to explore people's 'hunches' about what works in citizen engagement. Each of these sessions was run by different members of the co-investigator team and with members of the ARC.

The main purpose of the ARC was to identify and select mini 'ARC projects' to test and learn about ways to get more people involved in urban decision-making. We invited different ideas to be put forward and these were discussed in co-development workshops using methods such as Ketso (see Photo 3.1), a participatory brainstorming and planning creative method (Tippett and How, 2011). The ideas were then developed into formal proposals and put to the vote in a deliberative workshop. This was independently facilitated (see Chapter 2, Box 2.7, 'Facilitation – bringing methods to life') to try to de-privilege the power and authority of the academic research team in making the decision. Ten ideas were selected from a long list of project possibilities. An extended time was required to take the ideas through to implementation stage and to test the feasibility and deliverability of the ideas. Some projects were commissioned out to external delivery partners; others were delivered 'in-house' by people involved in Jam and Justice, including the academic research team. Each ARC member expressed their preferences and was allocated as a 'lead' to mentor and support at least one of the projects.

Opening up parallel tracks. Following the collective decision on which projects would go forward, a number of parallel processes opened up. Each project used a different approach to address the issue at hand (see the two Chapter 5 descriptions 'A method for making the everyday visible: photovoice and everyday politics' and 'Tapping hidden expertise: the model of the Inverted Citizens' Jury'). Project start up and delivery was staggered for different projects, depending on the duration of time from idea to practical implementation. As a result, the timelines and 'steps' diverged significantly. A flexible process was needed to accommodate these different temporalities.

The ARC also built wider networks and alliances in Greater Manchester and beyond to bring together people who were interested in addressing urban issues through co-production. Creative documentation was used to share this process with those not able to be involved (see Chapter 5, 'Closing the co-productive cycle: creative documentation as a method for multi-vocal representation'). This process was led by a sub-group of the ARC called the 'Coalitions for Change' group which was handed decision-making and budgets beyond those originally envisaged in the bid. This therefore represented a key opening of the scope for co-production in the project and significant redesign.

Photo 3.1 Using the Ketso method for participatory brainstorming on project ideas during the co-initiation phase of mini-ARC projects. (Photo by Beth Perry)

In addition, the co-investigator team forged a partnership, Developing Co-productive Capacities, with the Greater Manchester Combined Authority to look at the scope for co-production in policy development at the city-regional level (see Chapter 4, 'Exchange as method: the value of trans-local learning'). This included developing a single point of contact to lever policy influence, co-produce joint activities with policy officers and take responsibility for institutional learning within their organization. This was a further point of departure from the original bid, which had envisaged a standing group of local authority representatives to act as a sounding board to the ARC rather than play an active role in embedding findings.

As multiple openings emerged and the scope for co-production widened, ARC members were able to play different roles within the project, stepping into leadership roles and making decisions that were not previously on the table. The incomplete design – in which some things were unknown at the point of securing funding – enabled this flexibility and divergence in approach to accommodate different preferences and interests.

Coming together. Given the divergence of parallel project tracks we tried different approaches to building community and solidarity within the ARC. We organized meals and celebrations and made a 'socials' budget available for the ARC. A peer learning visit to Scotland proved especially effective in building group identity. It remained a challenge throughout to retain this collective identity given the multiplicity of activities that were being undertaken. Collective reflection was woven throughout the process. A collaborative 'quick reflection questionnaire' was developed using Google forms and self-administered by ARC members following key happenings and events. Academic researchers carried out 'welcome' and 'exit' interviews with ARC members. Two half-day participatory design trace workshops were organized to look back over the individual and collective journeys and identify critical incidents and moments. These workshops were important in offering closure on key moments and analysing the process.

Different projects marked their closure in different ways and at different times. Each project team developed their own forms of reporting and representation. Projects were able to access additional funds to boost their knowledge exchange and engagement with different groups. We also produced a collective report (Perry et al., 2019) which we launched at a final celebration event in a social venue in Greater Manchester in July 2019. We emphasized multi-vocality and diversity in outputs so that the coming together was not a flattening, but rather a celebration of difference. One mechanism for achieving this was the reallocation of budgets to make provision for ARC members to access their own individual knowledge exchange budgets.

Making a difference. Our incomplete design enabled the projects to create spaces for social innovation which had a high degree of autonomy and flexibility within a common framework. This approach also enabled wide reach across the city-region. Our ARC projects engaged over 400 discrete individuals and led to several evidenced changes to policies to bring urban justice issues into greater focus.

Each of the ten projects looked at a distinct urban issue: for example, how energy is produced for cities, how public money could be spent to produce more social value, how older people could be better supported to live a good life in their own homes, and what new roles local politicians could play to work even more productively with communities. We also explored routes of participation for women in urban decision-making, people who feel disconnected from formal politics, and for younger people. Other projects addressed how we can have better conversations about planning how cities develop, and new ways to model the economy for social benefit.

The projects acted as spaces for social innovation through *reframing* policy ideas, *seeding* new models or approaches, *infrastructuring* relationships through new or strengthening relationships, and *changing* mindsets by creating space for perspectives to shift.

Key findings

Our incomplete design generated many lessons for those seeking to embark on transdisciplinary research projects. For instance, we underestimated the time required to establish and explore group identity in the early stages of the projects; and the process of identifying project ideas introduced competition for funds among ARC members, which was not always productive. We also found that external pressures – for instance to complete the project within a finite time frame and budget – impacted on the quality and experience of the process at different moments. Acknowledging the antecedent power of the academics was a constant theme, promoting further inquiry into the nature of leadership in co-production projects (see Chapter 2, Box 2.6 'Leading transdisciplinary co-production'), and the extent of work in managing boundaries as academic 'active intermediaries' was unanticipated (see Chapter 2, 'Active intermediation').

A critical issue emerging is how we develop metrics for evidencing and evaluating the outcomes of complex, messy, distributed social processes, like social innovation and co-production. While we were fortunate to have staff and resources dedicated to tracking the impact of co-production, existing ways of measuring and evaluating co-production are inadequate (Durose et al., 2018). Long-term social processes enhance the importance of tracking impacts and outcomes to monitor both intended and unintended effects.

The CityLab programme in Cape Town

Warren Smit

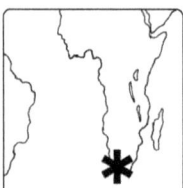

The CityLab programme was initiated by the African Centre for Cities (ACC) in 2008 as an interdisciplinary applied research programme on sustainable urban development, intended to deal with real issues in a way that overcame disciplinary divides and the policy-practice divide. When ACC became the anchor of the Mistra Urban Futures Cape Town Local Interaction Platform in 2010, the CityLab Programme became one of the main foci of the platform.

The CityLabs were essentially about bringing together relevant stakeholders to co-produce policy-relevant knowledge on the key urban challenges facing Cape Town. The topics of the CityLabs were identified through engagement with the two main government partners, the City of Cape Town (CCT), and the Western Cape Provincial Government. Funding from a range of sources, including Mistra Urban Futures, the City of Cape Town, and the Western Cape Provincial Government, was used to fund the CityLabs. In all, there have been nine CityLabs: the Central City CityLab; the Philippi CityLab; the Climate Change CityLab; the Urban Flooding CityLab; the Urban Ecology CityLab; the Healthy Cities CityLab; the Sustainable Human Settlements CityLab; the Safety, Violence and Inclusion CityLab; and the Public Culture CityLab.

Full-time researchers were recruited to co-ordinate the CityLabs (each researcher co-ordinated one or two CityLabs at a time). They were responsible for identifying and engaging with key stakeholders and facilitating the activities of the CityLab (seminar series, collective publications, collaborative research, etc). The CityLabs were all planned to have finite lifespans (typically of at least three years).

Various co-production methods were used, depending on the nature of the topic (for example, who the key stakeholders were, how importantly they regarded the topic, and what the local body of knowledge was). One common method that all the CityLabs used was bringing together different types of knowledge through seminar series and joint publications that reflect a range of experiences and views from academics, officials, and civil society. Field trips were also a useful way of helping people see issues in a different way and enabled participants to interact in a more informal way. The seminars, collaborative writing process, and field trips helped build 'communities of knowledge and practice' by bringing together academics, government officials, civil society, students, and others, to ensure participants were exposed to a range of perspectives and could build networks with a range of stakeholders. In addition, most of the CityLabs also involved one or more of the following activities:

- Undertaking collaborative research, for example, in the Healthy Cities CityLab, Urban Flooding CityLab, and Safety, Violence and Inclusion CityLab. Through bringing together people from different disciplines to collectively undertake research, this often ended up with methodological innovation/experimentation: for example, the body mapping methodology of the Healthy Cities CityLab and the Urban Flooding CityLab's mapping of the perspectives and technologies of key governance nodes involved in flooding in Cape Town. The body mapping methodology drew on the diverse experiences of the participants in the Healthy Cities CityLab, and involved community members, over the course of five-day workshops, tracing the outlines of their body, drawing their internal organs and then annotating these drawings to represent different aspects of their health and well-being and the areas in which they lived (Photo 3.2). These representations of the body and the neighbourhoods people lived in were then used to guide group discussions and interviews into issues of health and well-being and how these are affected by their living environments.

- Co-producing new policies was the focus of the Human Settlements CityLab, which involved collaboration with the Western Cape Provincial Government on a new human settlements policy called the Living Cape Framework.
- Co-designing and implementing innovative projects was the focus of the Public Culture CityLab, which implemented public art projects across Cape Town.

As with many similar endeavours, the experience of the CityLabs showed that co-production can be a time-consuming and complex process. Although the University of Cape Town (UCT) was very supportive of co-production as an approach, co-production doesn't fit in easily with academic performance evaluation systems, which value a high volume of high-profile research outputs, whereas the outputs of co-production processes take a long time to produce and are often not very academic (see Chapter 2, 'Active intermediation'). Getting government officials to participate was sometimes also a challenge, given that they are often very overstretched and caught up in dealing with constant crises. A final challenge was that of turnover of staff – this was a particular problem with officials involved in the CityLab programme, but in one case a CityLab co-ordinator resigned, which had a very negative impact on that CityLab.

Despite these challenges, the CityLab programme was very successful in bringing together different stakeholders in Cape Town, in integrating and expanding the knowledge base of key challenges in Cape Town and in contributing to policy development. The preconditions for this success were:

- Having a pool of very flexible funding that enable the CityLabs to have long-term and open-ended processes (i.e. identifying key stakeholders and bringing them together to decide on key issues and collaborative activities). Having an open-ended initial phase is crucial to understand the different perspectives and interests of participants in the process, and identifying a common agenda and common conceptual vocabulary may take a considerable amount of time.

- Recruiting the right staff who could straddle the academic research/policy and practice divide (most came from an NGO background).
- Strong support from the City of Cape Town and Western Cape Provincial Government. The partnership with the City later evolved into the Mistra Urban Futures Knowledge Transfer Programme (embedded researchers and exchange officials) (see Chapter 5, 'Building transdisciplinary capacities through the Knowledge Transfer Programme').

The CityLab model has subsequently been widely adopted as a way of co-producing policy relevant knowledge among key stakeholders in cities. For example, the Gauteng City-Region Observatory in Johannesburg, South Africa, adopted the CityLab approach in 2014 to explore and develop knowledge around implementing a green infrastructure approach in Gauteng. A CityLab is currently being explored at University College London (UCL) for green infrastructure planning and decision-making in London. Building on its experiences of the CityLab programme, the ACC further developed the model through an urbanization laboratory in Tanzania (TULab) that applied the same approach to issues of sustainability at a national scale (this was co-ordinated by a former co-ordinator of one of the CityLabs).

Suggested readings

Anderson, P.M.L., Brown-Luthango, M., Cartwright, A., Farouk, I. and Smit, W. (2013) 'Brokering communities of knowledge and practice: reflections on the African Centre for Cities' CityLab programme', *Cities* 32: 1–10 <http://dx.doi.org/10.1016/j.cities.2013.02.002>.

Culwick, C., Washbourne, C.-L., Anderson, P.M.L., Cartwright, A., Patel, Z. and Smit, W. (2019) 'CityLab reflections and evolutions: nurturing knowledge and learning for urban sustainability through co-production experimentation', *Current Opinion in Environmental Sustainability* 39: 9–16 <http://dx.doi.org/10.1016/j.cosust.2019.05.008>.

Smit, W., Lawhon, M. and Patel, Z. (2015) 'Co-producing knowledge for whom, and to what end? Reflections from the African Centre for Cities in Cape Town', in M. Polk (ed.), *Co-producing Knowledge for Sustainable Cities: Joining Forces for Change*, pp. 47–69, Routledge, London.

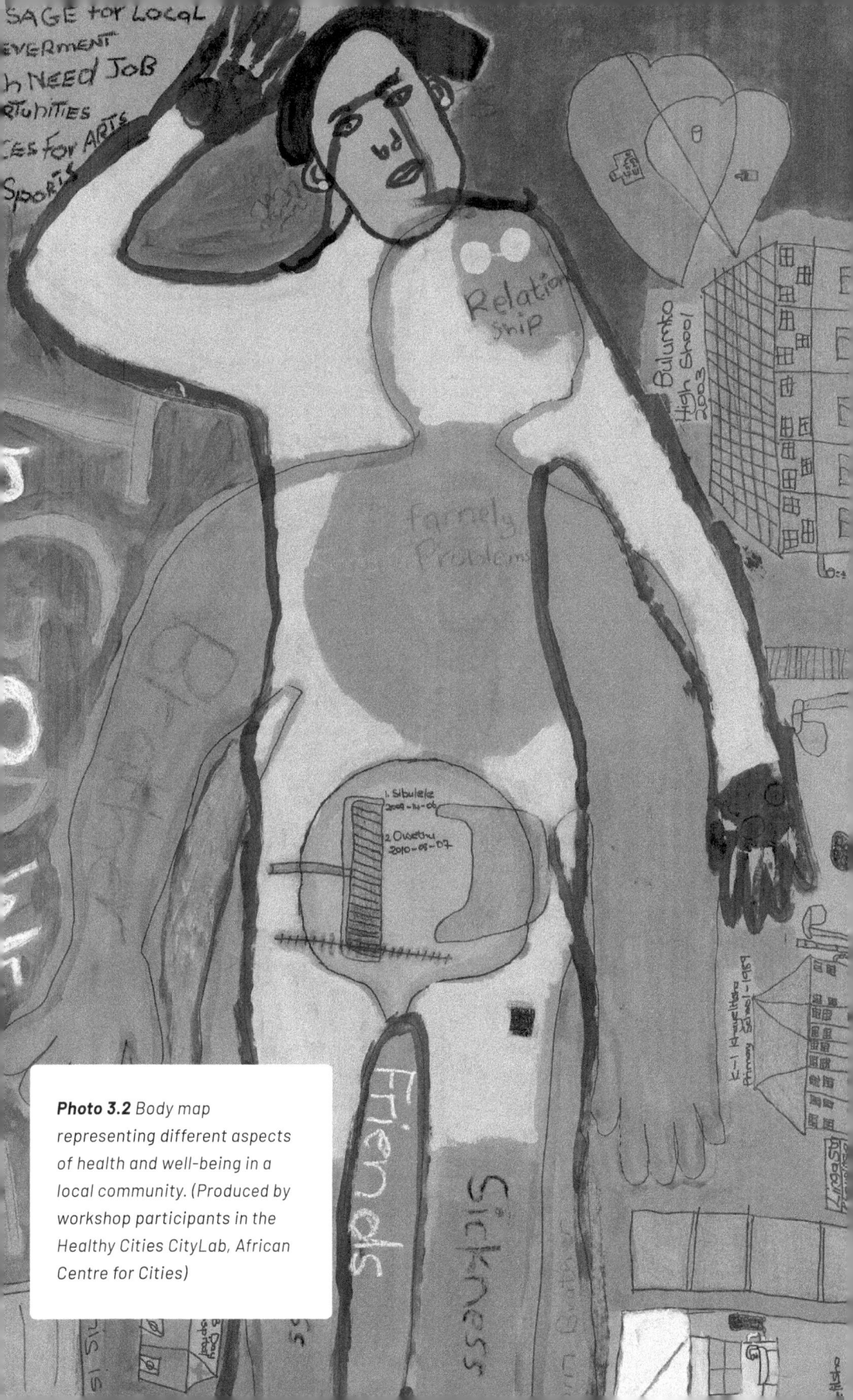

Photo 3.2 Body map representing different aspects of health and well-being in a local community. (Produced by workshop participants in the Healthy Cities CityLab, African Centre for Cities)

Establishing communities of trust through panels

*Barry Ness and
Kerstin Hemström*

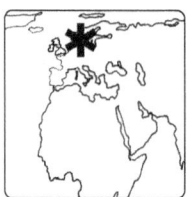

To harness local potential for co-productive research between academic and non-academic partners in southern Sweden, the Skåne platform arranged transdisciplinary expert *Panels* under three broad locally relevant urban themes: urban ecosystem services, migration and urban development, and sustainable neighbourhood development. The model is inspired by an earlier independent commission in Malmö (Stigendal and Östergren, 2010), which was created and appointed to understand and address the increasing health disparities and long-term social sustainability in the city. The work of this commission is known regionally as a good example of a cross-cutting approach to knowledge co-generation. It involved collaboration between researchers, citizens, public officials, civil society organizations, and industry, aiming to generate scientifically informed strategies for how the health inequalities in Malmö could be addressed.

The panels are an indirect outcome of the commission; they combine researcher and practitioner perspectives, mainly involving experts from the three regional universities and municipalities. The work of the panels was also augmented with members from regional authorities and/or the private sector, broadening the diversity of insights and promoting increased understanding of the particular urban challenge in question. Depending on the panel, their project work lasted from mid- to late-2018 through 2019 with ambitions to continue their respective project activities into the future. Each panel consisted of approximately 8–10 members. The three research themes were deemed those important to examine by Skåne platform leadership; platform leadership also selected a panel leader for each research theme based on their knowledge of key individuals working on the respective themes. The remaining panel members were then chosen by panel leaders based on their experience of working on the theme and through consultation with others. The panels were internally funded by the Skåne platform with matching funding from the Mistra Urban Futures project.

The aims of the panels were to gather and synthesize the disparate knowledge and experiences that existed on each of the targeted sustainable urban development themes. The ambition was then to disseminate this knowledge to actors both in and beyond the region in order to promote more informed and integrated sustainable urban development processes.

Each constellation worked as a knowledge cluster for its respective theme. The structure of the panels varied, and each panel organized its work and activities in different ways. They developed through collaborative processes among, and based upon the needs and desires of, their members. However, each panel also divided itself into even smaller, strategic sub-themes (e.g. experimental governance, development paths for children and youth), who worked collaboratively to produce deeper knowledge co-production into the targeted themes. The process of co-defining the knowledge needs in conjunction with participating in the different common panel activities has also fostered a community of trust and understanding among panel participants.

In each panel, members were jointly responsible for collecting, analysing, and synthesizing knowledge and experiences relevant to the theme. The work involved mapping knowledge gaps and demands in both research and city practice and locating a means to summarize and communicate critical insights in accessible ways. The work also included linking activities into ongoing policy and urban development processes, both within Malmö and throughout the broader region. Furthermore, the knowledge produced was disseminated via different media (e.g. social media, reports, peer-reviewed publications), aiming to promote the findings on sustainable urban development both in and beyond Skåne. These specific activities included, for example, co-writing of knowledge syntheses, common retreats and workshops with regional city planners, conference presentations, study visits, public presentations, and scientific publications. As another tangible example, one panel took the additional step of funding even smaller transdisciplinary projects, to stimulate development of ecosystems-based initiatives within the region.

According to most participants, panel collaboration proved rewarding. In addition to advancing the understanding of issues on the specific urban sustainability theme and sub-themes on which the panel concentrated, individual panel members benefited from the increased knowledge from the broader collaboration process and team of experts of which they were part. The insights they gained when interacting with other experts and perspectives of their field enabled participants to reflect upon and sharpen research questions and decisions in parallel research and practice activities. As such, there were co-benefits between the expert panel and the parallel decisions and networks that the members took part in.

Diversity of co-learning activities, frequent meetings with deliverables
As stated above, the structure, activities, and methods of each of the panels varied. All panels had a number of start-up planning meetings aimed for members to develop the broader project and the sub-themes within it. As the panel work progressed, the individual working styles evolved. As examples, the urban ecosystem services panel placed strong efforts on workshops with practitioners and how to better integrate ecosystem service thinking into

planning processes. The panel on migration and urban development had a more conventional academic approach with efforts focused on internal working seminars, where the specific sub-themes were presented and discussed by all panel members.

How the approach served to facilitate knowledge co-production
The different panel activities served as a worthwhile approach to facilitate knowledge co-production that probably would not have been possible with conventional academic or practitioner-specific knowledge creation processes. Notwithstanding that the duration of time the panels had to carry out their work was short (i.e. approximately one year), the different actions provided an opportunity for co-production to happen and created a basis for continued collaboration in the respective areas.

Key lessons from this applied approach – strengths and limits, unintended consequences
Despite the successes of the panels, there is room for improving the process. First, experiences from the panels demonstrated that co-production processes must be prioritized by participants and not seen as activities that have a lower priority than normal routines and responsibilities, especially academic research. In addition, the process of setting up the panels took significantly longer than expected, which had implications on the level of knowledge co-production that was ultimately achieved within the time frame. The key lesson is that ample time must be allotted for experts to form relationships and build communities of trust between themselves and the different organizations they represent. Furthermore, significant time can also be needed for the formation process to organize a common set of useful activities that promote interaction and knowledge sharing. While some panel members already had an established history of collaboration, other members were unfamiliar with the participants and the approach.

Finally, and as with all project activities, good panel leadership is essential. Leadership styles varied among the panels (see Chapter 2, Box 2.6, 'Leading transdisciplinary co-production'), which had strong implications for the level of success of the panels. Conventional academic project management is difficult; managing individuals from both academia and practice with their different priorities, outlooks, and work cultures requires leaders with the understanding, patience, and skills to guide the process down pathways that work for all participants. It is essential that these leaders are fostered for approaches such as panels to be fruitful.

A space for learners to lead and leaders to learn: Challenge Lab

John Holmberg and Johan Holmén

In this short description we provide an overview of the key elements of Challenge Lab: a space and process for strategic transdisciplinary university–society collaboration to navigate sustainability transitions in practice. Challenge Lab creates educational space for students from different master's programmes and cultural backgrounds to learn, exercise, and develop leadership for sustainability transitions. The work is oriented towards addressing local and regional sustainability challenges in leverage points, identified in the 'in-between spaces' that no single actor or organization can govern through their own activity. The students work in multi-stakeholder settings and apply a backcasting-from-principles-methodology (see below) and related tools including values-clarification and systems thinking together with dialogues and a focus on entrepreneurship.

Challenge Lab provides an opportunity for different societal actors to meet around master's students in a setting where complex sustainability challenges are put in the centre, rather than the needs of individual organizations or actors. The Lab is located on the border between the university and surrounding society, providing a complementary function to the university educations, exploring and engaging with sustainability challenges with a transdisciplinary approach. Characteristic for sustainability challenges is that they often sit in-between different organizations, demanding multi-actor collaboration. As achieving sustainability is rather a question of changing systems than change within systems, it is in these 'in-between spaces' that a potential for transition and system innovation can be identified.

The Challenge Lab methodology builds upon a backcasting approach. Students build trustful relations with different societal actors around a shared question of importance, by identifying root-causes and experimenting with leverage point interventions. The methodology acknowledges 'inner' as well as 'outer' dimensions of change, building upon the participating actor's own values, knowledges, and motivations as well as on systemic challenges, structures, and dynamics.

Below, reflections are provided on what is considered the core in the Challenge Lab methodology in three categories: the space, the process, and the people.

The Space
Challenge Lab is located at a science park (Holmberg, 2014). This location has been important for the Lab to serve as a boundary space between different societal actors. The intention is to create an experience of the Lab as a 'neutral', inviting,

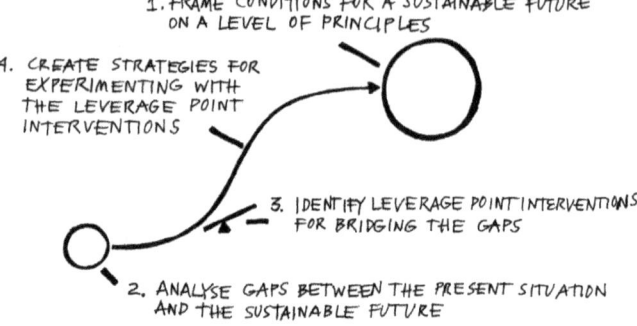

Figure 3.1
Illustration of the backcasting methodology used at Challenge Lab.

and 'open' space for all participants. Senge et al. (2015: 30) expressed the generative potential of creating truly engaged spaces in the following way:

> the conscious act of creating space, of engaging people in genuine questions, and of convening around a clear intention with no hidden agenda, creates a very different type of energy from that which arises from seeking to get people committed to your plan.

The Process

The backcasting methodology (Holmberg, 1998) provides an overarching structure/framework to focus the work and remove 'unnecessary uncertainties'. It seeks to generate knowledge and learning through the following steps (Figure 3.1):

1. Formulate guiding principles for a desirable and sustainable future ('What should be?')
2. Analyse the present situation in relation to the principles to illuminate gaps and challenges ('What is and why?', in relation to 'What should be?')
3. Identify leverage point interventions for bridging the gaps ('What could be?')
4. Create strategies for experimenting in the leverage point interventions ('What can be?')

The four steps are accompanied by different tools and methods, chosen and adapted depending on factors such as thematical orientation, scope, and context. In practice, the steps include both 'opening up' and 'closing down' time, allowing for brainstorming/exploration as well as condensing, summarizing, and prioritizing what has emerged. Results provided by the process, having gone through the four steps, are often strategic areas of intervention where coordinated efforts are needed to navigate sustainable systems innovation. Experience from working with the backcasting process is that it can support:

- thinking that goes beyond what currently is – starting from a sustainable and desirable future;
- thinking that is broad – acknowledging all sustainability dimensions;
- thinking that is together – for shared meaning and understanding.

The People

The facilitation of the process seeks to build capabilities for the students, through various methods and tools, to develop a leadership on three levels: leading oneself, leading together with others, and leading for humanity. It seeks to build on the students' intrinsic motivational factors of autonomy, competence, and relatedness. The learning process is further enriched by the heterogeneous group with students from different cultural and educational backgrounds.

The students then facilitate dialogues with people relevant for the challenge/question at hand, including researchers, public- and private-sector stakeholders, NGOs, and civil society representatives. The stakeholders are typically identified via snowballing methods, where many of them participate in the lab on a continual basis year after year, building trust over time. Through this process, the students become bridge-builders, challengers, and transition leaders. See Larsson and Holmberg (2018) and Holmén et al. (2021) for deeper reflections.

Suggested readings

Holmén, J., Adawi, T., and Holmberg, J. (2021) 'Student-led sustainability transformations: employing realist evaluation to open the black box of learning in a Challenge Lab curriculum', *International Journal of Sustainability in Higher Education* 22(1) <https://doi.org/10.1108/IJSHE-06-2020-0230>

Larsson, J. and Holmberg, J. (2018) 'Learning while creating value for sustainability transitions: the case of Challenge Lab at Chalmers University of Technology', *Journal of Cleaner Production* 172: 4411–20 <https://doi.org/10.1016/j.jclepro.2017.03.072>

Exploring TD methods in a PhD course: creating a TD 'learning space'

Henrietta Palmer and Merritt Polk

Despite growing attention to transdisciplinary research needs, transdisciplinary education programmes are still rare, and even fewer involve non-academic participants (Norris et al., 2016). During 2017–2019, the Gothenburg platform held a doctoral course (in two parts) for both doctoral students and practitioners. These courses were part of the platform's Urban Futures Open Research School. The overall aims of the research school were to have an international impact on the field of transdisciplinary research for sustainable urban development and to develop networks with 'realising just cities competencies' in academia as well as in the wider society. The main substantive areas were competences needed to promote the Centre's pivotal work with both transdisciplinary approaches and knowledge about what 'just cities' entail.

The aims of the research school were thus both to train PhDs with a solid experience and knowledge of transdisciplinary co-production (TD CP) for just and sustainable cities, and to contribute to urban development through educational activities that can be used within the professional mandates of the partner organizations. The courses targeted both PhD students and professional practitioners and were designed for both research and practice-based contexts. From these overall aims, the course conveners formulated learning goals following the student-centred learning approach in the Bologna process (University and College Council, 2019) (see Table 3.1).

Table 3.1 Learning outcomes for the doctoral course, Co-producing knowledge in transdisciplinary research – From practice to theory, 2017-2019

	After completion of the course, the student is expected to be able to:
Knowledge and understanding	• understand the complexities of urban challenges • be familiar with concepts of justice within the urban environment • apply knowledge on border management • understand transdisciplinary theory and relevant design theory, and be able to position individual research processes into a theoretical context
Competencies and skills	• design a transdisciplinary research project • practise a set of methods applicable in TD research • apply skills for facilitation of boundary projects
Judgement and approach	• evaluate and compare methods for transdisciplinary research • evaluate the scientific and practical impact of transdisciplinary approaches to urban problem solving in different substantive areas

Source: Course Guide, 'Co-producing knowledge in transdisciplinary research – From practice to theory' <https://www.mistraurbanfutures.org/en/course-co-producing-knowledge> [accessed 18 August 2020]

Approach

Two main narratives and learning approaches were used to fulfil the multiple goals and targets outlined in Table 3.1. The first narrative focused on the substantive knowledge needed to understand and problematize the theme of realising just cities. This narrative worked through scientific literature from a variety of disciplines that focused on the dilemmas, approaches, and theories surrounding the urban justice discussion. Practical and local examples from case studies of policy and implementation exemplified different equality topics and formed the practice-based core. The second narrative focused on gaining competencies in TD CP. Based both on methodological lectures and group work around several approaches, the students learned about and gained first-hand experiences with methods that are relevant for TD CP research (see Box 3.1). An additional learning approach was to develop a 'space' for collaboration and knowledge integration for different TD learning situations that included: learning within and across disciplines and thought-collectives (of both practitioners and academic researchers); learning across cultures of practices and 'silos'; co-learning from practice-based case studies; learning-by-doing, as reflection in action; student–teacher jointly co-learning; and teachers learning from students.

Sources of motivation for the course

One of the initial questions framing the courses was: Is there something we could call *transdisciplinary* learning? If so, what is it based upon and what does it entail? To answer these questions, the course conveners developed a TD pedagogical approach from current literature on TD CP research (Pohl et al., 2010; Lang et al., 2012), and references from adult development on societal change agents (Jordan, 2011). From educational theory, they used references from educating for sustainable development (Wiek et al., 2011) and TD pedagogy (Balsiger, 2015). Finally, they based the course design on three practical experiences. The first was the evaluation of research projects at the Gothenburg platform undertaken in 2015 (Hansson and Polk, 2017). The second was previous educational experiences from running a TD post-master's programme on urban futures in the context of an art academy (Palmer, 2014).[1] The third was the research framework of Mistra Urban Futures on Realising Just Cities.[2] In total these different departures formed a transdisciplinary base from theory and practice, identifying a wide set of competences and approaches that are relevant to teach within a course on TD CP research.

Course components and course description

The different course components were all framed and designed to include perspectives from both 'practice' and 'academia'. These components thus represented different ways of thinking and doing from both practice and academia. They included:

- Participants: course participants representing the dual target groups identified above.
- Lecturers: researchers, civil servants, and facilitators.
- Content: theoretical approaches; local case studies; methods for facilitation and collaborative knowledge production.
- Ways of learning: by doing collaboratively; by creating a reflexive space; by individually comparing; by creating joint voices.

The two courses were structured into four modules. Each module focused on a particular method and local case study.³ This structure enabled the unfolding of relevant skills and competences for a TD CP process, starting with joint visioning and ending with collaborative writing. Each module had particular theoretical concerns, which were reflected upon by both researchers and practitioners.

In terms of methods, trained competences, and ways of learning, the four modules contained the components outlined in Box 3.1.

Box 3.1   Methods, focus, and work modes used in the modules

Module 1: Challenges and holistic thinking for the urban future
Methods: Scenario thinking (anticipatory competences; competences of dealing with uncertainties; stakeholder awareness).

Focus: Wicked issues; urban justice; global frameworks; visions and visionary documents (normative competences).

Work mode: Case-study based group work; presentation as robustness test (interpersonal competences).

Module 2: Research practice and methods for transdisciplinarity
Methods: Perspective awareness; systems-thinking; designerly thinking; mapping (integrative competences of multiple knowledges and expertise; systems-thinking competence; competences of visualization).

Focus: Dealing with complex issues; multiple perspectives and conflicts (complexity awareness).

Work mode: Case study-based group work; presentation as deliberation (interpersonal competences; context awareness; self-awareness).

Module 3: Facilitation and border management
Methods: Facilitation and process design; learning history; context and power analysis (skills of process design; strategic competences; stakeholder awareness; context awareness).

Focus: Facilitation vs. research; institutionalization; power/knowledge; governance; Actor-Network-Theory; roles within TD CP research.

Work mode: Case study-based group work; presentation with case study-affected practitioners (interpersonal competences).

Module 4: Transdisciplinary theory and emerging epistemology
Methods: Collaborative writing as a research inquiry.

Focus: Reflexivity and knowledge production; normative perspectives of TD CP research; evaluation of TD CP research (competences of reflexivity).

Work mode: Writing in pairs (one practitioner/one PhD student); presentation as pair-reading.

Challenges and lessons learned
Each course ended by collecting oral and written evaluations from the students. Overall, their comments expressed great appreciation of the courses, reflected on the challenges for TD pedagogies, and offered different suggestions for improving the courses. Some of the comments that focused on normative competence as essential for TD CP research included: 'What are facts and what are values or opinions that different participants bring into the course?' 'We need agreements of certain concepts, such for example, what is the sustainable city?' Regarding reflexivity and stakeholder awareness and knowledge integration, the students pointed out the need to be conscious about which perspectives we are talking about when discussing: 'What is the "practitioner's knowledge" that I bring in as a practitioner' and 'We speak different languages and use different vocabularies.' An interesting remark addressed the role of confusion, where several students noted the importance of embracing uncertainty: 'I like the confusion! It makes me relax when everything is not clear. The process will take me somewhere.' Concerning the group work, the students emphasized the course space as a 'learning space' for TD CP processes: 'Group work gives a feeling of different vocabularies, different organizational problems and hierarchies.' More rules and pre-set standards around the group work were also required, for example to encourage training in how to listen, to build trust, and to be able to grow together. Overall, the evaluations reflected the radical set-up of the course, with the mixing of the different groups, which led to a simulated TD research situation that cannot be established in a purely academic context, nor achieved in a practice context.

The primary lesson learned from a PhD student perspective was the importance of being exposed to a 'real' transdisciplinary situation, before finalizing their studies. All of them noted that this does not happen within their academic programme, and if they create a TD research situation themselves, they are not trained as facilitators nor do they have a repertoire of methods to use. From a practitioner's perspective one main lesson was the importance of being grounded in theory to find arguments to break business as usual practices and to dare to cross silos. The experience of a TD learning situation gave them motivation to move beyond their standard practices and to meet wicked issues in a more grounded way. From a teaching perspective, there were many lessons, including the importance of creating a learning space and time for reflexivity. To plan time, to give space and tools for this in TD research and TD teaching situations cannot be underestimated.

Contributions to a TD pedagogy?

One concern for a TD pedagogy is how different pedagogical approaches to learning determine different outcomes. A *transformational learning* pedagogy, for example, requires having assumptions challenged in order to develop a different perspective from the one previously held. This points towards a situation where confusion is present, provoking a condition of 'liminality', where new perspectives can emerge (Land et al., 2014). But confusion is tolerable only when there is a sense of trust, care, and reciprocity. This shows the importance of establishing in-depth relationships in TD CP research.
The in-depth relationships in the courses were created by mixing practitioners and academics, and respective approaches and knowledge from both spheres. This TD learning space generated openness, curiosity, and care. It required the continuous presence by all, including us as teachers, to continually and jointly reflect upon our differences. All of these aspects contributed to creating trust. This is what we define as a liminal learning space.

Suggested readings

Balsiger, J. (2015) 'Transdisciplinarity in the classroom? Simulating the co-production of sustainability knowledge', *Futures* 65: 185–94 <https://doi.org/10.1016/j.futures.2014.08.005>.

Jordan, T. (2011) 'Skilful engagement with wicked issues: a framework for analysing the meaning-making structures of societal change agents', *Integral Review* 7(2): 47–91.

Wiek, A., Withycombe, L. and Redman, C.L. (2011) 'Key competencies in sustainability: a reference framework for academic program development', *Sustainability Science* 6: 203–18 <https://doi.org/10.1007/s11625-011-0132-6>.

Space-enabling co-production on solid waste management

Franklin Otiende and Michael Oloko

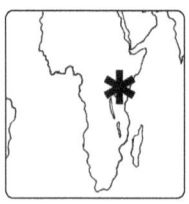

There have been several attempts to improve solid waste management in Kisumu, Kenya. Dependent on donor support, these have generally been unsuccessful in reaching sustainable solutions. Serious issues endure in a city overwhelmed by growing waste generation and limited resources and capacity to expand collection services. Most of the waste of the informal settlements is not collected, posing great health and environment hazards.

To move the situation forward, local researchers organized co-production research on waste management, concentrating the activities in specific urban areas and physical spaces. The overall objective was to improve the situation in the city by enhancing the waste management value chain and maintaining a clean and healthy environment. The solid waste management actors in Kisumu include both formal actors registered by city or government authorities, and informal non-registered individuals and groups handling waste through collection, transport, reuse, recycling or disposal. At the lowest level, these include individual waste pickers who scavenge valuable materials to sell to other operators in the waste management system.

Engaging stakeholders
Initially, the researchers identified relevant local waste actors and presented them with the overall research concept and objectives. This included the city Director of Environment, the directors of several local private companies, and the chairman of a local community-based organization handling waste. These actors were motivated to participate in the research by the prospects to find solutions to the waste situation in the city and enhance their benefits in/from the waste management value chain.

The selected waste actors were included in the research team and participated in all research activities. Overall, this included setting up pilot facilities for waste recycling and transfer, testing and developing new approaches and technologies for collecting and handling waste, collecting data through questionnaires, and validating results in workshops. Once the research activities were set up, the project team called a meeting with other local actors dealing with waste. This included informal (non-registered) actors and individuals earning their living by picking waste at dumpsites, collecting waste from households, selling materials for recycling, and transporting waste from one point to another. The few who attended the first meeting soon recruited new participants who also saw the potential to derive benefit from the outcomes of the research (Photo 3.3).

The significance of a temporary occupation licence
The research project set up experiments at a site managed by the local waste entrepreneur Kibuye Waste Management CBO. To ensure official recognition and safety of the work, the researchers requested a temporary occupation licence from the city authorities, which officially recognizes the use of space owned by the City, specifying the purpose and duration. Appreciating the benefits of the research as contributing to a clean and healthy city environment, the permit was approved and has been renewed annually.

While rendering a formal space for conducting research, the issuing of temporary occupation licences signalled a recognition of the informal waste actors and a commitment to the research by the city authorities. This was important to create trust between the involved actors and to motivate other waste actors to engage in the project. Other places earmarked for demonstration of waste management through

Photo 3.3 *Capacity building of Kibuye CBO members on briquette making process from market waste sourced from Kibuye Market in Kisumu. (Photo by George Kavulavu Ngusale)*

research activities included the Kachok dumpsite, which later was relocated, and Arina estate. These spaces provided the opportunity to set up research activities close to the community, rendering it possible for small-scale actors to take part. These served as testing and learning grounds for new technology, but also as spaces where different waste management stakeholders could meet.

An empowered network
The concentration of co-production research activities at a specific physical site where different actors involved in waste management could meet, opened new opportunities for collaboration. For example, individual waste pickers caught sight of benefits in co-ordinating their activities to share the costs of transport, while waste pickers could collaborate with those recycling waste to provide better quality materials. Learning from one another and co-developing better solutions, the waste actors soon formed a co-operative network – Kisumu Waste Actors Network Co-operative (KIWAN). This included both formal and informal actors and individuals involved in handling waste. The members selected leaders, who later were included in the research team.

As a co-operative, the informal waste actors and collective as a whole were in a better position to interact with, and champion their interests towards, the city officials who were formally responsible for keeping the city clean. Appreciating the benefits of the collective, the city duly registered KIWAN as a co-operative organization. KIWAN is currently at the forefront in discussing issues of solid waste with the city and county, as well as in mobilizing and organizing the waste actors' participation in the city waste management activities. In their monthly meetings, the members of KIWAN discuss individual and collective challenges and possible solutions. The elected leaders represent the members in meetings with city officials, lobbying for their interests. To mobilize resources for effective operations, the organization also provides loans to individual members. Loans are repaid on a monthly basis with interest that later is distributed to members as dividends at the end of the year.

Challenges
Through the opportunities for collaboration and dialogue, the solid waste management research resulted in longstanding relationships and the building of trust between university researchers, local waste actors, and city authorities. Initially, however, some city officials opposed the research, indicating that the issues addressed had already been exhausted. To convince these officials of the benefits involved, the researchers invited them to review and develop the project. To signify co-ownership of the research, city officials were also invited to co-author a paper together with academic researchers. In the process of doing so, both parties gained a deeper understanding of one another's viewpoints with respect to the issues addressed and the potential solutions. All results were also validated through workshops with relevant stakeholders. When waste actors contributed by collecting data, they would be called to a workshop where the researchers presented how they had analysed the data and what they had found. The waste actors would

then gain a better understanding of the situation and the outcome of the research, while discussing potential solutions. In other cases, preliminary results were validated through workshops with other actors than those included in the research, in order to get their direct feedback on the project. This also reduced the likelihood of hostility from city officials to project reports and proposals.

Suggested reading

Gutberlet, J., Kain, J.J., Nyakinya, B., Ochieng, D., Odhiambo, N., Oloko, M.O., Omondi, E., Omolo, J., Otieno, S., Zapata, P. and Zapata Campos, M.J. (2016) 'Socio-environmental entrepreneurship and the provision of critical services in informal settlements', *Environment and Urbanization* 28(1): 205–22 <https://doi.org/10.1177/0956247815623772>.

Academics and municipal officials co-writing in third space

Dianne Scott

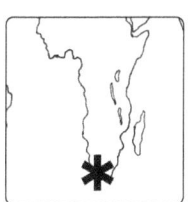

This section reflects on the co-production and co-writing of the book *Mainstreaming Climate Change in Urban Development: Lessons from Cape Town*, a product of a partnership between the African Centre for Cities (ACC), the University of Cape Town (UCT), and the City of Cape Town (CCT).[4] The aim of the book was to report on the progress of mainstreaming climate change into the various line functions of the CCT municipality. However, the book also aimed to produce knowledge co-written between CCT officials and UCT academics in the belief that this process would contribute to a more sustainable city. The municipal officials were enrolled through a selection process undertaken by CCT. The concept of 'third space' was used to design the support process for the authors and provide a metaphor that would assist authors from different frames of reference to collaborate with others.

Situation

The purpose of the book was to record the progress made and challenges to Cape Town's endeavour to facilitate sustainable development between 2015 and 2019 across various line functions of CCT through the process of mainstreaming climate change into urban policies, processes, programmes, and practices.

This challenge is set in a context of rapid urbanization, high inequality, and uncertainty about city-scale climatic changes. Mainstreaming is the process whereby climate change adaptation and mitigation are integrated into existing work being done by municipal practitioners (Uittenbroek et al., 2014).

Methods and activities

Overarching method. The method of co-producing knowledge through co-writing provided the overarching epistemological framework. In this case, theoretically, co-writing involves the incorporation of knowledge from the domain of both the municipality and the university as well as new knowledge to produce a co-written product through engagement, negotiation, exchange, compromise, and learning. The co-writing method was designed drawing on methods from previous exchanges, namely matching a city CCT official with a UCT academic with similar interests, and on facilitating preparation workshops for authors.

The preparation phase included three workshops. Importantly, the metaphor of 'third space' was introduced and employed as a heuristic tool. Rather than having an open choice as to the writing topic, the authors all had to focus on how they shifted their business-as-usual activities to mainstreaming climate change into their practices. City officials provided the empirical data about the mainstreaming process, while academics would provide relevant theory as a framing tool to analyse the empirical facts of the climate change issue.

The concept of third space as a heuristic tool. The concept of third space (Bhabha, 1994; Routledge, 1996; Wallace, 2004; Glasson et al., 2010) was applied heuristically as a means of getting the pairs of authors to conceptualize how they would engage with the frames of reference and forms of writing different from their own. The aim, as inherent in the concept, was to reduce the power differential between academic and practitioner. The power differential existed because of the asymmetry between the academy and the municipality as historically constructed sites of knowledge production. Third space, in this case, was proposed as a 'virtual' space to which authors would move from their home spaces (their spaces of expertise) to engage and produce knowledge. Figure 3.2 demonstrates the academics in first space (the most powerful space of academia) and the officials in second space (the less powerful space of the municipality). Once they have both moved to third space, negotiation in this space happens along the continuum of meaning-making between co-writers, and new hybrid meanings would be constructed (Scott et al., 2019). The burden of accommodation to produce an academic book lay therefore with the city officials who had to compromise their approach to writing (Canagarajah and Lee, 2013).

Process. Three workshops were designed to prepare partners for co-writing.[5] The process was designed to co-write a text conforming to the academic genre but at the same time written in an accessible form for practitioners and

Figure 3.2
The first and second spaces are 'home spaces', and academics and practitioners move from these spaces into the third space of co-production and co-writing. (Source: Scott et al., 2019: 66)

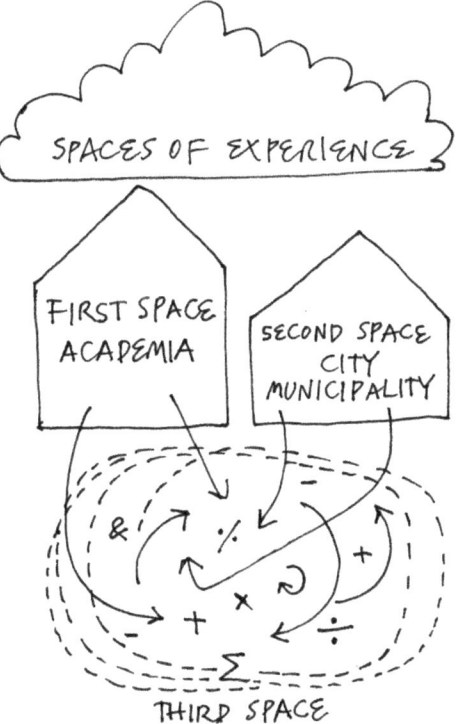

policymakers. The CCT, therefore, assumed that it was the officials who would need some support to write in the required academic style. However, the use of the metaphor of the third space in the workshops contradicted this assumption, as it introduced the idea that practitioners were not seen as needing 'writing development', but rather that both academics and practitioners would need to engage with new forms of writing together. This contradiction was therefore inherent in the project from the outset.

Workshop One: The concept of a *third space* was introduced in Workshop One as a framing concept to facilitate both officials and academics to position themselves in third space co-writing with their partners. In some cases, authors met each other for the first time. After an introductory session for all authors, the officials were introduced to the academic 'writing process' by the facilitators and critically discussed an example of the difference between academic writing and that of a city official. Finally, officials wrote abstracts for their chapters in a narrative form. On reflection, the academics should have participated in this exercise as well.

Workshop Two: The focus was on the application of theory in the writing up of the chapter which was for officials only. The veiled assumption here was that academics already know what theory is and how to apply it. This served to undermine the officials' confidence and position their knowledge as secondary to academic knowledge. The group interrogated an article using the concept of 'shadow spaces' to explain informal policymaking in eThekwini (Leck and Roberts, 2015).

Workshop Three: Due to administrative delays in getting the Memorandum of Understanding signed between CCT and UCT, this workshop served to get the process going again. After the presentation of contextual information about climate change and climate change policy in Cape Town, and the history of co-production between the CCT and ACC, officials and academics proceeded to critically compare an academic paper (Davison et al., 2015) with a policy text (City of Cape Town, 2001). The different forms of evidence, language used, and arguments raised the question of whose knowledge would prevail and in what form.

Peer Review. Each chapter was peer-reviewed by an academic and official in the same field as the authors in order to review the theoretical framing and argument and to ensure the contextual validity of the mainstreaming process, respectively. This was an important but difficult process, but it did ensure the academic theoretical language was made more accessible and officials became more rigorous in their referencing of empirical data. Chapters were revised to include reviewers' comments.

Survey. A short online survey was undertaken after the completion of the co-written chapters to understand how the authors had experienced co-writing and what impacts it had had on them. The survey revealed the prevalence of four different approaches:

1. The academic as a supervisor – the official doing the initial writing, after which it was then reviewed and augmented by the academic.
2. The interview approach – the academic commencing the writing based on initial discussions with the official.
3. The conventional co-authoring approach – each author writing different sections followed by putting their pieces together.
4. The 'iterative, constructive engagement approach' – the writing team conceptualizing the topic, structure, and narrative flow at the outset, and writing iteratively together.

The fourth approach, adopted by only 2 of the 10 writing teams, revealed that co-production had taken place from the start of the writing process. The first three approaches all started with a binary or hierarchical binary of 'supervisor/student', interviewer/interviewee, and official/academic writing separately, but experience shows that as the teams implemented their approaches, they shifted into a more 'constructive engagement' and co-productive mode of writing.

Key lessons

1. The key lesson is that power differentials between academics, coming from the first space (dominant space), and officials, from the second space (secondary space), must be adequately addressed before co-writing commences. The third space concept, if consistently applied, does aid in achieving this.
2. All authors need to attend the workshops together.
3. Officials and academics should at the outset engage to position themselves with regard to their frames of reference, values, and forms of writing. The workshops only partially achieved this.
4. Activities must be designed for the workshops so that the knowledge of natural scientists is recognized as equally important as social science, and academic knowledge is recognized as equal to practitioner knowledge. There was a feeling among officials that academic authority (power) sometimes overruled reason in the co-production process when co-authors did not reach consensus.
5. Participants must be willing and brave enough to create a *new language* with their co-writer. Working in the third space is not easy, as it involves compromise and negotiation. Natural scientists found it much harder than social scientists to collaborate as their positivist thinking locked them into thinking that natural science was the only way to know the world. Less than half the academics adopted a different way of thinking about their research. This suggests that both officials and academics did not adequately engage to co-write (see 3 and 4 above).
6. Plan for interim meetings during the writing process where the pairs of authors present their co-written work and explain how they produced it. These would provide the impetus for the authors to move forward in their work and provide additional learning opportunities. These were not held.
7. Adequate time is essential for preparing authors to co-write. The workshops were too few and too short.
8. Time was particularly inadequate for officials. They were always pressed for time due to work pressures at the municipality.
    - They were offered a space to work at UCT but hardly took the opportunity to do so due to time pressure.
    - Deadlines were often missed.
    - Although the contract allowed officials time off from work to write, when it came to asking for this time, it was denied.
9. Facilitators/editors need to plan for the tensions that are likely to crop up in the writing process. Provision needs to be made to assist writers at any moment when they experience difficulty. For example, the incompatibility between an official and an academic led to efforts to get a new academic partner enrolled, resolving the tension.

10. Provide for *two dedicated* authors to co-write the text. It is the case that some authors enrolled a number of their colleagues to work with them leading to:
    - Inefficiency and time delays in the reviewing and rewriting process.
    - The existence of 'ghost writers' who don't attend meetings or workshops.

Conclusion

Working with co-authors in the writing of the book was a lengthy but rewarding process, with many lessons learned. The presumption that only officials would need support in co-writing was incorrect. This set in train a series of workshops aimed mainly at officials, excluding the academics. This entrenched the power differentials between the two sets of knowledge producers. Academic knowledge then became more valued than practitioner knowledge. Thus, the main lesson learned was to set in place right from the very beginning the principles of transdisciplinary co-production and co-writing – that the knowledge of all authors must be recognized as being of equal value.

Application of this approach has proved very productive in the context of a university/municipality collaboration. A Memorandum of Agreement between the two institutions facilitated the process of collaboration and co-writing. It could similarly be used for co-writing between natural and social scientists or authors from different disciplines (thereby facilitating interdisciplinary co-production), or between members of different communities of practice. Not all co-writing outputs need to be geared towards producing an academic product. Policy briefs, working papers, and concept papers are just as relevant and useful in this context.

Notes

3.1 This post-Master's programme called Resources was conducted by Professor of Architecture Henrietta Palmer at the Royal Institute of Art, Stockholm, from 2005 to 2015. The focus of the different courses within the programme were cities of the Global South.

3.2 This framework was established in 2015, as a comprehensive research agenda for the research of all the local interaction platforms of Mistra Urban Futures.

3.3 Each with a weighting of 7.5 ECTS standardized units of the European Credit Transfer System.

3.4 This book was edited by Dianne Scott (ACC, UCT), Helen Davies (CCT), and Mark New (ACDI, UCT) and referred to from here onwards as Mainstreaming Climate Change.

3.5 The workshops were designed by Lucia Thesen and Mathilde van der Merwe from the UCT Centre for Higher Education Development and the author from ACC.

References

Balsiger, J. (2015) 'Transdisciplinarity in the class room? Simulating the co-production of sustainability knowledge', *Futures* 65: 185–94 <https://doi.org/10.1016/j.futures.2014.08.005>.

Bhabha, H. (1994) *The Location of Culture*, Routledge, London.

Canagarajah, S. and Lee, E. (2013) 'Negotiating alternative discourses in academic writing and publishing: risks with hybridity', in L. Thesen and L. Cooper (eds), *Risk in Academic Writing: Postgraduate Students: Their Teachers and the Making of Knowledge*, Multilingual Matters, Bristol.

City of Cape Town (2001) 'Integrated Metropolitan Environmental Policy (IMEP)', Cape Town, Environmental Management Department, City of Cape Town.

Davison, A., Patel, Z. and Greyling, S. (2015) 'Tackling wicked problems and tricky transitions: change and continuity in Cape Town's environmental policy landscape', *Local Environment: The International Journal of Justice and Sustainability* 21(9): 1063–81 <https://doi.org/10.1080/13549839.2015.1066321>.

Durose, C., Richardson, L. and Perry, B. (2019) 'Craft metrics to value co-production', *Nature* 562: 32–3.

Glasson, G.E., Mhango, N., Phiri, A. and Manier, M. (2010) 'Sustainability science education in Africa: negotiating indigenous ways of living with nature in the third space', *International Journal of Science Education* 32(1): 125–41 <https://doi.org/10.1080/09500690902981269>.

Hansson, S. and Polk, M. (2017) *Evaluation of knowledge co-production for sustainable urban development. Part I: Experiences from project leaders and participants at Gothenburg Local Interaction Platform 2012–2015*, Mistra Urban Futures, Gothenburg.

Holmberg, J. (1998) 'Backcasting: a natural step in operationalising sustainable development', *Greener Management International* 23: 30–51.

Holmberg, J. (2014) 'Transformative learning and leadership for a sustainable future: Challenge Lab at Chalmers University of Technology', in P.B. Corcoran, B.P. Hollingshead, H. Lotz-Sisitka, A.E.J. Wals, and J.P. Weakland (eds), *Intergenerational Learning and Transformative Leadership for Sustainable Futures* [online], pp. 91–102 <http://www.wageningenacademic.com/doi/pdf/10.3920/978-90-8686-802-5_4> [accessed 28 February 2020].

Holmén, J., Adawi, T., and Holmberg, J. (2021) 'Student-led sustainability transformations: Employing realist evaluation to open the black box of learning in a Challenge Lab curriculum', *International Journal of Sustainability in Higher Education*, 22(1) <https://doi.org/10.1108/IJSHE-06-2020-0230>.

Jordan, T. (2011) 'Skillful engagement with wicked issues. a framework for analysing the meaning-making structures of societal change agents', *Integral Review* 7(2): 47–91.

Land, R., Rattray, J. and Vivian, P. (2014) 'Learning in the liminal space: a semiotic approach to threshold concepts', *Higher Education* 67: 199–217 <https://doi.org/10.1007/s10734-013-9705-x>.

Lang, D.J., Wiek, A., Bergmann, M., Stauffacher, M., Martens, P., Moll, P., Swilling, M. and Thomas, C.J. (2012) 'Transdisciplinary research in sustainability science: practice, principles, and challenges', *Sustain Science* 7 (suppl. 1): 25–43 <https://doi.org/10.1007/s11625-011-0149-x>.

Larsson, J. and Holmberg, J. (2018) 'Learning while creating value for sustainability transitions: the case of Challenge Lab at Chalmers University of Technology', *Journal of Cleaner Production* 172: 4411–20 <https://doi.org/10.1016/j.jclepro.2017.03.072>.

Leck, H. and Roberts, D. (2015) 'What lies beneath: understanding the invisible aspects of municipal climate change governance', *Current Opinion in Environmental Sustainability* 13: 61–7 <https://doi.org/10.1016/j.cosust.2015.02.004>.

May, T. and Perry, B. (2018) *Cities and the Knowledge Economy: Promise, Politics and Potentials*, Routledge, Oxford.

Norris, P.E., O'Rourke, M., Mayer, A.S. and Halvorsen, K.E. (2016) 'Managing the wicked problem of transdisciplinary team formation in socio-ecological systems', *Landscape and Urban Planning* 154: 115–22 <https://doi.org/10.1016/j.landurbplan.2016.01.008>.

O'Rourke, M. (2017) 'Comparing methods for cross-disciplinary research', in R. Frodeman, J.T. Klein, and R.C.S. Pacheco (eds), *The Oxford Handbook of Interdisciplinarity*, pp. 276–90, Oxford University Press, Oxford.

Palmer, H. (ed.) (2014) *Access to Resources, and Urban Agenda*, Spurbuchverlag AADR, Baunach, Germany.

Perry, B., Durose, C. and Richardson, L. with the Action Research Collective (2019) *How Can we Govern Differently? The Promise and Practice of Co-production* [online], Project report, Creative Concern, Greater Manchester <https://jamandjustice-rjc.org/publications-jam-and-justice> [accessed 28 February 2020].

Pohl, C., Rist, S., Zimmermann, A., Fry, P., Gurung, G.S., Schneider, F., Ifejika Speranza, C., Kiteme, B., Boillat, S., Serrano, E., Hirsch Hadorn, G. and Wiesmann, U. (2010) 'Researchers' roles in knowledge co-production: experience from sustainability research in Kenya, Switzerland, Bolivia and Nepal', *Science and Public Policy* 37(4): 267–81 <https://doi.org/10.3152/030234210X496628>.

Richardson, L., Durose, C. and Perry, B. (2018) 'Moving towards hybridity in causal explanation: the example of citizen participation', *Social Policy & Administration* 53(2): 265–78 <https://doi.org/10.1111/spol.12481>.

Routledge, P. (1996) 'The third space as critical engagement', *Antipode* 28(4): 399–419.

Scott, D., Davies, H. and New, M. (eds) (2019) *Mainstreaming Climate Change in Urban Development: Lessons from Cape Town*, UCT Press, Cape Town.

Senge, P., Hamilton, H. and Kania, J. (2015) 'The dawn of system leadership', *Stanford Social Innovation Review*, Winter: 27–33.

Stigendal, M. and Östergren, P.O. (eds) (2010) *Malmö's Path Towards a Sustainable Future: Health, Welfare and Justice*, 3rd edn [online], Commission for a Socially Sustainable Malmö, Malmö <https://malmo.se/download/18.6c44cd5c1728328333211d32/1593519743583/malmo%CC%88kommisionen_rapport_engelsk_web.pdf> [accessed 18 August 2020].

Tippett, J. and How, F. (2011) *Ketso Guide*, Ketso Ltd, Manchester.

Uittenbroek, C.J., Janssen-Jansen, L.B., Spit, T.J.M., Salet, W.G.M. and Runhaar, H.A.C. (2014) 'Political commitment in organizing municipal responses to climate adaptation: the dedicated approach versus the mainstreaming approach', *Environmental Politics* 23: 1043-63 <https://doi.org/10.1080/09644016.2014.920563>.

University and College Council (UHR) (2019) 'The Bologna Process: the European Higher Education Area' [online] <www.uhr.se/internationella-mojligheter/Bolognaprocessen/> [accessed 16 July 2020].

Wallace, C.S. (2004) 'Framing new research in science literacy and language use: authenticity, multiple discourses, and the "third space"', *Science Education* 88(6): 901-14 <https://doi.org/10.1002/sce.20024>.

Wiek, A., Withycombe, L. and Redman, C.L. (2011) 'Key competencies in sustainability: a reference framework for academic program development', *Sustainability Science* 6: 203-18 <https://doi.org/10.1007/s11625-011-0132-6>.

CHAPTER 4
Designing processes to integrate knowledge

keywords
symmetrical leadership, design thinking, changes in outlook, urban station communities, urban girls movement, comparative transdisciplinary co-production, trans-local learning

As described throughout this book, it can be tricky to plan the sequence of steps necessary to bring a diverse group towards a common goal of shared interest. Knowledge integration can, and should, in one way or another, take place throughout the whole transdisciplinary co-production research process. There is no single blueprint for achieving this. Indeed, as the method contributions of this chapter demonstrate, each transdisciplinary team needs to work out its own approach according to the membership, objectives, topic, and desired outcomes. While the relational space, referred to in many of the method descriptions of Chapter 3, continues to be an integral component, the contributions of this chapter all describe a family of tools or the design of a step-by-step process that has enabled diverse participants to come together and broaden their perspectives, and co-produce knowledge around an urban challenge.

IN THE FIRST SECTION OF this chapter, we learn how a research process around well-being in sustainable cities was arranged to enable a balance between scientific and practice-based perspectives. Including roughly equal members of participants from different constituencies from the beginning, and maintaining the balance throughout the work, is one way of dealing with issues of power and representation within a transdisciplinary team (Norris et al., 2016). We then learn through a case study the sequence of steps taken to facilitate co-production through design thinking. Like the first example, the project referred to in the third case, on study circles and co-writing of 'changes in outlook', was co-led by an academic researcher and a practitioner but deployed a different path to integrate the two perspectives around the challenges in creating socially sustainable cities. Next, the descriptions on urban station communities and urban girls guide us through the steps taken to broaden the engagement in urban planning. Lastly, the final two descriptions both involve collaboration at international levels. The described framework and process for international and local co-production around the global Sustainable Development Goals (SDGs), and the design of trans-local learning, each exemplify how collaboration and understanding can be arranged across disciplinary, organizational, and contextual borders to improve knowledge integration.

Symmetrical leadership and participation for cross-learning in WISE

*Kerstin Hemström,
John Holmberg,
and Jonas Nässén*

In Gothenburg, the Well-being in Sustainable Cities (WISE, 2012-2016) project explored a focus on well-being as a driver for sustainable development. The project was based on identified knowledge needs among Mistra Urban Futures' local partners – to further the understanding of how the city can move towards low-carbon urban lifestyles without jeopardizing individual well-being. Altogether, it involved over 30 participants, with co-ownership and representatives from the City of Gothenburg, the Västra Götaland Region, the Swedish Transport Administration, Chalmers University of Technology, Gothenburg University, and the national Research Institutes of Sweden (RISE).

Setting the stage

The project work started with a two-day stay overnight workshop arranged by researchers, at which interested practitioners and researchers briefly introduced their perspective on the project theme, and interest to participate in project work. Based on this, individuals who retained interest in the project proceeded to co-develop the problem formulation, focus areas, research questions, and a project design of interest to all participants.

To maintain a balance between academic and non-academic perspectives throughout the project work, the project was co-led by a senior researcher and a high-level city practitioner. Research work was organized in five different sub-projects of varying scope, focusing on a set of sub-research questions relating to the overall aim of the project. All sub-projects involved collaboration between research and practice in different ways, depending on how much research was involved and how the sub-project related to ongoing processes in politics or public administration. One sub-project was led by a practitioner but involved several researchers, another was led by a researcher and developed through workshops with practitioners. A third sub-project was first led by a researcher and later by a practitioner, a fourth was led by a practitioner and a fifth by a researcher.

To build mutual trust and jointly reflect upon the progress of the project work, the project leaders organized regular meetings involving all sub-project leaders. These meetings took place monthly or bi-monthly throughout the five-year project period. The chairmanship alternated between the two main project leaders, to create an appreciated learning situation for everyone involved. In parallel, the sub-projects held workshops, seminars, presentations, and conferences with external participants and high attendance to discuss preliminary results. At times when it was difficult to bring about the joint project leader meetings, or when there were changes to the project design and organization, these contributed to retaining fellowship between project participants and their mutual interest to contribute to the overall progress of the project.

Key lessons
Project participants witnessed how the close-to-symmetrical representation of researchers and practitioners led to a balance between researcher and practitioner perspectives and needs throughout the project work, and that the repeated meetings with rotating chairmanship built a community of trust and a shared understanding of the different components and perspectives of the project. Also, the stay-overnight kick-off established a joint interest and enthusiasm for the project work which was kept throughout. The participants perceived the initial workshop as crucial for the relevance for practice, and for relating the project to ongoing processes in policy and practice.

There were continuous feedback learning activities during the project, both within the participant organizations and externally. The set of results generated through the project activities were communicated in various ways, including scientific and popular publications as well as decision-support models for planning practitioners; the development and incorporation of a consumption perspective in the city and regional climate strategies; a policy brief; and an interactive computer game targeting high-school students illustrating the connection between consumption and climate change.

Several things contributed to the high societal relevance of the research results. The project was well-funded, and participants experienced broad interest in the research theme from their home organizations as well as from public administration in general. The practitioners had long-term experience and could identify important knowledge gaps and issues in previous strategies and plans; and the participating researchers had a history of problem-driven research in relation to public agencies. Most of the team had also worked together previously.

Further, mutual respect for different perspectives and knowledges was considered a cornerstone of the overall experience of the process. Because of the joint problem formulation and the shared project ownership, design, and leadership, participating practitioners felt equally entitled to the process and worked proactively in formulating the research focus and questions. This changed their expectations on research collaboration. To achieve societally relevant results, these practitioners would expect equal entitlement to and responsibility for the research process.

Despite a general perception that experience-based knowledge was valued in the knowledge-producing process, concern was raised by a few participants regarding the discursive power of scientific knowledge and the exclusionary effects of, for example, semi-academic seminars. Thus, openness and motivation among researchers was regarded as crucial – but not a guarantee – for the status of experience-based knowledge. Maintaining practice-based credibility required constant vigilance on the part of practitioners.

Suggested readings

Hansson, S. and Polk, M. (2018) 'Assessing the impact of transdisciplinary research: the usefulness of relevance, credibility and legitimacy for understanding the link between process and impact', *Research Evaluation* 2018: 1–13 <https://doi.org/10.1093/reseval/rvy004>.

Westberg, L. and Polk, M. (2016) 'The role of learning in transdisciplinary research: moving from a normative concept to an analytical tool through a practice-based approach', *Sustainability Science* 11: 385–97 <https://doi.org/10.1007/s11625-016-0358-4>.

Joint problem formulation and solution through iterative practice: design thinking

Johan Larson Lindal

Design thinking (DT) is a challenge-driven innovation method developed at Stanford University using basic principles and tools from the design field to solve practical problems. Visualized as a 'double diamond', the design thinking process is shifting from specific to general and then back again, repeated twice. The double diamond goes through five stages: empathize (with the users), define (the problem), ideate (possible solutions), prototype, and test (selected solutions) (Figure 4.1).

Although design thinking was not a pre-assigned method for the Stockholm node, it was one of the preferred methods used repeatedly to plan and develop the joint work among the local partners. It was used successfully for initiating the work of applying for funding for the Stockholm node and for designing parts of the formation and application process. When the funding was received, the first steps of design thinking were used to help co-formulate a work plan. The events below account for these instances and show how DT becomes an efficient methodology for co-creation among actors from different sectors, facilitating a common understanding and way forward, addressing shared needs.

22 June 2016

A first workshop was conducted to generate ideas for the formation of a co-creation platform in Stockholm. Participants came from the City of Stockholm, Stockholm County Council, the Swedish World Wide Fund for Nature (WWF),

White Architects, JPI Urban Europe, the Mistra Urban Futures international secretariat, the local interaction platforms in Gothenburg and Skåne, and what became the Stockholm node partners (see Appendix). Two DT workshops were conducted later in the autumn, during which potential partners were asked to formulate their needs for a local interaction platform in Stockholm. Participants first interviewed each other about their reasons for joining the platform and what they wished to do. They then stated how they would contribute to the formation of a smaller Stockholm node of Mistra Urban Futures.

24 November 2017
DT was also used for understanding needs of actors within the Stockholm region regarding Agenda 2030 during a workshop facilitated by two DT coaches. Participants came from different municipalities in the region; the County Administrative Board; a public housing company; the Royal University of Technology and Stockholm University; the research centre Stockholm Resilience Centre; the research institute IVL Environmental Institute; the think-tank Global Utmaning, the WWF, and the non-profit organization Quantified Planet.

By treating the participants as 'users' or need-owners of sustainable urban development in the Stockholm region, the workshop functioned as an initial problem understanding and definition process, as well as jointly elaborating ideas for improvement, corresponding to the first three stages of DT (Figure 4.1).

Participants interviewed each other in pairs about their respective roles and challenges in sustainable urban development. Four groups then clustered and transformed the data into general insights and ideas on how to take on identified challenges, such as structures in public administration, conflicting goals in urban planning, and lack of co-ordination. Ideas included collaborative fora for politicians and digital tools for dialogue. Finally, each group recorded a video presenting their ideas. The outcome of the workshop anticipated a mapping of co-creation processes for social-ecological sustainability in the Stockholm region, initiated in 2018. Ideas for solutions, however, may have contributed less to the valuable outcome, as they could not be taken on into further operations at this stage of the Stockholm node.

Figure 4.1
The five stages of the 'double diamond', illustrating the iterative process of design thinking in 'opening up' to include knowledge vs. 'narrowing down' to define and test.

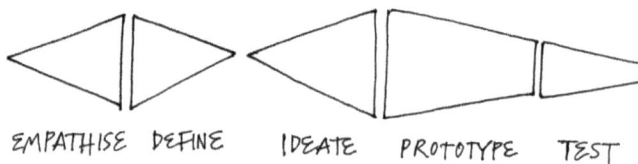

If DT had not been applied and with help from professional coaches, it is likely that a large proportion of participants would have proceeded with producing ideas for solutions at an earlier stage, leading to ideas being more individually formulated. Instead, the workshop created an environment where participants developed ideas only after having listened closely to one another, promoting cross-sectoral understanding and a joint production of knowledge.

13 February 2018

Finally, DT facilitated the writing of a legal agreement among partners of the Stockholm node, which the node's steering committee meetings used in February 2018. Two DT coaches also facilitated this meeting. During the meeting, ideas and wishes for future operations of the node were brainstormed iteratively, exchanged, discussed, and then agreed upon by the participants. Each participant provided what input they could contribute to realize the operational plan of the Stockholm node. Each partner organization had its own column on a chart divided into one square for each sub target of the operational plan. When assembled, the chart clearly displayed potential synergies, collaborative efforts, and joint vision among the partners, illustrating where different knowledge and resources could be used and how. Through this process, the steering committee gained a clearer view of their combined strengths and weaknesses and which parts of the operational plan would be most relevant to support.

In this way, DT facilitated the finding of a common understanding through addressing shared needs by using visual tools for clustering ideas among participants. After this, all of the partners were able to develop and sign the legal agreements. This would probably have been more time-consuming without a structured idea-generation process and professional facilitation. In conclusion, DT was a productive method for stimulating thoughts and discussions around how to form a node for co-creation.

Suggested readings

Conway, R., Masters, J. and Thorold, J. (2017) *From Design Thinking to Systems Change: How to Invest in Innovation for Social Impact* [pdf], RSA Action and Research Centre, London <https://www.thersa.org/globalassets/pdfs/reports/rsa_from-design-thinking-to-system-change-report.pdf> [accessed 29 February 2020].

de la Peña, D., Allen, D.J., Randolph, T.H. Jr, Hou, J., Lawson, L.L. and McNally, M.J. (2017) *Design as Democracy: Techniques for Collective Creativity*, Island Press, Washington, DC.

Manzini, E. and Staszowski, E. (eds) (2013) *Public and Collaborative: Exploring the Intersections of Design, Social Innovation and Public Policy*, DESIS Network, United States. Stanford d.school (no date) 'The Design Thinking Bootleg' [online] <https://dschool.stanford.edu/resources/design-thinking-bootleg> [accessed 29 February 2020].

Study circles and co-writing of boundary-breaking 'changes in outlook'

Birgitta Guevara, Kerstin Hemström, and Åsa Lorentzi

In Gothenburg, the transdisciplinary research project *KAIROS: Knowledge about and Approaches to Fair and Socially Sustainable Cities*, focused on the social dimensions of urban sustainability. The project was initiated and backed by five of the Gothenburg platform partners. From their representatives' point of view, the biggest challenges to social sustainability in the area involved increased segregation, local discrepancies in income and health, and lowering levels of political engagement. There was a sense of urgency to stop the city from falling apart.

The project was co-led by an academic researcher and a civil servant engaged in professional facilitation work within the city. It involved in-depth collaboration with some of the local city districts in the City of Gothenburg, the Human Rights Committee and Public Health Committees of the Västra Götaland Region, the Department of Social Sustainability within the County Administration Board, and the Swedish Association of Local Authorities and Regions. The project also collaborated with two local democracy and civil rights movements.

Initial methods for co-production

Three initial workshops, each involving 60–80 participants, most of whom were civil servants, laid the basis for the initial project plan. Based on the outcomes of these workshops, it was decided to focus on what driving forces, conflicting goals, and power structures could explain the discrepancy between political ambitions and the actual socio-economic development in the city. The guiding question became: 'Why do things turn out the way they do despite our good intentions?' To answer this, the project members addressed the following questions:

- What main driving forces, underlying conflicting goals, and power structures can explain the tendency towards increased segregation, social polarization, and discrimination, and the declining political participation in Gothenburg?
- How do these manifest themselves at the local level, and with what effect?
- How can these be managed or altered, to incite a more socially sustainable development?

These research questions were developed during open roundtable discussions or 'research circles' between all project members, on the preconditions for socially sustainable cities. The method of research circles aims to combine theoretically based scientific knowledge with the more tacit experience-based knowledge of practitioners in an explorative way. Co-production between participating researchers and civil servants was facilitated through an *abductive research approach*; moving back and forth between empiricism and theory by discussing key concepts and what they mean in theory and practice. To an outsider, these may be perceived as incoherent coffee breaks, lacking purpose and structure. In the project, however, these explorative open conversations were necessary to develop useful collective insights and knowledge.

Initially, the intention was for everyone involved to become familiar with the concepts, literature, experiences, and practice-based knowledge in the field. The researcher contributed, by help of theory, to demonstrate the driving forces behind and complexity of contemporary societal challenges, in a way that was meaningful to civil servants and the issues they were facing. At the same time, the practitioners contributed and demonstrated knowledge and perspectives from their organizations and experiences from working with these challenges on a daily basis on the strategic level. Going further, jointly agreed research questions, methodologies, and theoretical and conceptual starting points for the project work on how to achieve a socially sustainable development could be identified. All in all, this process took about a year.

Developing the research work
The project members divided the work between three sub-projects, in each of which issues were addressed through roundtable discussions on different themes. In parallel, project members conducted desk-based studies around specific topics, to enhance the theoretical anchoring of the sub-projects and facilitate the integration of previous research in the field. Some literature reviews were performed by master's students and one study was conducted by a civil society activist. All sub-projects included interviews and observations to improve the knowledge and empirical base in the research.

Bringing results to fruition
The main conclusion of the project work was that, to achieve sustainable urban development, those in power need to be open for political conversations with citizens, to co-create new pathways towards sustainability. A profound transformation is needed on several levels of society: and this transformation needs to be co-created.

To illustrate and communicate these points, the project members presented their results as eight mental shifts or *changes in outlook* (in Swedish *synvändor*), each identified as necessary to achieve socially sustainable development. The concept was coined by the Swedish author Elisabeth Hermodsson, her point being that to change the world, we need first to change our worldviews (Figure 4.2). They called attention to the need for new narratives and pathways to achieve necessary changes. The idea was to introduce new concepts of aspiration, to think and do things differently, in a manner mirroring the

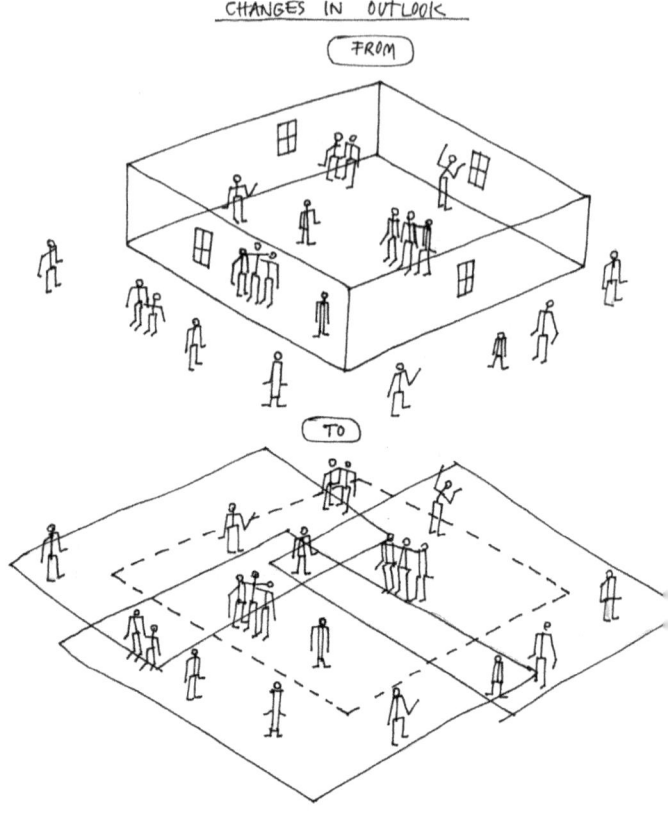

Figure 4.2
Illustration of the re-conceptualization of worldviews resulting from changes in outlook.

complexities we are facing, rather than improve or do more of what is done already. The intention was also to point out directions in which citizens, civil servants, and politicians can search their context for new ways to co-create, arguing that the concrete ways of putting this into practice would need to be co-created at local levels. Essentially, they meant, socially sustainable cities need to be built *with*, rather than *for*, people.

The changes of outlook were discussed and agreed upon within the project group and co-written between academic researchers and civil servants. Each of the changes of outlook – presented in text and video recorded as conversations in Swedish – aspired to include a broad range of perspectives and exemplify how co-creation between different actors can enable socially sustainable development. The co-writing itself was an important part of the project, in capturing and sharing the knowledge that had emerged throughout the three years of project work (see Chapter 3, 'Academics and municipal officials co-writing in third space'). The written output represented the collective insights of research and practice in the project with regards to what would be necessary to achieve socially sustainable development.

Challenges

Throughout the project work, the results were presented and discussed through workshops with different stakeholders (e.g. community organizations and networks) to verify conclusions. Regular workshops and seminars were also held with strategic representatives of the project partner organizations to discuss and reflect on the results. To disseminate results further, the final conference was organized following the principles of the OpenSpace method, where the project group presented the main results. The conference was prepared together with civil society organizations, to bring more perspectives on board and help disseminate the invitation. OpenSpace is a meeting method used in many contexts to promote exchange of experiences, change processes, and exploration of complex issues. Basically, it builds on self-organizing, where the participants are involved in setting the agenda, organizing discussions, and taking initiatives for future work.

Still, the main challenge was to bring and anchor the project insights among outsiders, as practical knowledge on *how* to operationalize them in local practice was missing. A following conclusion was that the implementation of broad transdisciplinary knowledge, in organizations characterized by divisional and siloed mandates and ways of working, needs to be backed and legitimized by leaders or institutional support structures. In this case, interfaces with local politicians would have been necessary to arrive at concrete and realizable suggestions.

As part of the research circles, the participants learned of the work conditions of one another. A challenge to the progress of the project work was the difference between academic researchers and practitioners. While their equal relevance was clear to those involved in the initial stages of the project, it was difficult to retain this balance later. This resulted in the following reflections:

- Public organizations are seldom organized to create space for problematizing, analysing, and critical reflection. This can undermine the equal position of researchers and practitioners, giving researchers the upper hand when it comes to interpreting results and reaching conclusions.
- The public sector represents a verbal and action-based culture, with the main task to bring about activities linked to political decisions, laws, and regulations. Activities are often developed through talking and doing and conversations held at meetings. One meeting is often followed by another, with limited time for reflection, reading, and writing. This makes it challenging for practitioners to contemplate the situations they encounter, and to prepare and substantiate their actions and decisions. Often, they are forced to act intuitively, on a fragmented knowledge base. Meanwhile, in a performance management context based on profitability criteria, the scope for risk-taking and uncertainty is reduced. The emphasis is placed on meeting superiors' guidelines, at the expense of other needs.

- Academics tend to generate knowledge through observations, reading, reflection, and writing. Often, the written output is at a generalizable and theoretical level; too abstract to have relevance and be applicable for practice-based decision-making. Meanwhile, they increasingly face uncertain terms of employment and are put under pressure to attain research funding and academic publications, to be measured by quantitative standards. The system rewards demarcation, scientific excellence, and measurability, at the cost of alternative and more comprehensive perspectives. This makes it challenging for academics to commit to transdisciplinary co-production.
- These circumstances leave little room for the in-depth, open, and confiding conversations that are necessary to reach new insights on the complex challenges faced by societies today, and limited leeway for expressing tacit and experience-based knowledge in writing.

Some practitioners perceived the theoretical frames as strict and misaligned with the concepts used in their daily work. In consequence, they did not experience shared ownership of the whole process and results. The power relations between academic and practical and tacit knowledge were perceived as unequal. Implementation in platform partner organizations was difficult mainly due to hierarchical structures, management, and leadership (following the principles of New Public Management). As a result of the process, however, the practitioners felt they had been strengthened in their professional roles.

Takeaways

- Co-production sometimes meets insurmountable demands on openness, active listening, and willingness to understand the perspectives of others. Generating co-understanding and new knowledge that can be transformed into relevant recommendations and proposals calls for strong pedagogical skills.
- Co-production puts high demands on comprehensive perspectives and thinking outside of the box. While researchers commonly are trained in critical thinking, many practitioners operate in a non-questioning work culture, within a given hierarchical structure. It takes confidence and courage to let go of the perspectives you've kept daily, to critically review and reassess reality.
- The aim, purpose, and results of the research need to be firmly established among the intended users. Although this project was initiated by public administration, the realization of results was limited by lack of support structures from within the same organizations. The way the project decided to present results, however, as changes in outlook, has proved useful in other urban contexts.

Suggested readings

Abrahamsson, H. (2013) *Power and Dialogue in Just and Socially Sustainable Swedish Cities* [pdf], Mistra Urban Futures, Gothenburg <https://www.mistraurbanfutures.org/sites/mistraurbanfutures.org/files/power_and_dialogue_in_just_and_socially_sustainable_swedish_cities_kairos.pdf> [accessed 30 January 2020].

Abrahamsson, H., Guevara, B. and Lorentzi, Å. (eds)(2016) Kunskap om och arbetssätt i rättvisa och socialt hållbara städer. KAIROS slutrapport [ebook, in Swedish], Mistra Urban Futures, Gothenburg <https://www.mistraurbanfutures.org/en/publication/kairos-slutrapport-som-e-bok> [accessed 30 January 2020].

Methods and tools for co-creation of urban station communities

Ulf Ranhagen

How can the urban planning process be improved by means of co-creative planning tools? A systematic and flexible working methodology has been the starting point for the development and applications of structured tools for co-creation in the urban station communities project. The project started in 2012 with a workshop focusing on sustainable densification around railway stations. This workshop resulted in a knowledge overview regarding R&D within the field. Successively, the project engaged multiple actors on national, regional, and local levels. In 2019, eleven municipalities in the western part of Sweden, two regional agencies, one county, the National Board of Transportation, and Mistra Urban Futures were involved.

The project is made up of different 'knowledge processes' where relevant cases are illuminated in co-creative workshops. This process has generated several specific R&D projects involving six universities. These projects dig deeper into topics such as spatial planning and urban morphology, noise and vibrations, small and medium sized station communities' digital tools supporting sustainable mobility patterns, and transport justice. The planning of stations and public transportation nodes in general can be a driving force for sustainable development in regions, cities, towns, and small urban centres. A condition for positive development is that integrated land-use and transportation planning is promoted including mixed-use densification close to stations. In our R&D we also have evidence of the importance of developing continuous paths for local public transportation, bicycling, and walking to surrounding urban and rural areas (Bertolini and Spit, 1998; Ranhagen et al., 2017).

The toolbox presented below has its roots in generic action research and research by design, but the applications discussed concern spatial planning of urban station communities in a wider sense. The tools can be combined, modified, adapted, and extended sequentially to fit the needs of a unique planning case. They have been used in transdisciplinary processes where practitioners from different municipal departments investigate relevant case studies representing typical planning situations in their region. The basic tools derive from a larger toolbox/model developed in practice-oriented R&D projects (Ranhagen, 2012; Ranhagen and Groth, 2012; Ranhagen, 2020a, b). A set of planning indicators was developed in a parallel project to facilitate investigations and evaluations of existing areas and their possible development. Below I will concentrate on experiences from the applications of specific tools rather than on the process as a whole, starting off with important tools for analysis of the prerequisites in the planning cases.

Mind-mapping combined with inspiration images and a working sheet for stakeholder analysis

Application 1: To inspire people to develop ideas and reflect on present and future urban station areas, 30–50 images with photos from different types of urban and rural environments were handed out to the participants. Each participant was asked to select three pictures that illustrated their reflections on urban station communities at present and in the future, as a basis for common discussions and conclusions. The same type of tool was also applied to generate ideas and reflections on what 'place identity' is for an urban station community. The tool helped participants to gain a deeper understanding of the unique features of existing areas around the stations. It also helped generate visionary ideas for what a future urban station community should be associated with.

Application 2: To identify stakeholders of key and secondary importance for a certain planning task, a worksheet was developed from which a mind-mapping could be facilitated. The worksheet was divided into four sectors following the quadruple helix principle that combines public sector, business sector, civil society together with academia, and the different levels of governance: municipal, regional, national, and international. This kind of mind-mapping helped participants to identify a wider range of stakeholders than is usually done in planning processes.

Walking tours for place and path analysis

This tool facilitates collection of participants' experiences of an urban station community. Routes and stops on walking tours are prepared on maps. Path protocols are used to facilitate teams' and participants' note-taking during walks. The protocols are divided into strengths/positive impressions, weaknesses/negative impressions, and ideas for improvement. The walking tours (including walk-shop, bus walk-shop, etc.) have been highly appreciated by the participants as they offer each participant an opportunity to experience personally the area being planned. Distinct from a walking tour, a walk-shop promotes active work while walking to capture and document strengths, weaknesses, and ideas for developing one or several areas. Bus walk-shops have been used in cases when the areas analysed were geographically dispersed.

After a walking tour, participants compile their impressions on maps and aerial photos using sticky notes. This tool has provided very useful bases for planning, as it enables the compilation of many different subjective perspectives. The compiled analysis and ideas can then be used for developing and evaluating different future scenarios.

Map- and indicator-based SWOT analysis
Indicators identified as important for sustainable urban mobility in a parallel R&D project have been used as a starting point for a map- and indicator-based SWOT. These indicators are arranged as a spider chart, divided into four groups: urban form, urban functions, urban connectivity, and urban public spaces. Participants then use the spider chart for proposing different indicator weights. These weights reflect the perceived importance of the indicators for achieving the station proximity effect on different distances from an actual railway station. The indicators perceived as most important within the group are then used as the basis for a map-based SWOT analysis of areas at different distances from the station. This experience-based and co-creative tool can be used as a supplement to technical and digital planning tools such as space syntax. The map- and indicator-based SWOT analysis facilitates an overall, yet systematic, compilation of both opinions and facts about a planning area.

Structured brainstorming
A structured brainstorming tool has been used to help define key issues in a planning task for an urban station community (Ranhagen, 2012). Participants start the process by reflecting individually on what they perceive are key issues in the planning task. These key issues are noted on sticky notes, which participants place on a wall. Successively, the participants then cluster the key issues into topical groups. Each participant then prioritizes the key issues by marking their top priority within each topical group.

This structured brainstorming tool has been valuable for structuring problems and obtaining ideas on what key issues are prioritized by local stakeholders. It helps participants to generate, compile, integrate, and prioritize their ideas to facilitate further work with planning alternatives. The compiled key issues can be used as the basis for formulating common visions, facilitated by the drawing of mind maps. The common vision can then be used to compare and link the issues prioritized with the group, to local, regional, national or international agendas.

Important tools for synthesis and research by planning and design are discussed below.

Backcasting combined with scenario-analysis (scenario matrix)

Tools for backcasting and scenario analysis (scenario matrices) are not commonly used in municipal planning but have proven to be valuable supplements to traditional planning tools. By encouraging the investigation of extreme alternatives, long-term scenarios help focus on critical future planning issues. Instead of making projections into the future from a present position, backcasting starts by sketching out images for the future that depict possible long-term solutions to a societal challenge for an urban station community. After delimiting interesting long-term images of the future, possible paths from the present situation to the future situation can be outlined (see also Chapter 3, 'A space for learners to lead and leaders to learn: Challenge Lab').

Within urban station communities, backcasting has been facilitated by a scenario matrix (Ranhagen, 2012). First, two important structural aspects are chosen as axes in the matrix (Figure 4.3). This facilitates the formulation and overall design of extreme case options, by combining extreme positions for each aspect. Examples of axes in the matrices are polycentric versus monocentric urban structure, mixed-used, dense paths versus nodes along paths, high density versus medium density, or a focus on public transportation versus bicycling as the main future transportation mode. One way of working is first to conceptualize two extremely different alternatives diagonally in the matrix, then supplement these with the other two. This type of matrix has facilitated the identification of totally different and extreme future scenarios, reducing the risk of locking into only one scenario. Thereby, several urban development options have been illuminated and discussed.

Figure 4.3
An example of a scenario matrix showing four possible futures of urban development as a combination of two variables: a concentrated monocentric development; a concentrated polycentric development; a linear monocentric development; and a linear polycentric development.

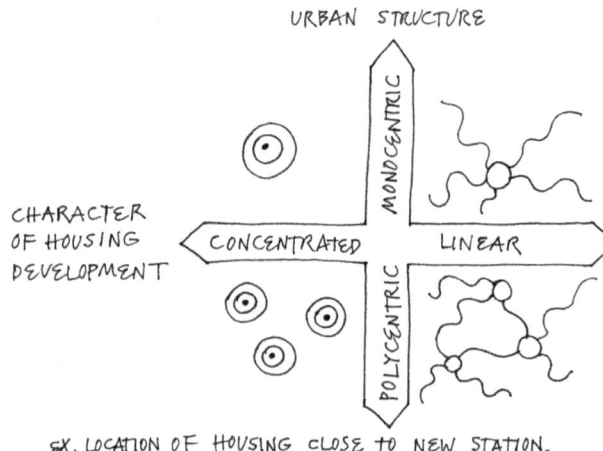

Evaluation and assessment of scenarios by evaluation tools
The evaluation and assessment of alternatives and scenarios comprises only one element of planning but is such a central activity that it permeates all parts of the planning process. Therefore, it is important to perform consequence analysis and assess different scenarios successively. Thereafter, a reduced number of alternatives can be re-evaluated using additional criteria and indicators. In the urban station communities project at least three tools have been introduced, tested, and evaluated by the municipalities:

- effect profiles for ranking alternatives;
- value rose (spider diagram) for qualitative assessments, comparisons, and ranking;
- multi-criteria analysis (MCA) for more streamlined and specific comparisons of alternatives.

MCA has been the most widely used method in the urban station community project (Ranhagen et al., 2017). It includes both the ranking of alternatives for each chosen evaluation criterion or indicator, and the weighing of the chosen criteria/indicators in relation to each other by distributing 100 points (or an alternative number suitable to the situation). By using an Excel chart for the MCA process it is easy for the participants and the working group as a whole to put in numbers for both these components, while also making a robustness analysis. The latter is performed through testing whether a certain alternative keeps its position when the weights of the criteria/indicators are changed. This is important given that the numbers are not absolute but represent a relative judgement of how well the alternatives fulfil the chosen objectives.

It has been useful to combine several evaluation tools, such as MCA and the effect profile. The effect profile illustrates an overall ranking of the alternatives. By adding the weighting of indicators, it is possible to build an understanding of how robust an alternative is when changing the distribution of weights. Applying this tool has deepened insights on the implications of different localizations of stations. It has thereby facilitated decision-making in complex planning situations, contributing to more elaborated bases for decisions.

Application of a decision tree for analysis of strategic choices
The planning tasks related to the location of stations and the planning of surrounding areas are usually complex. For that reason, the decision tree for analysis of strategic choices is useful (Figure 4.4). For example, there are two options for the location of a station, each with totally different implications for future development. Starting from the present situation, a decision tree presented on a working sheet admits a first decision between two options in the short term, four new options mid-term, and finally eight different long-term decisions. The tool's design can be varied in many ways. Each decision can be visualized

Figure 4.4
An example of a decision tree for the analysis of strategic choices. The tree presents decision options based on positive or negative responses, in the short term, the midterm, and in the long term.

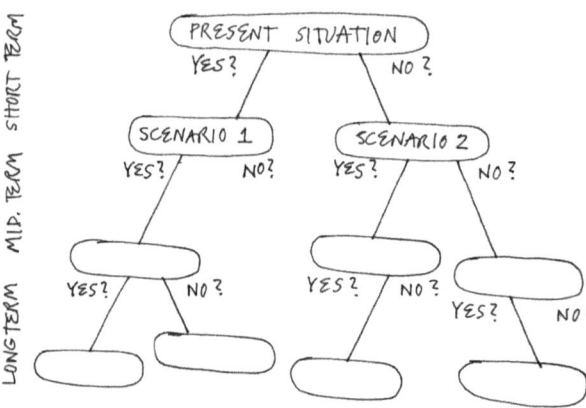

principally on maps or aerial photographs, among others. Finally, different choices can be compared by discussing pros and cons, ranking or performing MCAs (see above). The outcome illustrates the consequences of decisions that had not even been touched upon initially. Often, the participants have been surprised by how one short-term decision can result in very large deviations from the intuitive imagination of future options.

Key lessons from the applied tools in co-creative processes
The processes initiated in the urban station communities project and related R&D projects have supplemented ordinary planning processes by adding new perspectives on the planning tasks. The tools have been applied for improving both existing and planning new urban areas, and have been especially useful for administering major, strategic planning issues on regional, municipal, and district levels. Applying the toolbox has directly influenced the strategies, planned development, and location of stations, in several urban centres. Beyond supplementing formal planning procedures, the tools have encouraged creativity and improved the capacity for collaboration between different stakeholders. Stronger networks have also been developed between national, regional, and local stakeholders, contributing to mutual understanding of different planning approaches.

The activities in this project have been carried out in a transdisciplinary process with participants from the public sector, but also from business sector and civil society. The role of the two process leaders has been twofold: to organize and lead the interactive action research and to document and analyse the outcome of the processes. The participants' opinions have been collected via questionnaires and interviews (see Ranhagen et al., 2017; Ranhagen, 2020b). Further evaluations and reflections on the tools and the huge empirical material collected through the research are in process.

Suggested readings

Ranhagen, U. (2017) *Process Tools in Co-creative Processes*, Working Paper 2017:4, Mistra Urban Futures, Gothenburg.

Ranhagen, U. and Groth, K. (2012) *Symbio City Approach: A Conceptual Framework for Sustainable Urban Development*, SKL International, Stockholm.

Ranhagen, U., Dahlstrand, A. and Ramstedt, A. (2017) *Co-creation in Urban Station Communities: Findings from Working Seminars Involving the Collaboration of Transdisciplinary Agents 2015-2016*, Report 2017:2, Mistra Urban Futures, Gothenburg.

A method for participatory public space planning and design: Urban Girls Movement

Elin Andersdotter Fabre and Tove Derner

The starting point for the Urban Girls Movement (UGM) is the notion of 'plan a city for girls, and it will work for everyone'. The hypothesis has been successfully tested in a pilot in the municipality of Botkyrka, in the Stockholm region, and contributes to advancing the practice of feminist urban planning (Andersdotter-Fabre et al., 2019: 8). Sustainable urban development is recognized in the 2030 Agenda and aims to, among other things, 'create cities for all' (ibid.: 14). The approach is developed to fit any public space regeneration project but particularly meets the needs of deprived neighbourhoods, focusing on health and well-being; gender equality; and reducing inequalities through multi-stakeholder participation and partnerships in the public spaces of a local community.

Recent action research (Andersdotter-Fabre et al., 2019: 10-13) shows that highlighting young women's experiences and needs early in an urban planning phase, such as girls' integration, educational opportunities, and work opportunities, significantly enhances inclusion, health, and well-being among all inhabitants of the area. The independent think-tank, Global Utmaning, has been studying good practices of public space participatory governance, planning, development, and design. They show that a successful participation process is one that responds to the actual needs of the population living in and around the area. Involving marginalized actors and other relevant stakeholders early on, creates both legitimacy and quality to the process and outcomes. They also show that such a process is not difficult to achieve, but rather facilitates implementation and keeps costs down as the right priorities are made. However, process owners need to believe in a true multi-stakeholder approach, bringing all actors to the table equally and in the earliest stage.

Based on a global mapping of good participatory practices, UGM has developed a method and a toolbox for gender- and age-sensitive participatory planning and design, providing a multi-sectoral and multi-level urban governance model. The outcome of this model delivers a visionary yet integrated solution to increase citizens' health and well-being. The cross-sectorial nature of the participating group and a mainstreamed understanding about intersectionality and equality ensures solutions that address social, cultural, economic, and environmental determinants of health and well-being. In practice, by gathering knowledge about how the built environment affects access to public space for the most vulnerable inhabitants, this method becomes a useful tool for the end users (planners, architects, construction companies, etc.) to improve the living conditions of this group.

The Urban Girls method consists of nine steps where girls and young women participate with other multi-stakeholders and experts (i.e. researchers, planners, private sector, civil society, civil rights activists, etc.). For each step a workshop is organized (see Photo 4.1). In general, each step consists of an innovation lab producing concrete results which becomes the basis for the following step. Each step contains a range of tools which are gathered in the toolbox for urban girls and local leaders. This method for community involvement is designed to establish the needs and priorities of different groups in order to address these in the course of programming social, economic, and physical space interventions:

1. *Context*: In the first workshop the concept of feminist urban development is introduced; we examine the relation to the Sustainable Development Goals; good examples of feminist urban planning; and the urban site in question. Urban walks are practised, inspired by Plan International and UN-Habitat's Safer Cities for Girls checklist.
2. *Challenges*: In the second workshop we consider concrete tools available within urban development; identify challenges and highlight needs; and brainstorm around the potential of the space. We use Method Kit decks of cards, a method used to summarize people's thinking and talking about different topics, as guidance in the discussion.
3. *Possibilities*: In the third workshop we explore the existing potential of the space with the goal of formulating a vision for the space; sketch concrete ideas; and initiate the first illustrations of our ideas. Again, we use Method Kit.
4. *Illustrations*: The fourth workshop, based on the outcome of the first three participatory problem-solving workshops, focuses on testing solutions, illustrating them in 3D and further developing the details. We work with the Block by Block-tool developed by UN-Habitat and Mojang inspired by the computer game, Minecraft.
5. *Input*: The fifth step takes the form of a presentation of results or an exhibition with the aim of sharing the mid-term results and draft designs. We collect more

knowledge about the local needs to be addressed through the valuable input from citizens and additional experts.

6. *Recommendations*: In the sixth step we discuss what is required for the proposal to be implemented. The target group of girls and young women and professionals work together to develop concrete policy recommendations for decision-makers as well as supporting guidelines for implementation.

7. *Plans*: In the seventh step external input is taken into consideration and professionals continue to work on the proposals together with architects, starting to turn the draft solutions into sketches, models, and plans for the area. We use Sketchup, 3D glasses, and 3D prints and models of the space.

8. *Sharing*: The eighth step is about presenting the final outcome to local, regional, and national decision-makers together with other stakeholders. Other national and international actors are invited to discuss and take part in the lessons learned in order to maximize outreach and up-scaling.

9. *Evaluation*: In the last and ninth step we evaluate the process, report the project, relate to indicators, and make sure that the lessons learned are shared with others.

The primary objective of the initiative is to provide capacity building and urban solutions to different actors with different needs. UGM creates an open source interactive platform to make all results accessible. The Urban Girls publications have further become a catalogue for anyone interested in building cities for girls. A research council is linked to the project where the researchers participate in the innovation labs and a research network meets in connection with the lab to discuss their ongoing research in related areas.

Suggested reading

Andersdotter Fabre, E., Anneroth, E. and Wrangsten, C. (2019) *Urban Girls Handbook: A Global Guide to Participatory Public Space Planning & Design*, Global Utmaning, Stockholm <https://www.globalutmaning.se/rapporter/urbangirls-handbook/> [accessed 18 August 2020].

Andersdotter Fabre, E., Anneroth, E. and Wrangsten, C. (2019) *Urban Girls Catalogue: How Cities Planned for & by Girls Work for Everyone*, Global Utmaning, Stockholm <https://www.globalutmaning.se/rapporter/urbangirlsmovement-catalogue/> [accessed 18 August 2020].

Her City toolbox (2021) <https://hercity.unhabitat.org/> [accessed 18 January 2021].

Photo 4.1 Workshop activities involving the Method Kit decks of cards and the Block by Block-tool developed by UN-Habitat and Mojang, during step 2 of the Urban Girls method.
(Photo © Global Utmaning, 2018)

A framework for comparative transdisciplinary co-production around the Sustainable Development Goals

Sandra Valencia

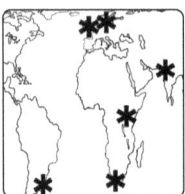

During the years 2017–2019, a research project involving seven cities around the world aimed to follow and analyse the implementation of the United Nations (UN) Agenda 2030 and its Sustainable Development Goals (SDGs) and UN-Habitat's New Urban Agenda (NUA) at the city level. The cities involved were Buenos Aires (Argentina), Cape Town (South Africa), Gothenburg and Malmö (Sweden), Kisumu (Kenya), Sheffield (UK), and Shimla (India). Covering four continents, these represent a variety of contexts, ranging from small to medium-sized cities, one being a capital (Buenos Aires), and very different socio-economic, political, geographical, and cultural conditions. The cities were motivated to participate in the research by the opportunity to compare local work with other cities across the globe; to position local sustainability work in a global context; and strengthen international relationships with other cities. While the project aimed to address both the SDGs and the NUA, Buenos Aires was the only participating municipality to engage at all with the NUA. Accordingly, the relationships between the two agendas could not be studied as planned, so the focus was essentially on the SDGs. During the project, several practices proved useful to maintain a coherent and comparable approach across the cities, to facilitate cross-city learning, and to extract lessons relevant beyond local contexts.

Set-up

The project involved a core research team with at least one academic researcher in each case study city, collaborating and co-producing research with officials of their respective municipality. The academic researcher in Gothenburg also led the international component of the project and drew up guidelines and reporting requirements to be followed by each city team. The teams then adapted that methodology to their local interests and needs.

Each city researcher established a local working group with municipal officials. Given the comprehensive and cross-sectoral nature of the SDGs, most of these involved individuals at strategic and leading offices such as the planning office, city executive office, or, in smaller municipalities such as Shimla, the head of the municipality (see a description of the set-up in Kisumu in Box 4.1).

Most local processes started by setting a common working agenda, discussing overall project goals and timelines, and adapting them to the municipality's interests. Nearly all cities started by mapping relevant targets and analysing which departments should co-ordinate the SDGs, and which actors should be involved.

Box 4.1 Local co-production around the implementation of SDGs in Kisumu

Michael Oloko and George-Mark Onyango

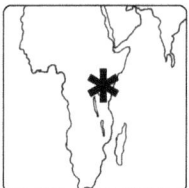

The set-up of the local research on the implementation of SDGs in Kisumu, Kenya, was facilitated by a previous pilot study focusing on developing and testing SDG 11 targets and indicators. The pilot study revealed critical needs for collaboration and co-ordination between local and national governments, as well as difficulties in accessing key data for local planning purposes. The primary focus of the local research activities was therefore to identify and contact key actors relevant to engagement with the SDGs and find out how the necessary data collection tools and procedures could be developed.

Having been part of the pilot study, the City of Kisumu was interested to continue collaborating at the local level to develop their work on the SDGs. Seeing the objectives of the international comparative project, they also saw benefits in sharing experiences with and learning from other cities. Accordingly, the researchers took concrete steps to involve other relevant public authorities. At the local level, this included county officials who had previously not engaged actively with the SDGs. At the national level, connections were made with the national SDG implementation team in Nairobi. This team involved representatives of critical actors responsible for the implementation of SDGs in Kenya, including the National Bureau of Statistics, the National Treasury, the Ministry of Planning and Devolution, and the private sector. In formal visits to these, the researchers presented the results of the pilot study and the objectives of the comparative research project. All of the actors could see benefits in collaborating across administrative levels and were interested in developing the necessary data to work with the SDGs. Although already actively engaged with the SDGs, the national team had not yet worked to localize SDG-related processes. The Kenya national delegation was also able to meet the international project leader during the 2018 UN High Level Political Forum to discuss project activities and the localization of the SDGs implementation in Kenya. This helped clarify the overall objectives and relevance to Kenya as a whole and prompted subsequent joint functions between the local government departments and the national team.

Given their overlapping responsibilities and geographic coverage, the local team comprised representatives of both the City and County of Kisumu, and an academic researcher. This team held monthly face-to-face meetings to discuss progress and challenges in how the city was implementing the SDGs. When relevant and possible, other actors, such as the directors of the water supply and sewerage and energy supply companies in Kisumu, were also involved. Similar discussions were held every four months in meetings between the local team and the national SDG team. To learn more about the research and the local activities, the national team also organized a workshop with city and county officials in Kisumu.

Local lessons
The international comparative component of the research provided opportunities for exchanging data and experiences, as well as building a peer network with counterparts in other cities. Locally, the research facilitated the continuous engagement of the City and County of Kisumu in the issues involved in implementing the SDGs and reinforced the capacity to work with the SDGs on both city and national level. The local work was applauded nationally as a good initiative, successfully drawing attention to how the local SDG work in Kenya can be improved. The research successfully highlighted challenges of the localization process, such as the need to strengthen the collaboration between different government levels and revise the policies of different agencies in order to ease the sharing of data and information. It also influenced the national team to put more emphasis on SDG 11, which has an urban focus. Following from the research, the local County has created an SDG unit with representatives from all departments. Similar to the national SDG group, their ambition is to also include researchers and representatives of non-governmental organizations. Overall challenges to the progress of this collaborative research relate to the lack of time and availability of personnel in the respective public offices in the city, county, and national institutions, and the costs associated with getting different officials together in organized workshops.

For example, in Buenos Aires, the researcher established a working team with three main actors: academia (the Observatory on Latin America, hosted by the University of Buenos Aires), civil society (the NGO Centre for Legal and Social Studies), and the public sector (the General Directorate of Strategic Management and Institutional Quality, in charge of the SDGs in the City of Buenos Aires). They discussed and agreed on the research focus, taking into consideration the diverse objectives of each institution. During the first year, the teams focused on habitat issues covering housing, access to water, transport, and electricity. Work tasks were divided between the researchers, NGO partners, and city officials and later reviewed in monthly meetings.

Monthly online meetings between the researchers. Monthly conference calls were set up within the core research team. This open and regular channel for sharing progress in each case study city, discussing challenges and opportunities of doing co-production with city officials, and planning the next steps, was critical for the project to run smoothly and for maintaining cohesion and coherence. The meetings were an opportunity to discuss necessary changes to the content and focus of the project following the needs of each city, and for finding a balance between these and the needs of the research project. Meanwhile, they helped the local researchers to keep the process going, share and get ideas from each other, and plan subsequent reports.

Annual face-to-face meetings. Annual face-to-face meetings between all researchers and at least one practitioner from each city were important to strengthen the local-global dynamic of the project. A first meeting was held in Kisumu early on between the researchers only. This helped develop good working relations and jointly decide and agree on the expected outcomes and outputs of the project. The following two years allowed week-long, face-to-face conference meetings involving all researchers and officials from most municipalities. This helped establish new relations among them, enhance trust and group cohesion, and legitimize both the local and international components of the project. Throughout the week, the respective teams could share experiences and learn and be inspired from others. In consequence, city officials were interested in maintaining contact and sharing experiences between meetings.

City-city peer review. To further facilitate city-to-city exchanges in a concrete manner, the project established a process in which each city team prepared a proposal (peer-review request) outlining a challenge being faced or a process being developed in relation to the SDGs. The project leader then randomized peer-review cities, one municipality being principal reviewer and a second preparing a shorter commentary.

Reviewers commented on the peer-review request in writing based on their experiences of working with the SDGs or compatible sustainability initiatives. Apart from a four-page limit, there were no detailed requirements or guidelines for outlining a proposal or writing a review, allowing each city team to focus on the issues most important to them. The idea was to keep it informal, avoiding bureaucratic processes requiring approval from high level managers, or diplomatic issues. Since the process mostly involved individuals who had met face-to-face and were already acquainted, who could explain the process to other city team members, the group could maintain a certain level of informality.

The peer-to-peer review process was deemed interesting and a good way to share knowledge and experiences and reflect on local challenges and processes. Some city teams submitted documents they were already planning to submit to managers for approval, others prepared proposals from scratch. Preparing these proposals was also useful for reflecting and agreeing on a working agenda moving forward. In Buenos Aires, for example, the exercise was believed to strengthen the officials' commitment to the project. In Kisumu, preparing the request and reviews provided opportunities to assess the entire SDG implementation processes in the city and county, revealing both strong and weak areas.

The SDGs serve as boundary concepts

The focus on the SDGs as uncontested boundary crossing concepts was paramount in comparing and drawing upon the lessons and experiences of the participating cities, at both local and global levels (Figure 4.5). In general, the Agenda 2030 and its associated SDGs, targets, and indicators cater for a common language and frame of reference beyond the contexts of individual municipalities. This enables discussions and disclosure of disparate interpretations, and concrete similarities and differences at the local level.

Using the SDGs as a guiding framework allowed the research to be practice-oriented, grounded in local realities, while also enabling the sharing of knowledge and experiences between municipalities. It has exposed them to perspectives that might not have surfaced had the project been designed by individual local authorities. The specific strategies being taken by each to localize the SDGs vary significantly, particularly because their respective mandates (i.e. which aspects they control), institutional, and financial capacities are quite diverse.

Figure 4.5
How knowledge co-production between government and academia in the adaptation of a global sustainability agenda to the city level interplays with the implementation and monitoring of the agenda at other levels.

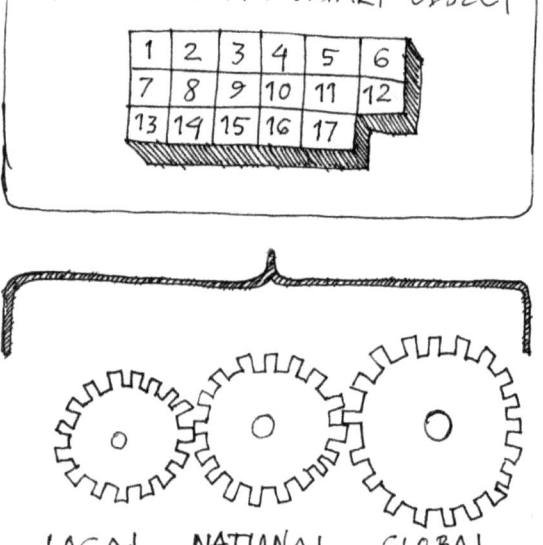

Meanwhile, the municipalities have gone through similar processes when reflecting on how to adapt this global agenda to the urban level in their respective city. Comparing these has both facilitated reflection on local processes and strategies and informed global discussions. Reflections concern not only the adaptation and implementation of the SDGs, but also aspects such as SDG communication strategies, monitoring mechanisms, and guidance received from the regional and national level (or the lack thereof, as has been the case in several cities), as well as issues on how to integrate the SDGs into existing planning mechanisms, such as municipalities' development plans and budgets. The project submitted evidence to several different UN agencies and national reviews, responding to calls for SDG reviews and good practices.

Challenges
During busy administrative times, such as the run-up to the end of the financial year, elections or city development plan preparations, officials were less likely to engage, thereby delaying the project. During these times it was important for the researchers to adapt and try to maintain contact and produce relevant documentation so that the municipal officials continued to see added value rather than regard the research as a burden. For example, meeting the deadlines of the city-to-city peer review was a challenge for most municipal officials because these fell at times when pressing issues such as budget planning took precedence. For several officials, their busy schedule meant a more limited engagement than was originally anticipated. A more relaxed schedule might have ensured deeper engagement.

In future international comparative co-produced urban research involving municipal officials, involving a smaller number of cities could help the respective teams to gain a better understanding of one another's contexts, thereby facilitating more in-depth suggestions. In this seven-city project, the monthly virtual meetings were limited to the academic researchers. Involving fewer cities may allow regular virtual exchanges between both officials and researchers within each team.

It was challenging for the researchers involved to find a balance between supporting the SDG localization process and maintaining independence and critical reflection on the process itself. Setting up clear expectations, dividing the work, and building trust between the partners has been crucial for the ability to jointly develop project work while also maintaining some independence for individual reflection.

Key messages
- Finding a boundary object such as the SDGs, that surpasses local institutional, economic, political, and social differences can be an effective mechanism for international co-production projects. Being part of an international project where all cities are attempting (to different extents) to localize the SDGs has

- been useful for municipalities to enhance the legitimacy of the process locally as well as feel part of a greater project where the local sustainability work can be set in a global context.
- Co-producing research in this way requires flexibility and being cognizant of the time limitations of the municipal official counterparts.
- Given that this project was not requested by city officials, it was up to each local researcher to find a suitable counterpart at the municipal administration and establish a working relation and work plan, which takes time. The flexibility of the central project, in terms of both time frames and content, allowed the local teams to achieve good working dynamics, with jointly agreed agendas that were relevant to both the city and the comparative project.
- Face-to-face interactions allow participants to get to know each other better and prevent misunderstandings during virtual meetings. They also enable both deeper discussions on methods, theory, and processes not easily done through online tools, and informal discussions providing opportunities for new collaborations between city pairs working on similar challenges.

Suggested readings

Ministry of Devolution and Planning (2017) 'Implementation of the Agenda 2030 for Sustainable development in Kenya' [online] <http://genderinkenya.org/wp-content/uploads/2017/12/Kenya-HLPF-report-June-2017.pdf> [accessed 18 August 2020].

Simon, D., Arfvidsson, H., Anand, G., Bazaz, A., Fenna, G., Foster, K., Jain, G., Hansson, S., Marix Evans, L., Moodley, N., Nyambuga, C., Oloko, M., Ombara, D.C., Patel, Z., Perry, B., Primo, N., Revi, A., Van Niekerk, B., Wharton, A. and Wright, C. (2015) 'Developing and testing the Urban Sustainable Development Goal's targets and indicators: a five-city study', *Environment and Urbanization* 28(1): 49–63 <https://doi.org/10.1177/0956247815619865>.

Valencia, S.C., Simon, D., Croese, S., Nordqvist, J., Oloko, M., Sharma, T., Taylor Buck, N. and Versace, I. (2019) 'Adapting the Sustainable Development Goals and the New Urban Agenda to the city level: initial reflections from a comparative research project', *International Journal of Urban Sustainable Development* 11(1): 4–23 <http://dx.doi.org/10.1080/19463138.2019.1573172>.

Valencia, S.C., Simon, D., Croese, S., Diprose, K., Nordqvist, J., Oloko, M., Sharma, T. and Versace, I. (2020) 'Internationally initiated projects with local co-production: Urban Sustainable Development Goal project', in D. Simon, H. Palmer, and J. Riise (eds), *Comparative Urban Research from Theory to Practice: Co-production for sustainability*, Chapter 6, pp. 113–131. Policy Press and open access, Bristol.

Exchange as method: the value of trans-local learning

Beth Perry and Bert Russell

Advocates of transdisciplinary knowledge co-production propose that 'impact' and 'knowledge exchange' are hard-wired into the research process, cultivated through specific methods and modes of operationalizing a commitment to participation in research. Yet even in such projects, certain aspects of the research process can often remain closed to participants without paid academic positions. Specifically, resources can be limited for co-researchers from outside the university setting to engage in comparative work or trans-local learning.

We wanted to challenge traditional ideas about the purpose of comparison being only to *generalize*, and centre the need to *learn* instead, through creating spaces for exchange and opening the horizons of possibility for more participatory cities (May and Perry, 2010; McFarlane, 2011). Our aim was also to subvert the usual linear model of knowledge *transfer* – whereby formally recognized 'knowledge producers' are seen to transmit information to 'knowledge consumers' – through designing an active process of knowledge *exchange* to engage decision-makers in real-time learning.

To address this challenge, we developed a pilot method to engage urban decision-makers in Greater Manchester in the co-production of relevant and useful lessons to support local democracy and participation, through creating formal and informal spaces for the exchange of ideas and developing joint platforms and processes (for more information, see Perry and Russell, 2020).

What do we mean by trans-local learning?

To exemplify co-productive design principles, it is important to challenge the idea of an 'end-user' who receives a final report (Perry and May, 2010). This means rethinking what impact looks like and how it can be achieved. Trans-local learning is an important element in opening up spaces for exchange and dissemination often reserved for academics. Trans-localism is more than just cities learning from each other across or within national boundaries. It points to the need for meaningful interactions between networked individuals and groups of similarly thinking people beyond the local. What is at stake is a sense of belonging through shared perspectives and concerns that transcend local boundaries.

Exchange as method

This method was developed by researchers in the Sheffield-Manchester platform. Our first objective was to create a coherent 'gateway' for decision-makers in the Greater Manchester Combined Authority (GMCA) to collaborate with a wide range of co-production projects. The GMCA is an organization which supports joint decision-making and action for the 10 local authorities in the metropolitan area, in selected areas of urban policy, such as transport and housing.

The need to have a single 'gateway' was important for two reasons: first, the GMCA was a relatively new organization, and structures and entry points were initially unclear; second, our portfolio of projects cut across multiple policy domains. We were mindful that individual researchers would have their own policy relationships; but equally we did not want multiple, parallel discussions with the GMCA about the relevance of our findings to undermine a collective impact. There were many different moving parts on both sides of the partnership.

We developed a process we called Developing Co-productive Capacities to enable knowledge exchange and to facilitate the engagement of officials in the portfolio of our work (see Chapter 3, 'Designing the Action Research Collective: embracing incompleteness'). Basket funding for the process was secured from impact funds allocated by participating universities (Sheffield, Manchester, and Birmingham) and by aligning existing local spending for knowledge exchange within a range of projects. Matched in-kind funding was agreed by GMCA in the form of officer time and the provision of venues.

The negotiation of this year-long process took over three months, with high-level sign-offs required to enable city officials to participate in activities and the identification of key personnel to take part. While delaying the initiation of some parts of the process, this led to strong buy-in and credible commitment, as well as high interest in the results of analysis. The resulting partnership agreement enabled better access and enrolment of senior decision-makers and set out mutual expectations. One agreement, for instance, was that participants would write blogs on their reflections and commit to internal workshops as a first step to enabling learning to be embedded in their respective institutional contexts.

The agreed process of *Developing Co-productive Capacities* included:
- the joint planning and delivery of two internal workshops with GMCA officers to share existing practices around co-production;
- the identification of tools and resources that could support learning about the principles, practices, and pitfalls of co-production;
- three international learning visits (see below), including the preparation and delivery of joint presentations;
- co-organizing and hosting an international policy exchange workshop, with attendance from senior politicians (see Photo 4.2);
- an interview programme with senior decision-makers and politicians;
- internal workshops organized by GMCA staff to share and embed learning and identify next steps.

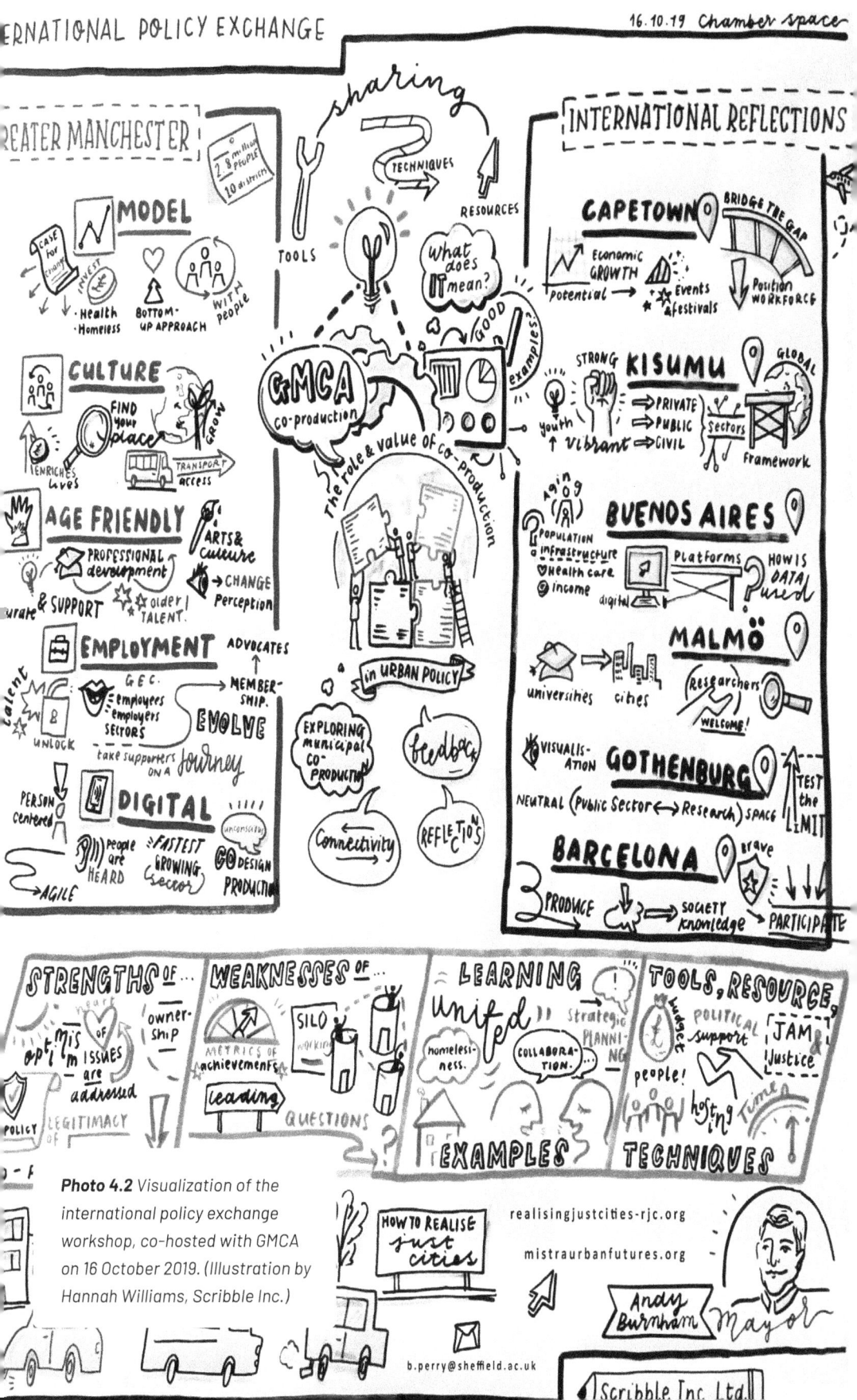

Photo 4.2 Visualization of the international policy exchange workshop, co-hosted with GMCA on 16 October 2019. (Illustration by Hannah Williams, Scribble Inc.)

Our second objective was to support trans-local learning through three learning visits. The first learning visit was to the Mistra Urban Futures' Annual Conference in Cape Town in November 2018, during which Greater Manchester and Gothenburg officials – alongside academic and non-academic researchers – were invited to present their urban contexts and governance arrangements. The second visit shortly thereafter involved a mixed delegation from Greater Manchester to the International Observatory of Participatory Democracy meeting in Barcelona. The third was a three-day learning visit to Gothenburg with a wider delegation including citizens, third sector representatives, activists, and local officials from Greater Manchester, as well as from the West Midlands Combined Authority. These different contexts provided diverse points of learning and engagement – enabling Greater Manchester decision-makers to meet:

- other co-production scholars and practitioners (Mistra Urban Futures networks/ Cape Town);
- local governments involved in participatory democracy (IOPD/Barcelona); and
- metropolitan and city officials (Gothenburg).

After each visit, we undertook different forms of reflection, including group discussion, individual reflection, and interviewing.

In keeping with the ethos of 'doing with' and 'not to', involving urban officials and stakeholders in the generation of comparative insights through the learning visits enabled learning from the outside-in. By this, we mean using insights from other urban settings to better understand conditions, constraints, limits, and possibilities in one's own context.

The trans-local visits enabled *learning about citizen involvement in decision-making* through direct engagement with specific tools, techniques, approaches, and methods. Delegates *reflected on policy and practice* in their own context, through honest consideration on the strengths and limitations of existing approaches. Rather than looking for 'quick fixes' or models that could be transferred from context to context, comparative learning enabled context-specific lessons to be drawn, building on pre-existing understandings of institutional constraints and possibilities. Looking from the 'outside-in' meant that progress could be then *grounded in international experiences and perspectives*. This enabled better understanding of where there were learning opportunities and where Greater Manchester had a distinctive offer to make. Importantly, the experience started to open up discussion on different *horizons of possibility* for action and the necessary institutional and cultural changes required to bring them about.

Space was created for urban officials and stakeholders to think outside their usual constraints. One delegate referred to such learning as a 'luxury' not afforded in their everyday professional settings. In the reflective dialogue, delegates prompted, questioned, and challenged one another, for instance in relation to ideas of what was or wasn't deemed 'possible' in Greater Manchester. Members of the same local governance organization had the opportunity to engage with one another's ideas and perspectives in ways that were not seen to be feasible at work. Stimulating critical thinking and space for reflection was as valuable as concrete tools and actions.

Lessons learned
By negotiating a process to facilitate exchange between researchers and decision-makers and to enable participation in processes of trans-local learning, we extended the logics and principles of transdisciplinary co-production beyond the production of data and empirical research. The process facilitated the co-production of usable findings and practical tools and simultaneously generated new insights about the contexts in which knowledge is received and implemented. To this extent, enabling local stakeholders to participate directly in comparative learning activities accelerated the transfer of relevant lessons which could support the realization of more just cities.

The negotiation of the process depended on longstanding, embedded relationships between senior academics and gatekeepers in the organization, without which it is unlikely that agreements with such high levels of access would be granted. This needs to be taken into account when considering the replicability of the process to other contexts. In addition, while the original aspiration was for decision-makers themselves to be the active carriers of knowledge back to their organization, the academics ended up playing a key role in sharing internal learning with GMCA. At one level, this was a deliberate shift in tactic, in order to mobilize the legitimacy and position of 'international' academics to establish credibility and independence in mobilizing for internal change. However, it also undermined 'ownership' of the lessons learned.
A further issue related to the different qualities of the reflection: group facilitated reflection provided greater insights than independently written blogs. Indeed, there were limits to the 'soft power' of the academics to ensure that such expectations were delivered on.

Collective experience and discussion had other impacts, in strengthening relationships among delegates. Rather than a critical agenda owned solely by academics, a greater shared problem space and critical lens started to develop among delegates. Learning together built trust, which had an impact on the quality of the local co-productive relationships.

References

Andersdotter Fabre, E., Anneroth, E. and Wrangsten, C. (2019) *Urban Girls Catalogue: How Cities Planned for and by Girls Work for Everyone* [pdf], Global Utmaning, Stockholm <https://www.globalutmaning.se/rapporter/urbangirlsmovement-catalogue/> [accessed 28 February 2020].

Bertolini, L. and Spit, T. (1998) *Cities on Rails: The Redevelopment of Railway Station Areas*, Taylor & Francis, London.

McFarlane, C. (2011) *Learning the City: Knowledge and Trans-local Assemblage*, Wiley Blackwell, Oxford.

May, T. and Perry, B. (2010) 'Comparative research: potentials and problems', in T. May (ed.), *Social Research: Issues, Methods and Process*, pp. 243-67, Open University Press and McGraw-Hill, Maidenhead, UK.

Norris, P.E., O'Rourke, M., Mayer, A.S. and Halvorsen, K.E. (2016) 'Managing the wicked problem of transdisciplinary team formation in socio-ecological systems', *Landscape and Urban Planning* 154: 115-22 <https://doi.org/10.1016/j.landurbplan.2016.01.008>.

Perry, B. and May, T. (2010) 'Urban knowledge exchange: devilish dichotomies and active intermediation', *International Journal of Knowledge-Based Development* 1(1): 6-24 <https://doi.org/10.1504/IJKBD.2010.032583>.

Perry, B. and Russell, B. (2020) 'Participatory cities from the outside in: the value of comparative learning', in D. Simon, H. Palmer, and J. Riise (eds), *Comparative Co-production from Theory to Practice*, pp. 133-54, Policy Press, Bristol.

Ranhagen, U. (2012) *4 Big Leaps and 20 Small Steps: Conceptual Guidelines on Sustainable Spatial Planning*, Swedish Energy Agency ET 2012:14, Eskilstuna, Sweden.

Ranhagen, U. (2020a) *Co-Creation in Urban Station Communities: Summary of three lectures with a presentation of findings from the project 2017-2019*, Mistra Urban Futures Report 2020:5, Gothenburg.

Ranhagen, U. (2020b) 'Densification of station areas in order to promote sustainable mobility, health, well-being and energy efficiency - opportunities and obstacles. The case study of Mölnlycke urban centre in Gotenburg region', *IOP conference series*, 2020, Vol 588.

Ranhagen, U. and Groth, K. (2012) *Symbio City Approach: A Conceptual Framework for Sustainable Urban Development*, SKL International, Stockholm.

Ranhagen, U., Dahlstrand, A. and Ramstedt, A. (2017) *Co-creation in Urban Station Communities: Findings from Working Seminars Involving the Collaboration of Transdisciplinary Agents 2015-2016*, Mistra Urban Futures Report 2017:2, Gothenburg.

CHAPTER 5
Blurring boundaries to facilitate understanding

ords
ledge transfer
amme, research forum,
ovoice, social inclusion,
ens' jury, FunkTek,
tive documentation

In one way or another, all method descriptions in this book refer to the act of crossing or managing boundaries following from disparities in, for example, ways of expression, types of knowledge, rationales, and organizational cultures. Sometimes these boundaries are evident and known, sometimes hidden. It is not certain that the critical boundaries assumed (e.g. between academic researchers and civil servants) are those that matter most to the participants in the process. The contributions of this chapter each set out various tools to consider when engaging different communities in transdisciplinary co-production. Several of them involve redefining which roles and tasks different stakeholders take on in the research process. By doing so they aspire to generate learning and understanding and the acceptance of all knowledge as being of equivalent value, for example through addressing power differentials between academic and lay knowledge, and between the knowledge of city administrations and citizens.

WE FIRST LEARN HOW THE KNOWLEDGE programme in Cape Town was set up to facilitate learning and knowledge integration between the university and city administration. The following description on the Research Forum also engages in critical boundaries between researchers and practitioners and provides a framework for different types of interaction. The next four contributions all describe tools to engage hidden voices that often are excluded in knowledge production. Here, we learn how Photovoice can be used to engage and raise the voices of community members in a co-production process, and how a community playground became a means of boosting social inclusion. The description of the inverted citizens' jury then takes us through how the model can facilitate learning across boundaries and bring in new testimonies of relevance to urban decision-making. The FunkTek method then illustrates how participants can be engaged through a norm-critical approach, and how the method itself sometimes becomes the solution. The chapter concludes with a description of creative documentation as a method to record and represent multiple voices.

Building transdisciplinary capacities through the Knowledge Transfer Programme

Warren Smit and Rike Sitas

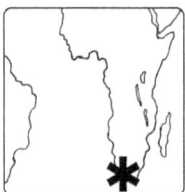

Since its establishment in 2007, the African Centre for Cities (ACC) at the University of Cape Town had closely partnered with the City of Cape Town and had identified a number of key topics for collaboration between City officials, University researchers, and other stakeholders. This resulted in the establishment of the CityLab programme (see Chapter 3, 'The CityLab programme in Cape Town'). Although very successful in producing new research and developing new policies, obtaining the long-time commitment of City officials was a continual challenge, due to understaffing and constant crises that officials needed to deal with. After the ACC joined Mistra Urban Futures as the anchor for the Cape Town Local Interaction Platform, it was decided to develop a more structured programme to create a cohort of researchers that could straddle the worlds of academic research and local government policy/practice and thus help contribute to the development of both policy-relevant research and research-informed policies. The Knowledge Transfer Programme was therefore launched in 2012.

The first component of the Knowledge Transfer Programme was the embedding of PhD researchers within the City of Cape Town for three years at a time, to work for the City (typically for 50–60 per cent of their time) on policy/research on a particular theme while simultaneously doing academic research on the same theme. In this way, the researchers help to inject cutting-edge research into local government policy processes (and significantly add to local government capacity), while also helping ensure that research on local government is based on the realities that officials face. In all, seven PhD researchers were embedded in the City of Cape Town, four of them for three years each and three of them for two years each. The topics they have worked on are: climate change adaptation and mitigation; the green economy; energy governance; the implementation of the Sustainable Development Goals; understanding the urban economy spatially; transport justice; inclusionary housing; and cultural planning.

The second component of the Knowledge Transfer Programme was an official exchange programme for City of Cape Town officials to get up to two months of 'academic leave' each to spend at the University of Cape Town writing up and reflecting on their practical experiences at the City, and undertaking reviews of relevant literature so they could relate their work to theory and the existing body of knowledge. There typically were six officials in each round of the exchange programme, and they each were given six weeks of 'academic leave' by the City to spend at the University of Cape Town. Officials were paired with relevant academic writing partners to write journal articles and book chapters on their work (see Chapter 3, 'Academics and municipal officials co-writing in third space').

Many journal articles have been produced, as well as a book. The officials exchange programme enabled officials to document and reflect on their work and enabled them to engage with the academic literature and think about the implications for their daily practice.

Through the Knowledge Transfer Programme, the ability of the City to grapple with and address many of the complex issues it faces was enhanced, and academic research on Cape Town was greatly enriched through exposure to many of the realities of local government that are generally not well understood in academia. All the embedded researchers and exchange officials found the process personally very valuable for their own growth and knowledge, but it was also very challenging. The embedded researchers had competing demands on their time, having to do research and policy work for the City while simultaneously researching and writing a PhD thesis. Doing research in a very fluid institutional environment with frequent institutional restructuring and frequent changes in policy priorities was also a challenge. As a result, some of the embedded researchers struggled to complete their PhDs. For the exchange officials, the main challenge was academic writing, but through providing support (such as writing workshops) and through pairing with academic writing partners, this challenge was quickly addressed. Some of the exchange officials subsequently re-applied for the exchange programme, and two City officials ended up participating twice in the programme.

Given the advantages of the embedded researcher model, other organizations have shown great interest in replicating and adapting the model. The Future Resilience for African Cities and Lands (FRACTAL) project, coordinated by the Climate Systems Analysis Group at the University of Cape Town, adopted the embedded researcher model in 2016 (its embedded researcher programme was coordinated by a former embedded researcher from the first phase of the Knowledge Transfer Programme). In order to help city governments in Southern Africa to be able to effectively tackle climate change, a total of six researchers were embedded in five different city governments: Lusaka (Zambia), Windhoek (Namibia), Harare (Zimbabwe), Maputo (Mozambique), and Durban (South Africa). Also, in 2016, one of the other Mistra Urban Futures partners – the Skåne Local Interaction Platform – initiated a municipal PhD project that drew on the experiences of the Knowledge Transfer Programme. Although broadly the same as the Knowledge Transfer Programme in that it has created a cohort of researchers who straddle local government and academia, the different context has resulted in the details of the project being quite different. As part of this project, four officials from various municipalities have had time freed up to undertake part-time PhDs at the three universities in the region. The PhD students are supported by main supervisors from the universities and co-supervisors from the municipality.

Suggested readings

Miszczak, S.M. and Patel, Z. (2018) 'The role of engaged scholarship and co-production to address urban challenges: a case study of the Cape Town Knowledge Transfer Programme', *South African Geographical Journal* 100(2): 233–48 <http://dx.doi.org/10.1080/03736245.2017.1409649>.

Patel, Z., Greyling, S., Parnell, S. and Pirie, G. (2015) 'Co-producing urban knowledge: experimenting with alternatives to "best practice" for Cape Town, South Africa', *International Development Planning Review* 37(2): 187–203 <http://dx.doi.org/10.3828/idpr.2015.15>.

A model for co-production of knowledge: creating a Research Forum

Mirek Dymitrow and Karin Ingelhag

Transdisciplinary collaborations based on academic–practitioner interactions are not always straightforward. In this text, we would like to share some insights from our work with the project 'Urban Rural Gothenburg', within which we have launched the *Research Forum* model as a means of co-producing new transdisciplinary knowledge.

Urban Rural Gothenburg and the associated Research Forum

'Urban Rural Gothenburg' was a three-year (2017–19) EU-sponsored project for sustainable development with the overarching aim to create improved conditions for green innovation and green business development between the city and the countryside. Operating in five testbeds in four so-called local hubs in socially deprived areas of Gothenburg, the project sought to develop and implement new low-carbon approaches to local development, with linkages to food, logistics, tourism, and ecological business models. This involved combining innovations for social improvement with reduced environmental and climate impact, for Gothenburg to become a sustainable city of globally and locally equitable emissions. The project was based on a so-called 'penta-helix model' methodology, which involved creating new knowledge through consistent cross-border cooperation between local authorities, the business sector, residents, civil society, and academia.

The *Research Forum 'Urban Rural Gothenburg'* constituted the academic component of 'Urban Rural Gothenburg' penta-helix model. Basically, it was meant to serve as an incubator and accelerator of various initiatives concerned with understanding, testing, and implementing ecologically oriented solutions that may arise through academic–practitioner interactions. The Research Forum (RF) was thus not a 'place' but a collaborative effort of two coordinators – one practitioner and one academic – who actively pursued and facilitated new ways of extracting knowledge.

Different types of interaction

Identifying and successfully matching different perspectives and pools of knowledge is a difficult challenge. This is mainly because interactions are seldom based on the same principles; different people have different foci, incentives, and agendas, while understanding how they work out in practice is key to successful implementation of the RF model. Figure 5.1 depicts four of the most common modes of interaction encountered during our work with the RF, and a description and analysis follows.

Academics to practitioners. It seems easier to attract academics to ongoing municipal, regional, and national projects than vice versa. Academics have the confidence and personal motivation to engage outside of academia, as such engagements are condoned and rewarded by the current academic discourse. From our experience, many approaches by academics have been motivated by a desire of adding a feather to their cap, or – more commonly – to obtain funding. In our case screening an academic's ongoing work and a simple question 'Do you have funding for your work?' was usually enough to deter the most disingenuous approaches. Instead, we understood that for an academic to engage wholeheartedly in a project there must *true* rather than *tangible* academic interest in the given topic, or the academic in question must be in need of a case study that sits well with the design of their research. Sieving out these intricacies early and quickly has proven an important step of running a RF.

Practitioners to academics. Engaging practitioners in systematic academic collaboration, on the other hand, has been inextricably more difficult in this

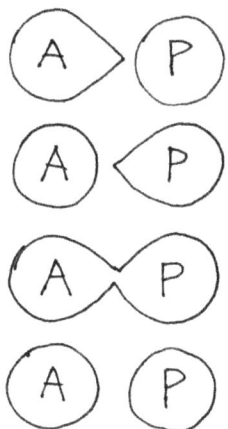

Figure 5.1
The Research Forum model with different forms of academic–practitioner interactions, referred to in the text. From the top: academics to practitioners, practitioners to academics, academics with practitioners, and academics without practitioners.

case, and for the opposite reasons. Practitioners usually lack the incentive to move beyond their comfort zone, but also lack the confidence to face an open discussion with academics. The internalization of academic knowledge as 'superior' relative to other forms of knowledge is so strong that breaking the confidence barrier is a time-consuming process that requires motivation, considerable help, and systematic inoculation. Running a RF thus involves making it a goal to systematically send out practitioners to various academic conferences, seminars, and workshops, and make them accustomed to the particularities of academic discourse. By committing to this intentional practice, it is easy to quickly see the results; practitioners feel more confident, engaged, and boosted on a personal level, feeling comfortable giving advice to academics, receiving critique, and sharing knowledge. Another important incentive in this direction is the use of steering documents that encourage co-production of knowledge. In some cases, academics are 'lured' into practitioners' projects in order to add superficial legitimacy to the latter. Running a RF also involves protecting 'the project' by spotting and averting such conduct.

Academics with practitioners. For successful co-production to take place, a few important rules need to be obeyed. We suggest the following. First, integrate academics and practitioners *early on* and avoid adding people to established projects, as this may cause an 'imposter effect' and disrupt a functioning power balance. Second, attach academics and practitioners to concrete and manageable *tasks* within the project, not the project in general; this is crucial to instil a sense of *responsibility*, rather than merely a sense of belonging. Third, always depart from *real-life problems* rather than from formal (written) *project goals,* as these are often significantly different. Fourth, stay sensitive to collaborations that wander off into the realm of 'sustainability clichés' without significant amount of criticism. Clichés are socially inculcated, and thus tend to be similar for practitioners and academics. This also means that no new knowledge will be co-created. Lastly, only account for meaningful *interactions* between academics and practitioners, rather than merely *encounters*.

Academics without practitioners. Co-production of knowledge is not always desirable. Put simply, sometimes expertise should be given authority before calling for a diversity of knowledge. This is especially the case whenever a project task does not require new ways of problem-solving if traditional approaches can do so in their own right. Another important insight is that co-production can take place without the different pools of knowledge being aggregated, but rather *superimposed*. Sometimes, two ingredients taste better one by one than in a hotchpotch. Throughout the process, pay attention to personal traits and 'chemistries', as not all people are made for each other and should not be encouraged to work together at any price. Also, make sure that responsibilities of practitioners and academics are comparable yet *different* in terms of workload and importance. It is unlikely that new knowledge will arise if people emulate each other or when a disruptive social hierarchy manifests itself. Lastly, stay vigilant of excessive routines or 'repertoires' (although not necessarily *working methods*) that both practitioners and academics take with them to the project. If we truly want to embrace co-production as way to obtain *new* knowledge, we inherently must concede part of our individuality towards a homogeneous goal. Put simply, we must constantly remain open to change.

Suggested reading

Dymitrow, M. and Ingelhag, I. (eds)(2020) *Anatomy of a 21st-century Sustainability Project: The Untold Stories*, Mistra Urban Futures, Chalmers University of Technology, Gothenburg.

A method for making the everyday visible: photovoice and everyday politics

Daniel Silver and Sarah Whitehead

What does everyday politics look like? There are some obvious things that people can do to participate in politics – voting, standing for election, joining a political party, or responding to consultation. But what about the less formal ways that people participate in everyday politics? This was a central question selected by the Jam and Justice Action Research Collective (see Chapter 3, 'Designing the Action Research Collective: embracing incompleteness') to be the focus of a small community research project in Greater Manchester, UK, in 2018-2019.

Revealing the everyday is a key challenge for research. It requires us to value and make visible things that can seem mundane or be taken for granted. This is a political task. Traditional methods, such as interviewing, are often inadequate in generating new insights or perspectives, especially when the questions have already been set by trained academic researchers.

Documenting the everyday through working with 'everyday makers'

Two academic and two community researchers from the Action Research Collective formed an action research team to work together to design a project working with 'everyday makers' to make everyday politics visible. 'Everyday makers' are people who get involved in local and concrete projects with a do-it-yourself ethos, who make a real difference to people's lives and benefit the local community (Bang, 2005). They are well-known, well-networked, and trusted across their communities, working either as part of a community-led action group or by themselves. Everyday makers create tangible changes that make a difference to their communities.

Training 'everyday makers' as community researchers
Addressing the question 'what does everyday politics look like?' demands a transdisciplinary approach – centring on the experiential knowledge of everyday makers themselves. With this co-production project, we wanted to value the knowledge and skills of different participants and ensure that there were open spaces for participants to contribute their opinions, be listened to, and influence the process.

Eight 'everyday makers' were recruited by the action research team to take part in the project. Over eight months they became community researchers to bring their knowledge and experience to explore how they participated in everyday politics. We decided to use a method called photovoice, a community-based research method that uses photographs as a basis for discussion.

The tradition of photovoice
The academic researchers brought knowledge of how photovoice could be used as a community-based participatory method (Wang and Burris, 1994) to enable everyday makers to share their experiential knowledge. Photovoice is based on a rich literature, including Paolo Freire's ideas about education for critical consciousness, feminist theory's recognition of the value of subjective experience and expertise, and the tradition of documentary photography and its attempt to give visual expression to the social conscience. British photographer and educator, Jo Spence, famously described 'community photography' as a way of thinking about how ordinary people could appropriate the camera for social change (Evans-Agnew and Rosemberg, 2016).

The method in action
Our photovoice project started off with the action research team, with the community researchers from the Action Research Collective providing critical grassroots knowledge and access to recruit and set up the project. Once they recruited the everyday makers, the action research team organized a workshop to discuss the idea of 'everyday makers' with them, and how participants felt this related to their work. They then explored the photovoice method and the use of cameras. At the end of the workshop, participants were asked to go away and capture photographs that could illustrate how they felt about formal politics, and the ways in which their practices as everyday makers produced an alternative.

Photo 5.1 Photographs taken as part of the photovoice method showing everyday encounters of community researchers Saraswati Sinha, Jane Gregory, Pete Simms, and Tony Wright (clockwise from top left). (© each named photographer)

The 'everyday makers' then went about their daily lives and took photographs (see examples in the collage in Photo 5.1). When they felt they had enough photographs, academic researchers interviewed each everyday maker to discuss the meaning of the images. Wide-ranging one-to-one dialogue took place that was rooted in the experiences of the participants.

After all the dialogues had been completed, another workshop was organized and led by the academic researchers, where the participants came together to explain their photographs to each other. This drew on the mnemonic of SHOWED (Catalani and Minkler, 2010), which included the following reflective questions:

- What do you (S)ee here?
- What is really (H)appening here?
- How does this relate to (O)ur lives?
- (W)hy does this concern, situation, strength exist?
- How can we become (E)mpowered through our new understanding?
- And what can we (D)o?

As each participant explained their photographs, the others listened and wrote down the key themes that they felt were being explored. Through this process, an early coding framework was created. The rest of the workshop involved refining and discussing this framework. The coding framework that had been discussed through the workshop was then used by the researchers to analyse the interviews to understand the everyday politics that inform the work of participants.

Five themes were identified and then presented back to participants at the final workshop and discussed. These themes about what 'everyday makers' do are:

- *Valuing*: recognizing and building on the strengths in our communities.
- *Connecting*: bringing communities together.
- *Questioning*: challenging the status quo to put forward alternative approaches.
- *Reasoning*: learning within communities to create shared understanding.
- *Developing*: working with communities to come up with solutions.

Key outcomes and results
Participants decided that key audiences for the work were other community workers and activists, so that they could recognize the work that they do as everyday politics. The community researchers and the action research team co-produced a touring exhibition and a booklet: *Everyday Politics*.

This booklet illustrates positive ways in which everyday makers are making a difference in their communities.

We had begun with a negative premise that many people had lost faith with formal political institutions. The touring exhibition and resources presenting *Everyday Politics*, produced by the 'everyday makers', helped recognize their work and show that everyday politics can help people to make change collectively.

Pete Simms, one of the participants, reflected that the project showed how real change can be achieved and sustained at a micro level, allowing for wider conversations to happen which can and do influence change on a regional and national level.

The exhibition has toured across Greater Manchester, from community centres to museums. Everywhere the exhibition has generated new conversations about the invisible, lesser valued, but important work undertaken by 'everyday makers', challenging assumptions that people just 'don't care'.

Lessons learned
Photovoice was an effective method to engage people working in communities but who don't engage with formal politics, in a research project about politics. The emphasis on creative, participatory research meant that the project delivered its aims and also built relationships that are fundamental in supporting the textured fabrics of our communities.

Two key challenges arose. The first relates to the pre-defined short time frame for the project which made it hard to go at the 'natural speed' of participants. The second related to the mismatch between the university's administrative processes and the need for flexibility and lightness in interactions with participants (see Chapter 2, Box 2.11, 'Facilitating supportive administrative relationships for co- production' in the Sheffield-Manchester region and Gothenburg). Paying participants, underpinned by an ethical commitment to recognize different forms of labour in knowledge production, meant working at the edges of accepted processes within the university and finding ways to be creative and think outside the box. This meant that the administrative load of the project was greater than initially imagined.

Nonetheless, photovoice enabled the project to be truly inclusive and accessible to a wide range of people, regardless of age, education or ability – giving a deeper insight into the radical grassroots led social change that is taking place across the UK.

Suggested readings

Calver, S., Graham, A., Gregory, J., Minocha, N., Nkrumah, D., Simms, P., Sinha, S., Unegbu, E. and Wright, S., with Durose, C., Silver, D., Whitehead, S., Asumu, J. and Bickerton, A. (2018) Everyday Politics, Project report, Dan Farley Designs, Greater Manchester <https://jamandjustice-rjc.org/sites/default/files/J%26J_Everyday-Politics_web-edition.pdf> [accessed 21 July 2020].

Perry, B., Durose, C. and Richardson, L. with the Action Research Collective (2019) How Can We Govern Differently? The Promise and Practice of Co-production, Project report, Greater Manchester: Creative Concern <https://jamandjustice-rjc.org/publications-jam-and-justice> [accessed 21 July 2020].

Playing for social inclusion

Lillian Omondi, George Mark Onyango, and John Sande

The concept of social inclusion implies a level playing field, with every individual in society having an equal opportunity to participate in self and societal development. Achieving this in the developing world is quite complex. This is because the issues lie at the intersection of several interrelated variables which determine the level of inclusiveness of the populace. Enhanced economic capacities, neighbourhood accessibility, and planning have to be juggled in order to find a balance in societal inclusion.

Dunga in Kisumu County, Kenya, is one such community struggling with creating an environment for all its members to feel included. Lying in the informal belt surrounding the city centre and on the shores of Lake Victoria, Dunga is one of the popular sites for settlement of rural-urban migrants into the city. Most of these new entrants end up in the informal sector of employment.

This example from Dunga tackles a number of related but discrete urban issues by making the physical space of a playground into a common boundary object for co-production.

Process
Engagement with this community through the platform in Kisumu (see Appendix) began with the aim of assessing the challenges and opportunities presented by urbanization processes. This was executed through round table discussions involving the resident groups, members from the city council, and researchers. Through the discussions, it became evident that the community had different

segments of people, whose participation and inclusion in community activities was nuanced by issues that were very specific to their different identities. This encouraged more engagement with these specific groups using participatory techniques which provided an arena for the discussion of some of the issues that were plaguing the area and promoting segregation of the different groups.

A priority of the women involved in the sale of fish, for instance, was the fact that their engagement with the labour market was reduced due to role conflict. Most of them with young children had to cut working hours to take care of their children. During a visioning exercise, these children were asked to close their eyes and describe what they could see their community look like. The engagement with these two groups brought out the lack of play spaces within the locale. Even though Dunga's landscape provides a perfect natural environment for children to explore, climb, and imagine, the race towards urbanization has forced children to play on or near the road. Other issues that came up during the engagement included the political tensions, especially during the national election periods which have in the past led to ethnic balkanization, and the unplanned nature of the settlement, which made waste management complicated.

The community members, the city authorities, and the researchers held further sessions to identify and prioritize some possible solutions to these challenges. High on the list was a solution addressing multiple challenges to ensure effective and efficient use of existing resources. The process gave rise to the idea of erecting a playground. The community members had to certify minutes of meetings to show that they were all in agreement and then put in an application to the city government to get approval for construction.

Successful outcomes

The project, dubbed 'Building on the Children of Dunga', was the construction of a play area for children (Photo 5.2), with the intention of enhancing social inclusion and addressing social justice by responding to the aforementioned issues. By introducing the space and activity, some of the noted successes so far include:

- *Increased inclusion and engagement with the labour market*. A safe area for children to play and interact means the mothers could engage more efficiently in their daily fish sale activities as they did not have to worry about where to leave their children while at work. It also acted as an attraction to the area, thus increasing the numbers of visitors and subsequently customers.
- *Strengthening the ideals of social cohesion*. Childhood memories are very strong in us and these can be used to get participants in touch with the past and present environments. These experiences can be used to reduce ethnic divisions. As children play together, they form a 'tribe' of their own that knows no ethnic, social or religious boundaries. This consequently creates a community that is bonded together and strives to include all its members.

Photo 5.2 A playground working as boundary object bridging different interests and issues at Dunga beach. (Photo by John Xavier Chweya)

- *Inculcating principles of environmental conservation.* The idea of using locally available recycled material such as old car tyres and plastic reinforces on the children and community at large the principles of reduce, reuse, recycle. The community members were amazed that something as beautiful and useful could come from what is considered as waste materials.

The achievement of the above objectives in both the short and long term, if sustained, should move Dunga community towards achieving social inclusion by improving different aspects of social, economic, environmental, and urban governance. The project shows how multi-stakeholder engagement in a space devoted to something as everyday as the playing of children can address multiple and complex societal issues.

Challenges
One of the main challenges, however, is management of the playground. The playground was officially handed over to the Dunga Beach Management Unit once construction was complete. The demand for the play area has been overwhelming, with the children overloading the existing facilities, which has led to some of the swings breaking. Essentially, it was agreed that all the children of Dunga should be able to use the facility free of charge so as to ensure that no child is left out. A small fee would, however, be charged on children who were visiting the area to ensure that there was money for repairs. This has not been executed and therefore even minor repairs have so far not been made. As engagement with the community is still ongoing, there is intention to address ownership and maintenance as soon as practicable.

Tapping hidden expertise: the model of the Inverted Citizens' Jury

Jez Hall and Amanda Preece

An Inverted Citizens' Jury on Care at Home
The Jam and Justice Action Research Collective (ARC) aimed to develop ideas for action research projects that would test and learn from different approaches to citizen engagement and deliberative democracy (see Chapter 3, 'Designing the Action Research Collective: embracing incompleteness'). Jez Hall, a director of Shared Future Community Interest Company (SFCIC) and member of the ARC, proposed that social care – and in particular the care of elderly people within their own homes – would be a critical area for engagement. Greater Manchester's health commissioners were undertaking a service re-design to rethink how to provide elder care at home – so it felt timely to do something that might work alongside an existing policy process and test a new approach.

Truly person-centred co-production is notoriously hard to achieve within traditional top-down 'medical' care models. We developed an Inverted Citizens' Jury on Care at Home, to see if the deliberative processes used for citizens' juries might unlock a more responsive person-centred set of healthcare recommendations. Our aim was to tap into emotional, practical, and professional knowledge, and shift the traditional power imbalances from a medical model of healthcare towards a more social model.

Adapting the model of the citizens' jury
SFCIC is a recognized leader in the field of facilitating citizens' juries. These structured deliberative processes create a panel of lay citizens using random selection from the general public, who are then set a challenge around an issue of public policy. The citizens' jury hears expert testimony around the topic and produces recommendations. A final 'stakeholder' event is essential to disseminate the citizens' jury recommendations, and to influence power holders to change practice.

Citizens' juries are a well-respected model of deliberative democracy and are increasingly used to develop policies more free of institutional or political bias. Their design goes back to original Greek democracies, where citizens were chosen by lot to form the governing body of their city (SFCIC, 2017). They also mirror the use of juries in legal processes.

Our suggested approach was therefore a model of 'collaborative service re-design', using the approach of the citizens' jury but inverting it in an innovative manner. A conventional citizens' jury would have a randomly selected sample of citizens, from whom around 12–25 people are chosen. Instead we used (almost) randomly selected health professionals.

Turning an apple cart on its head?
Our idea was that, often, the most appropriate knowledge is already locked up within the public system, segmented into different departments and specialisms. In the absence of good communication and deliberation, health commissioners can propose top-down interventions which are inappropriate for very vulnerable but 'not yet ill' individuals and are resisted by their families and by frontline care staff. Shifting the organizational culture through traditional service planning can be fraught with blockages, dominated by institutional needs, and can end up with largely the same outcomes.

By recruiting a random sample of health professionals of different disciplines and seniorities, and facilitating an open and equal exchange through structured deliberation, we hoped to shift these institutional blockages and produce recommendations that might be directly taken up by decision-makers. Taking health professionals out of their daily work contexts was intended to enable different ideas to be generated which would get traction with their colleagues through the use of a well-established model of deliberative policy design. A further aim was to enable a more emotional, holistic, and empathetic response among professionals by enabling them to hear expert testimony from patients and service users.

Enabling knowledge co-production through good design
We designed the inverted inquiry to deliberate and co-produce a set of recommendations that attempted to answer the following question: *What would it take to help people to have a good life at home for as long as they choose?*

The citizens' jury methodology is very rigorous and we knew we had to be inventive. We kept many core design features, such as an oversight panel who advised on recruitment and set the challenge question; a panel of participants who represented the diversity of the health economy; the use of structured facilitation techniques; bringing in expert testimony; and the development of recommendations presented by participants directly to a panel of change makers and influencers.

Where the process differed slightly was in the recruitment of the participants. This was done through an open call. We made sure that the chosen participants did not know one another prior to taking part, had very different levels of seniority, participated as individuals rather than organizational representatives, and gave their time freely outside of their paid work. They were volunteers, committed to the topic, and free to express themselves openly and as equals. Time and budget constraints meant we also ran a slightly shorter process than some citizens' juries.

SFCIC trained two facilitators to follow a well-tested method for building deliberation and co-production between strangers. During six two-and-a-half-hour evening sessions (15 hours in total) jury members:

- explored their own responses to the challenge question and mapped out the problem using a range of visual methods;
- agreed on the underlying structures and drivers that blocked change within the healthcare system through a mixture of small and large group work;
- heard and questioned the testimony of those with 'lived expertise', positioning people who have direct experience of the care at home system as the witnesses or experts;
- received training and support to question the 'witnesses' in an open and empowering manner to explore new perspectives and unearth relevant information;
- came up with their recommendations for change using a structured process.

The project team, led by SFCIC, turned the recommendations into a report, ran a feedback event where recommendations were presented to commissioners and other stakeholders, and facilitated action-planning workshops to map pathways to implement the recommendations.

The project team included an academic lead from Jam and Justice as well as a social researcher who attended all of the sessions to capture the experiences of participants. The academic team helped shape the programme design, attended oversight meetings, and significantly brokered relationships with commissioners at the Greater Manchester Health and Social Care Partnership. Academic involvement brought trust in the process for commissioners and probably improved the recruitment of participants for the same reason. It also provided opportunities for ongoing reflection and learning, offered free meeting spaces in which to hold inquiry sessions, and contributed to the design and dissemination of reports and other visual materials. This process was run on a budget significantly less than a standard citizens' jury. In-kind support and encouragement by the academic team was essential to achieve the objectives and a good example of co-production between academics and practitioners – each side utilized their skills and knowledge in a collaborative and innovative way, while also working alongside public policymakers.

What we learned surprised us

Our Inverted Citizens' Jury showed that the deliberative model that works for lay citizens also works within an organizational setting, if good process is followed, and the underlying values enable the building of trust and reciprocity. Feedback from participants showed they had been personally moved by the experience. Jury members also came up with some powerful and innovative recommendations that were very well received by commissioners. Commissioners valued it highly, as they also felt blocked by the institutional culture they were operating within and could use the independent recommendations of the 'care at home citizens' jury' to sell their own transformational model.

The process opened doors. Health commissioners promoted the process as a good model of co-production within their wider organizations. They also sponsored a follow-up national conference, attended by many different health boards from across the UK to explore both traditional citizens' juries and the inverted model within the context of healthcare. They invited SFCIC to present the model internally on several occasions to policymakers as an example of best practice in co-production, as well as inviting inquiry participants to a follow-up meeting to demonstrate their impact on the ongoing policy process.

Our experience suggests that the model of the citizens' jury can be applied in innovative ways to support co-production through valuing different skills and expertise. The Inverted Citizens' Jury enabled caring, and doing with, not to, through co-producing recommendations drawing on diverse expertise and challenging traditional notions of the 'expert'.

Other large organizations could run an inverted citizens' jury, using staff recruited within their own 'community of practice'. This would allow them to bring in expert testimony from service recipients as a way of creating new products or services and new approaches and releasing hidden knowledge around seemingly intractable issues. However, independent facilitation (see Chapter 2, Box 2.7, 'Facilitation – bringing methods to life') will always be required to ensure that participants feel free to speak openly and honestly and so that the process remains trusted and rigorous. When enabled by expert facilitation, the model of the inverted citizens' jury could be used to support knowledge co-production and address a wide range of complex issues.

Suggested readings

A full report, including the recommendations and process description is available on the website of Shared Future at <https://sharedfuturecic.org.uk/inquiry-in-the-challenge-of-care-at-home-final-report/> [accessed 28 February 2020].

Bryant, P. and Hall, J. (2017) *Literature Review of Citizen Led Deliberation Processes* [online], Shared Future CIC, Manchester <https://sharedfuturecic.org.uk/literature-review-citizen-led-deliberation-processes/> [accessed 29 February 2020].

Degeling, C., Thomas, R. and Rychetnik, L. (2019) 'Citizens' juries can bring public voices on overdiagnosis into policy making', *British Medical Journal* 364: 351 <https://doi.org/10.1136/bmj.l351>.

Engaging people of different needs to create a better city for all: FunkTek

Kerstin Hemström,
Per Myrén,
Daniel Gillberg,
and Magnus Eriksson

Cities should work for everyone, regardless of functional variations and needs. In Gothenburg, the project FunkTek (2014–2017) was engaged in the challenges faced by people with different functional variations when taking part in cultural activities in the city. The project was based on a norm-critical approach, setting out that cities and their institutions – not the people who live in and use them – have disabilities. Norm criticism is about analysing, understanding, and questioning the privileges, exclusions, and power imbalances norms can create. The purpose of the project was twofold:

- To evaluate and improve the accessibility of the Museum of Gothenburg and its accompanying activities.
- To develop a method for participatory design for accessibility in urban environments.

The FunkTek method
The FunkTek method was developed to evaluate places and information and improve urban environments from an accessibility perspective. The principal idea was to collect knowledge and experience from a broad spectrum of visitors, to which an area or activity should be accessible.

Focusing on accessibility, people with different functional variations were hired as FunkTek pilots, to scrutinize and evaluate the public activities and exhibitions of the Museum of Gothenburg from an accessibility perspective. The pilots were recruited through digital advertising in the network of one of the projects partnering non-profit organizations and employed with salary from the project. In the recruitment, a group of people comprising broad representation of as many functional variants as possible was sought.

Each recruited FunkTek pilot was considered an *expert*, tasked to evaluate environments, locations, and activities from an accessibility perspective. When conducting an evaluation, the pilots spent about 15 minutes in a setting to assess different aspects by help of a questionnaire. To communicate their respective findings to one another, they also took photos with their mobile phones. The results were then summed up and reviewed in smaller groups. Finally, joint discussions were held during a shared coffee break. This planned time for relaxed socializing was important for the kinship and feeling of togetherness within the group. It was during the coffee break that most new ideas and insights appeared. Together, the participants could discuss different conditions and experiences of the researched places and identify challenges and potential developments. This created a learning situation for everyone involved of the conditions of the environments investigated, and whose needs they actually did speak to.

Initially, the FunkTek method was used to evaluate cultural events and exhibitions from a functional and norm-critical perspective, focusing on accessibility in urban environments (Photo 5.3). As the project evolved, however, the method also came to include participatory design of solutions. Based upon the evaluations, the FunkTek pilots were invited to co-design and develop new solutions in collaboration with museum staff. This work evolved in an iterative process with several cycles of prototyping and testing, evaluation, and design, before landing in a solution. The overall purpose was to change the way cultural exhibits are envisioned, planned, and built, in order to incorporate accessibility in the design from the start. In other words, the goal was not to find separate solutions for some but develop broad solutions that work and improve experiences for everyone.

When to use it
The FunkTek method has been used to evaluate several cultural activities in Gothenburg, including city walks, public baths, and the design and placing of

Photo 5.3 Group of FunkTek pilots testing the city accessibility together with project co-ordinator Lisa Wahle, on the streets of Gothenburg, 2015. (Photo by Daniel Gillberg)

historical information in the city. All in all, over 80 workshops were held within the scope of the project, focusing on different specific issues and activities. Each lasted for two to four hours and involved between 5 and 20 participants. All were held at the Museum of Gothenburg.

The installed transformations of the Museum of Gothenburg would not have happened without the FunkTek pilots. For the project members, the method has created an understanding of what working with accessibility means: familiarizing and engaging in mutual learning with people of different needs, particularly those who know what it is like to be excluded. As such, the method became the solution.

Overall, the FunkTek method draws attention to the fact that cities are perceived differently from different perspectives, and that the design of places and activities often is based on limited notions of, and norms for, how they should be used. Using the FunkTek method enables a discussion of the preconditions of different urban environments, and who they create opportunities for. Although the project focused on evaluating spaces and activities from marginalized perspectives, the method could similarly be used to explore, create a mutual understanding of, and incorporate other users or diversity perspectives in urban development work.

Challenges
- The main funding of the project was intended for developing and testing new technical solutions according to the principles of *design for accessibility*. Soon, however, the project members realized that the solution was not to be found in new technology, but in new ways of approaching accessibility. The developed method became the solution itself and the main takeaway from the project. However, communicating this to financers was challenging.
- The uneven distribution of working hours between the museum employees and other participants was an impediment to interaction. Had the museum staff had more time to interact directly with the FunkTek pilots, more concrete solutions could have been reached. Lacking this opportunity, the recommendations of the FunkTek pilots were sometimes perceived as criticism rather than a support to museum operations.

Takeaways
- The cultural environment is part of our collective resources, our environment in its broadest sense, and must be managed in a socially responsible manner.
- Increased accessibility often improves conditions for everyone, including the majority.
- The most trustworthy informants of inaccessibility are those who have experience of it.

- The FunkTek pilots had large influence over the design and use of the questionnaire and evaluations and were employed with salary at a similar level as the project manager.
- Make sure to have time for laidback chit-chats after your workshop! It will enhance the feeling of togetherness and comfort in the group, enabling participants to share thoughts and impressions.

Closing the co-productive cycle: creative documentation for multi-vocal representation

Alice Toomer McAlpine and Beth Perry

The Jam and Justice project brought together a diverse group of stakeholders to explore and take action around the topic of participation in urban governance in Greater Manchester (Perry et al., 2019). The Action Research Collective (ARC) – a group of academics, activists, community leaders, and citizens – worked together on several co-production projects (see Chapter 3, 'Designing the Action Research Collective: embracing incompleteness'). Beyond this, a wider network of groups and individuals with a stake in some or all of Jam and Justice's work were brought together to form broader 'coalitions for change' and support peer learning and knowledge exchange.

Capturing and sharing a collective story

Usually the emphasis in knowledge co-production is on how questions are set, how research is undertaken, and what impact work can have. However, it is equally important to close the co-productive cycle and consider how the voices and perspectives of different participants are represented and shared in the findings and outputs of the research.

The need to capture a diverse range of voices and build a collectively owned story across multiple 'languages' was identified early in the lifespan of the ARC. The project had to produce the usual academic outputs to meet funding requirements. However, following discussion, it was clear that not everyone was interested in writing these and the audiences were often limited and specialist, particularly if academic outputs are not open access.

We wanted to find other ways of giving voice and ownership of the collective story to ARC members. We also wanted to open the process, in 'real-time', to allow other people outside the ARC to see our inner workings and share in our journey. Drawing on the skills and expertise brought by ARC members, we decided to test a creative documentation method.

What is creative documentation?

Creative documentation is a method of recording, making sense of, and sharing the outputs of collective activity. The idea is that creative documentation goes beyond both the typically internally focused, formal, 'meeting minutes' format, and the typically externally focused, glossy promotional marketing content often produced during or (more often) at the end of an event, process or activity. The key principles are inclusivity and diversity; encouraging convergence while holding space for conflict, divergence, and questions; creative and alternative modes of communication; and the action reflection cycle.

The method draws on a number of existing practices, including graphic facilitation, generative listening, and intentional harvesting, which sits within a wider approach to collaborative leadership called the 'Art of Hosting': 'there is no point in doing work in the world unless we plan to harvest the fruits of our labours. Harvesting includes making meaning of our work, telling the story and feeding forward our results so that they have the desired impacts in the world' (Corrigan, 2012).

The method in action

Creative documentation of the ARC involved the production and dissemination of several digital outputs including graphic designs, audio and video content at various key points throughout the project. These included:

- using creative minutes to capture ARC workshops and developing mini-pitches to share key lessons from the ARC with imagined external audiences. These were video recorded, along with stills/animations of the workshop materials;
- recording workshops and seminars to capture learning and ensure that those not able to attend could still find out what happened, for instance at the International Observatory of Participatory Democracy in Barcelona;
- developing video provocations to help develop common understanding among new project teams and provoke discussion; for instance, in our project on digital democracy, gender, and participation – *GM Decides*;
- capturing video footage to feed into a collective design process about how to engage with different audiences and ensure impact from our research;
- documenting the process of building coalitions for change with wider stakeholders and audiences through creative documentation to stimulate interest and engage others in the process;
- narrating the overall 'story of the ARC', drawing on and adapting Marshall Ganz's 'Public Narrative' methodology (Ganz, 2011).

We developed five functions of creative documentation: planning, documenting, sense-making, analysing, and representing. Importantly, these functions feed into each other and interact, rather than necessarily being linear steps in a process.

A good example is the use of creative documentation to support our aim of building wider coalitions for change in Greater Manchester, beyond the ARC. First, video interviews were used at various stages of the process as a way of bringing more of the ARC's voices into spaces where decisions were being made by smaller groups on behalf of the whole. Our three main coalitions for change events were documented through graphic design and video outputs. This content offered different ways of synthesizing and sharing information and summarizing complex ideas and processes. The documentation was then woven into an ongoing process of action and reflection, often planned alongside the design of workshops and meetings and co-ordinated as an element of the facilitation process itself, as opposed to an additional activity separate to process design and delivery. This also supported subsequent analysis. For instance, in one session we had a workshop with multiple groups from Greater Manchester about the purpose of a co-production network. Participants moved around the room to stand close to statements which captured their aspirations, such as whether a local network could support political movement building, a platform for marginalized voices, or sharing best practice. By graphically animating this movement, creative documentation captured group dynamics and responses/reactions to provocations from the facilitators that would otherwise be outside the data record of the project.

Supporting knowledge co-production: participation, translation, and multi-vocal narration

Creative documentation is an important method in supporting knowledge co-production for three reasons.

First, creative documentation supports *participation* through enabling people's inputs to a collaborative planning and design process even when they cannot be physically present. The role of the creative documenter is not only to record, but to engage in different levels of listening (downloading, factual, empathic, and generative) in order both to summarize and also to generate collective learning (Sharmer, 2018).

Second, creative documentation supports *translation* between different meanings and linguistic registers, for instance the different 'sectoral languages' or jargon that different groups use. This makes processes accessible to participants not from academic or institutional backgrounds. The outputs produced were intended to straddle the line between internal and external communications and were created with an audience of 'potential participant' in mind, meaning that individuals with little to no technical knowledge on the subject could engage with the content and see how they might be able to contribute to the project's subsequent stages.

Third, creative documentation retains the diversity and richness of participants' voices in multi-vocal narratives that are not flattened by neat formulaic 'findings'. Unlike traditional outputs, the ongoing documentation process of the ARC and its surrounding activity aimed to acknowledge and give attention to moments of conflict and divergence, while highlighting commonalities across the diverse range of perspectives. The aim was to identify opportunities for collective action, such as the 'Stories of the ARC' video project using the public narrative storytelling method to move from a personal to a shared story, towards an ultimate aim of collective action for change.

Lessons learned, questions emerging

The creative documentation method used throughout the lifespan of the ARC was not explicitly planned from the beginning, and instead emerged from within the ARC itself as an opportunity to try out different ways of communicating both internally and externally. The approach benefited from the flexibility of the Jam and Justice project leaders, who welcomed these alternative forms of documentation as they were offered and managed to realign available resources to support them.

Taking a more creative approach to documenting complex processes can be more labour intensive than traditional minute taking. Having a clear documentation plan that is developed alongside the process itself can mitigate this by ensuring that the most valuable information is being harvested for specific purposes.

This then raises issues of who 'owns the story'? The creative process itself potentially puts more power in the hands of whoever produces the outputs. In the case of the ARC, any outputs which attempted to tell a collective story sought feedback and consent from all ARC members. However, we realized the value of creative documentation to knowledge co-production in the course of undertaking it. The ability to influence the telling of one's personal and collective story is an integral part of power sharing.

A valuable lesson would be to include creative documentation as an explicit part of the wider process design from the beginning to the end. This would enable movement beyond 'consent' and 'sign off' on a multi-vocal narrative, towards ownership. This could be enabled, for example, through facilitated listening sessions to explore ideas of collective narrative together and make decisions on how and what the group felt would be valuable to capture. Group members would be able to contribute more consciously to the ongoing development of a shared story with a clear idea of how, why, and which parts of the process would be documented.

Suggested reading

If you would like to view the creative documentation of the ARC's journey, please visit <https://jamandjustice-rjc.org> for updates.

References

Bang, H. (2005) 'Among everyday makers and expert citizens', in J. Newman (ed.), *Remaking governance: Peoples, Politics and the Public Sphere*, pp. 159-79, Policy Press, Bristol.

Catalani, C. and Minkler, M. (2010) 'Photovoice: a review of the literature in health and public health', *Health Education & Behavior* 37(3): 424-51 <http://dx.doi.org/10.1177/1090198109342084>.

Corrigan, C. (2012) 'From consultation to participatory engagement: a concept paper and design plan for creating ownership and activating leaders in community engagement initiatives' [online] <http://www.artofhosting.org/wp-content/uploads/2012/10/100921ParticipatoryengagementCCorrigan.pdf> [accessed 28 February 2020].

Evans-Agnew, R. and Rosemberg, M. (2016) 'Questioning photovoice research: whose voice?', *Qualitative Health Research* 26(8): 1019-30 <http://dx.doi.org/10.1177/1049732315624223>.

Ganz, M. (2011) 'Public narrative, collective action and power', in S. Odugbemi and T. Lee (eds), *Accountability through Public Opinion: From Inertia to Public Action*, pp. 273-89, World Bank, Washington, DC.

Perry, B., Durose, C. and Richardson, L. with the Action Research Collective (2019) *How Can We Govern Differently? The Promise and Practice of Co-production* [pdf], Project report, Greater Manchester: Creative Concern <https://jamandjustice-rjc.org/publications-jam-and-justice> [accessed 28 February 2020].

SFCIC (2017) *Citizens Jury Literature Review*, Shared Future Community Interest Company, Manchester <https://sharedfuturecic.org.uk/wp-content/uploads/2018/01/Literature-review-on-Citizen-Juries-25.5.2017.pdf> [accessed 12 May 2020].

Sharmer, C.O. (2018) *The Essentials of Theory U: Core Principles and Applications*, Berrett-Koehler, Oakland, CA.

Wang, C. and Burris, M. (1994) 'Empowerment through photo novella: portraits of participation', *Health Education Quarterly* 21(2): 171-86 <https://doi.org/10.1177%2F109019819402100204>.

PART 3

Conclusions

166 CHAPTER 6
Concluding reflections and recommendations

169 APPENDIX
The contexts – Mistra Urban Futures Local Interaction Platforms

CHAPTER 6
Concluding reflections and recommendations

keywords
transdisciplinary co-production, methods, context sensitivity, reflexivity, sustainable urban development, Mistra Urban Futures

In this final chapter, we summarize the rationale for, and principal features of, this guide. The book sets out the broad methodological approaches to transdisciplinary co-production and explains individual methods and tools to facilitate this type of collaborative research, developed or modified by Mistra Urban Futures. Detailed contextual explanations and recommendations will enable readers to adapt methods to become locally appropriate and hence useful in co-producing more just and sustainable urban areas and societies as a whole.

AS THIS GUIDE EXEMPLIFIES, the practices of transdisciplinary co-production draw upon a broad combination of methods and tools stemming from different scientific disciplines and diverse professional experiences, including those specializing in learning between different communities of knowing and practice. Giving examples of methods and how these were combined and enabled in diverse urban settings through the work of Mistra Urban Futures, the aim of this book has been to share knowledge on how to address urban challenges collaboratively.

The conditions under which transdisciplinary co-production research is undertaken vary in terms of the substantive challenges addressed, how the research is initiated and led and by whom, what stakeholders and/or decision-making levels are involved, and how the research process is designed. They also differ in what institutional arena(s) the research is undertaken, and in what way the research itself is managed, organized or enabled. As noted throughout, these methods have been developed in or adapted to one or more urban contexts. Despite this urban focus, we make no claim to urban exceptionalism and hope that these methods can be adapted for use in various non-urban contexts.

Altogether, the authors of this book have addressed many aspects of the practice of transdisciplinary co-production, while illustrating that the specific means by which and purposes for which transdisciplinary co-production is undertaken need to be based on a nuanced understanding of each situation. In order to make the book as useful as possible across geographical and socio-cultural settings around the world, we have presented descriptions of the respective methods as well as taken care to provide contextual information and guidelines that enable our readers to understand the rationales and objectives as well as share our understandings of what made each method helpful in its particular setting. This process was challenging and valuable in itself. Encouraging the respective authors to debate, clarify, and unpack important issues related to their methods made the text clearer and more explicit as the work progressed. We hope that these efforts make this book useful as a guide to practice and helpful as an aid to adapting the methods to your own local contexts and training future participants in transdisciplinary co-production. As noted in several descriptions, some methods have already been replicated. In relation to the cross-city comparative research that informs part of this book, relevant methods had to be adapted or newly developed to work in multiple local contexts.

During its 10 years as a transdisciplinary centre, Mistra Urban Futures became an important boundary crossing organization in its own right. Both conceptually and in practice, such institutional spaces are difficult to position within academic research contexts and practice-based organizations alike, as they don't 'fit' neatly anywhere. Nevertheless, as this volume attests, endeavours like Mistra Urban Futures are increasingly essential and need to be embodied as an institutional presence in order to move transdisciplinary co-production research beyond the intriguing but limiting conditions of eternal 'experimentation'. In practice this means that we need to continue to create institutional conditions around such research that can better promote the spaces needed to support boundary crossing engagements in society today.

Finally, we offer a few reflections and recommendations for transdisciplinary co-production. These are arranged in a logical sequence to help you plan and launch your research:

- Even more than with other forms of social research, methods for transdisciplinary co-production cannot simply be transferred from one setting to another in a mechanistic way. Context is everything and it is therefore essential to start by reading and reflecting on the contextual information and guidelines provided regarding what the authors see as key factors or attributes that make the methods successful where they were developed.
- Then we advise that you select a shortlist of potentially useful methods in your context and consider how the conditions and objectives of each compare with the situation you are seeking to address.
- Reflect and discuss with team members how each might appropriately be adapted to your context. A certain amount of trial and error will be inevitable, and it could be worth experimenting with more than one possible method to test practicability and even acceptability to the various participants.
- Even before commencing implementation, it is essential to provide training and to ensure that everyone is clear about the objectives and particular purpose, the sequence of steps and what would constitute a successful outcome.

Remember that, in this kind of research, success is usually not defined as a simple yes or no kind of answer, but tangible progress towards building shared understandings and perspectives, and the most acceptable or preferred outcomes or 'solutions' in the specific context.

- One of the biggest challenges in practice is dealing with implicit or embedded power relations. It is easy to assume that all participants in the process are equal as individuals and, therefore, provided normal rules of courtesy (like not interrupting, insisting on speaking first, or being directly or indirectly rude to others) are observed, that the proverbial playing field is level for all participants. This is rarely true. Merely agreeing to participate in co-production does not mean that people leave their personalities and privileges or disadvantages at home. We have all witnessed numerous cases where underlying social norms or supposedly acceptable local practices privilege or inhibit people on the basis of differences in age, gender, ethnicity, religion, home language or which community, professional qualification, institution or stakeholder group they come from or represent. The group or a facilitator or moderator needs to be aware of these issues, to make them explicit at the outset, to remain vigilant, and to have the trust and authority to ensure that all voices are heard in a constructive atmosphere.

- Schedule time for joint reflection, not only towards the end, but throughout the process.

- Finally, don't be afraid of failure and do be prepared to learn by doing because there is no ideal experience or perfect exercise. Even the same experienced facilitator or moderator is almost certain to have very different experiences using the same method in the same city and context but with different participants simply because of the personalities and characters involved, and how power relations are interwoven with those.

Good luck and try to have fun during these very worthwhile but challenging processes!

APPENDIX
The contexts – Mistra Urban Futures Local Interaction Platforms

The Cape Town Local Interaction Platform

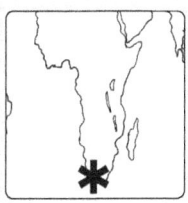

The Cape Town Local Interaction Platform was established in 2010. It is anchored at the African Centre for Cities (ACC), an interdisciplinary urban research institute based at the University of Cape Town in Cape Town, South Africa. The platform involves a partnership between the ACC and the City of Cape Town, the municipality that governs Cape Town. There is a formal Memorandum of Agreement between the ACC and the City of Cape Town, and the partnership is overseen by a Steering Committee with three members from each of the partners.

Cape Town is the second-largest city in South Africa, with a population of over 4 million people. Established by Dutch colonists in 1652, it is a diverse and complex city, with a long history of segregation and inequity. The city continues to be characterized by high levels of inequity, most tangibly manifested in the presence of informal settlements. Much of this inequity is along racial lines as a result of enforced spatial segregation during colonial and apartheid times. Since South Africa's transition to democracy in the 1990s, the city has continued to evolve, with significant urban regeneration initiatives and with major governance reforms (with the 57 local government bodies and regional government body that existed in the early 1990s being merged into one local government body, the City of Cape Town, in 2000).

The Cape Town platform work has focused on the co-production of knowledge, initially through the CityLab programme, which brought together different stakeholders to create policy relevant knowledge on a range of key challenges faced by Cape Town. To strengthen this collaboration, in 2012 the platform initiated the Knowledge Transfer Programme, a programme to help bridge the divide between academia and local government, through embedding academic researchers at the City of Cape Town and through hosting officials at the University of Cape Town on writing fellowships. Part of ACC's Africa-wide work, for example developing the research and policy capacity of research institutes in Africa and comparative research on urban food security in Africa, has also formed part of the platform activities. The main thematic focus of platform work has been on the transformation of Cape Town to make it a more integrated and just city.

This has included work on land, housing, informal settlement upgrading, urban violence, urban food security, and public culture.

Through extensive knowledge co-production work in Cape Town, the platform was able to greatly expand the bodies of knowledge on several key challenges facing Cape Town, has helped expose key stakeholders to diverse views on these challenges and potential solutions, and has facilitated building the capacity of government to engage with other stakeholders and address these challenges. On a number of topics, for example housing and flooding, the Cape Town platform was able to also have a direct impact on policy development.

The Gothenburg Local Interaction Platform

The local interaction platform in Gothenburg was inaugurated as part of Mistra Urban Futures in 2010, based on a history of collaboration within the region; between political parties, between the city and local business communities, and between academia and private and public sector actors. With 13 municipalities and a population of about 1 million, the Gothenburg city region is the second largest in Sweden. Located by the river Göta with its industrial heritage, surrounded by forest and agricultural landscapes, and as part of Västra Götaland region, connections between the urban and the rural are tangible at both the local and the regional level in Gothenburg.

From the inception until 2019, the platform was hosted by Chalmers University of Technology and organized as a consortium of seven partners, representing four regional and local authorities, two universities, and one research institute. Together, these partners represent the main political, administrative, regulatory, educational, and research institutions in the region. The same consortium co-funded and shared ownership of the Mistra Urban Futures centre as a whole, overseeing overall operations and expenditures.

Over the years, the Gothenburg Platform evolved into a visible actor and an active arena for new knowledge on sustainable urban development, where local parties could meet outside established structures to critically review processes and changes in the region. Through regular meetings, the platform staff collaborated closely with representatives of the partnering organizations to plan and develop platform activities. One of the most complex and persistent problems in the region is social polarization and segregation. Other critical urban challenges and opportunities for improvement, identified by the platform partners, included transformation of the economy, migration, climate change adaption, and ecology.

Through the years, the platform facilitated over 70 research projects with different actor constellations, initiated by platform partners or other stakeholders. Research project topics relate to, for example, culture and cultural heritage, governance for sustainability, urban-rural relations, climate change and wellbeing, participatory planning, social sustainability, sustainable lifestyles, and transport development and planning. Many of these projects have also involved national and international collaboration. The platform also hosted an open research school on transdisciplinarity and co-production for PhD students and experienced practitioners, and several thematic networks to promote knowledge exchange between researchers and practitioners. Network themes range from pedagogy for sustainability to urban food, sustainable mobility, socially sustainable transport planning, co-creation and facilitation, climate-smart vacationing, and migration in relation to urban development. A series of activities and events, hosted by the platform, contributed to communication of results and mediation of research-practice collaborations.

From 2020, an eighth former associated partner joined the former seven partners in the establishment of the co-owned Centre for Sustainable Urban Futures, hosted by Gothenburg Centre for Sustainability (GMV). The ambition of the new centre is to continue collaborating for sustainable urban futures, through transdisciplinary co-production.

The Kisumu Local Interaction Platform

With a population of about half a million, Kisumu is the third largest urban area in Kenya. It is situated on the shores of Lake Victoria – the largest freshwater lake in Africa and third largest freshwater lake in the world – near the borders of Uganda and Tanzania. Despite a long history of trading and a growing economy Kisumu has one of the highest poverty levels in Kenya. Rural migration contributes to rapid population growth, unmatched by infrastructure development and service expansion. Unemployment rates are high, among young people in particular. Following Kenyan independence from colonial rule, years of rivalry over national and local resources along with political tension left Kisumu a largely unplanned and underdeveloped city, characterized by peri-urban informal settlements lacking basic urban services and requisite infrastructure. In the 1990s, the city became largely ungovernable and a bedrock for Kenyan oppositional politics. Elections often lead to destruction of property and loss of lives, coupled by fear of losing private assets. This situation poses great challenges to the city authorities. Some of the most pressing ones relate to the political situation, migration and population growth, poverty, transport, planning, and waste. The transport system is derelict, flash floods strike the residential areas and city streets during rainstorms, and poor solid waste management and discharges from public services and industry cause environmental degradation.

In this context, the Kisumu Local Interaction Platform was established in 2010, bringing different actors and sectors together for dialogue on the challenges within the city and in western Kenya. The platform initially operated under the umbrella of the Kisumu Action Team, a group established by the Municipal Council in 2008 – in part spurred by community members and civil society campaigning for better governance and living conditions. It has since been transformed into a trust representing a broad circle of stakeholders, including the public and private sectors, civil society, and academia. The trust oversees all platform operations, driven by the two local universities, Jaramogi Oginga Odinga University of Science and Technology and Maseno University, in partnership with the City of Kisumu, the County Government of Kisumu, and the local community.

With time, the Kisumu platform has become a key driver for local co-production of knowledge between citizens, city managers, practitioners, and academia. Research activities have addressed solid waste management, food security, cultural heritage, community-based ecotourism, the Lake Victoria water hyacinth situation, and the revitalization of railways and lake transports. These projects emerged from research work in the early years that focused on two thematic areas, namely ecotourism and marketplaces, and were prioritized by the research team and approved by the Trustees for research during 2016–19. The project locations were influenced by ease of access, proximity to the city, the concentration of ongoing activities, and consideration of how the activities would contribute to realization of a just Kisumu City. The co-productive activities around the local implementation of the global Sustainable Development Goals (SDGs), enabled by the platform, has caught the attention of both the Kenyan national SDG implementation team and County Government of Kisumu. The process in Kisumu is carefully observed, with the intention of replicating it in other Kenyan cities.

The Skåne Local Interaction Platform

Skåne is the southernmost region of Sweden, known for its coastlines, farms, and castles. It is also a dynamic, growing, and culturally rich region home to 33 municipalities and over 1.3 million inhabitants. The urban centre of Skåne is Malmö, located in the southwest end of the province. However, the region also has a variety of medium-sized cities including Helsingborg, Lund, Kristianstad, Landskrona, and Trelleborg. The region is also a part of greater Copenhagen with its connection to Denmark located just over the sound.

Despite the region's strong cultural and physical appeal, urban areas in Skåne face many challenges for decision-makers. There is a shortage of affordable housing and working spaces in the region, in many cases creating pressures of urban sprawl onto the country's most agriculturally rich soils. As Skåne is the entry point into the rest of the country from mainland Europe, the region also faces numerous challenges around shaping sustainable, inclusive immigration processes. Furthermore, Skåne's labour market faces significant challenges as nearly 30 per cent of the unemployed do not have a high school education and half are born outside Europe. Augmenting this challenge, a large percentage of the unemployed are youth.

The Local Interaction Platform in Skåne was formed in 2016 and has promoted and harnessed transdisciplinary research for sustainable urban development both in and beyond the region. Its roots are in the transdisciplinary Commission for a Socially Sustainable Malmö (2010-2013), an independent group that had the aim of developing co-producing strategies to reduce health disparities among the residents of Malmö. The initiative was the first of its kind in Sweden, involving expertise from several public and private actors, academic disciplines, and community organizations. Following their work, the platform has a robust academic presence, consisting of a consortium of three institutions: Malmö University, Lund University, and the Swedish University of Agricultural Sciences in Alnarp; with solid support and co-operation from the City of Malmö. Additionally, the platform has had support from other municipalities, organizations, and private sector actors, including the co-operative housing developer, HSB, Helsingborgshem, among others. The participating organizations view the collaboration as a way of fostering more robust knowledge on the urban challenges the region faces that could not be done by each of them individually.

The platform in Skåne has supported a variety of innovative transdisciplinary urban sustainable development projects under an umbrella of three broad themes: urban ecosystem services, migration and urban development, and sustainable neighbourhood development. Examples of individual project themes include fostering planning processes around the topic of ecosystems services in smaller urban areas, enhancing apartment building renovation processes through broader actor participation, and knowledge exchanges between Skåne and Kisumu to promote more sustainable urban solid waste management systems. The platform flagship activities are transdisciplinary expert panels focusing on each of the themes, consisting of, for example, academics, city officials, and representatives from the private sector. The panels have been responsible for collecting and systematically analysing the knowledge and experiences generated on the diverse activities in the region on each theme, and broadcasting that knowledge, in different manners, to help promote sustainable urban development throughout Skåne and beyond.

The Sheffield-Manchester Local Interaction Platform

The Sheffield-Manchester Local Interaction Platform (SMLIP) was developed as a cross-city platform in 2016, with the expansion of Mistra Urban Futures' work across the North of England. It was anchored at the Urban Institute, University of Sheffield.

The Urban Institute is an interdisciplinary research centre which examines how cities are responding to intensified urbanization, injustice and marginality, technological innovation and ecological change. With embedded critical social science expertise, the institute's projects bring together the multidisciplinary and cross-sectoral knowledge needed to understand and support sustainable urban change in the UK and across global contexts. Cross-cutting themes include controlled environments, urban robotics and automation, life at the margins, climate urbanism, infrastructure inaction, urban humans – and co-producing urbanisms, within which the SMLIP's programme of work was located.

The SMLIP involves a number of distributed partnerships, each with negotiated autonomy and devolved responsibility. These partnerships are governed by different partnership agreements and collaborative arrangements, through memoranda of understanding, terms of reference and sub-contracts for instance. The platform worked with more than 60 partner organizations, with over 300 co-researchers involved in 14 projects. The projects have all responded to climate change, economic injustice, social inequalities, spatial planning, and knowledge-based change.

One of the platform's key priorities has been to develop transdisciplinary approaches to rethinking wider processes and structures of urban governance. Several English metropolitan areas have gained additional powers and responsibilities through new city deals with central government since 2012. SMLIP researchers were keen to explore whether and how the devolution deal in Greater Manchester could be an opportunity for more radical change. The ESRC Jam and Justice project, co-funded by Mistra Urban Futures, set up an Action Research Collective to co-initiate a series of projects to test and learn about how to make devolution matter, and support more participatory urban governance <https://jamandjustice-rjc.org>. The insights, methods, and approaches contributed to this book all draw from this project or its underpinning ideas.

Overall, SMLIP's portfolio of work has enabled researchers to work closely alongside policymakers, civil society groups, and residents, through creating intermediary spaces that break down boundaries and enable recognition of diverse forms of expertise. The platform sought to facilitate residents to develop their own ideas and explore creatively how different procedures and methods can open up knowledge processes. The SMLIP's multiple impacts include shaping policy processes and opening up imaginations about more creative approaches to producing knowledge; enabling trans-local learning, exchanges, and networks, and stimulating infrastructures for action and building co-productive capacity. For instance, the platform worked closely with the Greater Manchester Combined Authority to support the public sector reform agenda and increase citizen engagement in the Green Summit. It supported community and activist groups to table options for community-led housing and a new network called GM Savers, a charitable women-led network spreading the word about how savings enable community-led change <https://gmsavers.org.uk>. You can read more about the platform's work in its final report available at <https://realisingjustcities-rjc.org/reports-and-briefings>.

The Stockholm Node

Stockholm was the first city ever to be appointed European Green Capital (2010). It is a leading city in greenhouse gas emission reduction. However, many challenges remain: climate change, air quality, diminishing green areas, and the tremendous pressures on the Baltic Sea on the eastern fringes of the region are examples of potential threats to both human well-being and ecosystems in the region. It is also important to consider the great social and economic divides between different areas. For example, in the City of Stockholm life expectancy is eight years higher in a wealthy district of the inner city compared with a less prosperous district in the southern suburbs.

In June 2016 a large group of actors working with sustainable development in the Stockholm region organized a workshop around the requirements for collaboration for meeting the needs of the region, such as the ones described above. The conclusion from the workshop was that there is a role for collaborative arenas between sectors, actors, and levels in the region. The Stockholm Node was founded in 2017 with the goal of creating a regional forum for co-production and knowledge exchange for sustainable urban development between actors in the Stockholm region.

The final consortium of the Node consisted of representatives from Openlab (also hosting the project team), Stockholm University, Stockholm Resilience Centre, IVL Swedish Environmental Research Institute, the independent think-tank Global Utmaning, the non-profit organization Quantified Planet, and KTH Royal Institute of Technology. Openlab is a challenge-driven 'innovation community' providing courses for professionals and master's students, co-working space, innovation projects, and a conference centre. The consortium representatives agreed that Openlab represented an ideal neutral arena for the Node since it is a joint undertaking of many key stakeholders and is situated at the entrance to the KTH university campus, thus making it highly accessible to participants from all partners. Several ideas emerged regarding both content and process of a Stockholm node. The Node eventually became a partnership with a unique set of expertise involved, as all of them worked with co-production in some form or other and had interest in learning from and enriching one another. As an initial step towards realizing this goal, the Stockholm Node determined one of its activities as focusing on gathering information about successful co-production processes aiming at social ecological transformations in the Stockholm region.

www.ingramcontent.com/pod-product-compliance
Lightning Source LLC
Chambersburg PA
CBHW040423100526
44589CB00022B/2809